OEDIPUS AT THEBES

Bernard Knox

OEDIPUS AT THEBES

*Sophocles' Tragic Hero
and His Time*

Yale University Press

New Haven and London

Library of Congress Cataloging-in-Publication Data

Knox, Bernard MacGregor Walker.
    Oedipus at Thebes: Sophocles' tragic hero and his time / Bernard Knox.
        p.   cm.
    Originally published: 1957. With new preface.
    Includes bibliographical references and index.
    ISBN 0-300-07423-9 (alk. paper)
    1. Sophocles. Oedipus Rex. 2. Oedipus (Greek mythology) in literature.
    3. Thebes (Greece)—In literature. 4. Heroes in literature. 5. Tragedy
    I. Title.
PA4413.07K55 1998   97–18471
882'.01—DC21   CIP

Printed in the United States of America.

A catalogue record for this book is available from the British Library.

The paper in this book meets the guidelines for permanence and durability of the Committee on Production Guidelines for Book Longevity of the Council on Library Resources.

TO ROWENA WALKER KNOX

CONTENTS

When this book was first published by Yale University Press in 1957, it received favorable notices in the *New Yorker* and the *New York Times* but only two serious reviews in scholarly publications. They were written by two brilliant classical scholars, Cedric Whitman and D. W. Lucas; both were generous in their praise of what they saw as the book's originality and sharply critical of what they considered its extravagances. But apart from these two thoughtful and substantial assessments, the scholarly press avoided comment. When later, in Vienna, I met Albin Lesky, the Continental doyen of studies in Greek tragedy, he told me, with a paternal smile, that it was "a young man's book." I refrained from telling him that I was over forty when it appeared, because in a sense he was right. Between 1936, when I received my B.A. from Cambridge, and 1947, when, fresh out of the U.S. Army, I enrolled as a graduate student at Yale, I had done no serious work in the classics; my only contact with them had been teaching elementary Latin in a private school in Connecticut. The rest of the decade had been spent fighting in two wars, working at odd jobs, emigrating to America, and getting married. And there were indeed some features of the book that called up the image of a young man in a hurry and that seemed calculated to set the teeth of the classical establishment on edge.

The polemical tone of the original Preface, for example, seemed to suggest (though it was not my intention) that I was accusing my fellow classicists of "exclusive technicality" (I had been dismayed by the appearance of an article, extended over two successive issues of a periodical, entitled "The Carrot in

Classical Antiquity"). Further, my decision to transliterate my frequent citations from the Greek text was an expedient scorned by the profession at that time. Whitman, for one, complained that some transliterated sentences had the "unhallowed look of jabberwocky." This was true, but because the use of Greek script would have made it next to impossible for the Greekless reader to follow an argument based on a demonstration of the repetition of key words, it was a blemish I was prepared to accept.

Such close attention to verbal patterns was, of course, a characteristic of what was then known as the New Criticism. Studying and soon teaching at the same university as Robert Penn Warren and Cleanth Brooks (though I had not yet meet either of them), I read with enthusiasm and absorbed the insights and techniques of their influential textbook *Understanding Poetry.* (I still have the battered volume, annotated by its enthusiastic undergraduate owner with such marginal notes as *PATHETIC FALISI* and *FALIC SYMBALL,* which I had bought secondhand when, at the age of thirty-two, I started graduate work at Yale.) My first article, "The Serpent and the Flame," which appeared in print in 1950, acknowledged its indebtedness to the New Criticism not only in the flamboyance of its title but also in its subtitle: "The Imagery of the Second Book of the *Aeneid.*" This was followed in 1952 by a study of an image in Aeschylus, "The Lion in the House," and later by an article on the *Hippolytus* of Euripides, which, though it had comparatively little to say about imagery, based its argument on repeated verbal patterns. But the genesis of this book was a public lecture given at Yale in 1951, the opening lecture of a series entitled "Tragic Themes in Western Literature," in which I was one of seven participants, all drawn from the Yale faculty. The lectures were published by Yale University Press in 1955.

My lecture, which dealt with both Oedipus plays, presented a preliminary treatment of the main thesis of this book: that the language of the *Oedipus Tyrannos* invests its protagonist with all the great qualities and achievements as well as the tragic flaws of fifth-century Athens and, beyond that, of all humankind, as pride in the superiority of its intellect tempts it to forget its inferiority to the gods. But much fuller evidence was needed to buttress the claim that "the language of the play suggests a comparison between Oedipus' speech and action in the play and the whole range of sciences and techniques which have brought man to mastery, made him *tyrannos* of the world."

As an undergraduate at Cambridge I had been awestruck by a statement of Walter Headlam, a brilliant Cambridge scholar whose career was cut short by his early death at the age of forty-eight in 1908. He claimed that when embarking on the elucidation of a Greek poetic text, the scholar should first learn the text by heart and then read the whole of Greek literature looking for parallel passages. I cannot claim to have lived up to this Olympian formula (though Headlam seems to have done so for his uncompleted edition of the *Oresteia*), but I did read though all the extant Greek literature, early or late, that might help me understand the resonances of Sophocles' words and phrases. I looked for parallels not only in the works of poets, historians, and philosophers but also in the court-room speeches of the orators, the Hippocratic medical texts, the writings of mathematicians, Xenophon on hunting, and a good many odd treatises of Plutarch. I was looking for evidence that Sophocles had chosen words for his mythical characters, and for Oedipus above all, that called to mind the political and legal context of contemporary Athenian life and the many facets of the intellectual fervor of the age, as well as the stages of humankind's progress from savagery to the civilization of the city-state.

The suggestion that Oedipus, a royal member of a mythical accursed Theban house, could be seen as a figure symbolic of Athenian democracy is not so strange as might at first appear. Such glaring anachronisms are far from rare in Athenian tragedy, and they are often much more specific than the impression conveyed by Sophocles' choice of vocabulary. In 463 B.C., for example, Aeschylus has the unnamed king of Argos tell the fifty daughters of Danaus that he will not grant them asylum without the consent of his people; the matter must be submitted to the assembly. When Danaus comes back from Argos, the chorus leader asks him, "What is the final decision? On which side is the empowered hand of the people in the majority?" Danaus gives them the good news that they are welcome. He does so in a recognizably Athenian democratic formula: *edoxen Argeioisin* (resolved by the Argives) and describes "the air bristling with right hands held high as the proposal was ratified." There is, of course, no suggestion in Sophocles' play that Thebes is a democracy. Oedipus is a benevolent ruler, but he is in full control of the city. He is *tyrannos,* autocratic ruler, and the effect of the language he uses is to suggest a likeness to Athens, the *polis tyrannos,* as its enemies called it; it was a designation accepted as exact by both Pericles and Cleon in speeches to the democratic assembly.

This insistence on locating the play firmly in its historical context was not, of course, something I had to learn from the New Criticism, which was, in one of its many aspects, a hostile reaction to a common tendency not to teach poetry "as poetry" but to substitute for the poem as an object of study other things, among them "biographical and historical materials." I had, however, chosen history as my special field in my last year at Cambridge, and though I could see the play as a literary construct and attempt to pay full attention to tone, imagery, and theme, I was equally interested in its roots in and attitude toward its time and place. The resultant combination of methods was a sort of new critical historicism. But emphatically not the "new historicism" of recent years, which insists on viewing the historical circumstances of the poem as limitations on interpretation and often rejects claims of enduring significance over the centuries as mere illusions, the raw material of *Rezeptionstheorie.* A play, however, which suggests that, for all its great achievements, human ingenuity may be fatally flawed, does not seem irrelevant for an age that lives in dread of atomic and biological warfare, not to mention the nightmare possibilities offered by the latest developments in genetics.

One passage in this book has met with total rejection even from authorities I respect: my decision (on pages 7–8) to reject Brunk's emendation of verse 376. I still think that the reading of the manuscripts (including the oldest among them, a papyrus of the fifth century A.D., makes good sense, and that interpreting Oedipus' preceding lines as a contemptuous rejection of punitive action against Tiresias is much more convincing than understanding it as a claim that Tiresias cannot harm him, something Tiresias has never spoken of doing. I am lonely in this stance, but not quite *Athanasius contra mundum;* Gilbert Murray reads the Greek this way (though for the wrong reason), and the ancient scholia announce that the lines can be read either way (*diploun to noema*).

This book is addressed to the classical scholar and at the same time to the " Greekless reader," a category which, once treated with scorn by the professors of more educated ages, now includes the overwhelming majority of the inhabitants of the planet. The book is therefore condemned from the start to fall between two stools. But since the two stools in question often turn out to be those of exclusive technicality on the one hand and bodiless generality on the other, I may perhaps be excused for declining to sit squarely on either one of them.

I am optimist enough to think that the educated reader of today will follow a discussion of Sophocles which deals with the actual words of the poet rather than those of a translator, for it has been demonstrated that he will do so for a book on Rimbaud, Goethe, or Dante without much knowledge of French, German, or Italian. But to superimpose on the barrier presented by an unfamiliar language an extra hurdle in the shape of Greek letters is too much; the Greekless reader will feel, with some justice, that he is being excluded, as I myself feel when confronted with the Chinese ideograms of Ezra Pound's latest Cantos. True, most people know some Greek letters, but it is my experience that few of them can, and even fewer will, puzzle out the words of the printed Greek text. For this reason I have throughout the body of the book trans-literated the words of Sophocles into the letters of our own alphabet. I know that many of my fellow scholars will find this intolerable; all that I can do is to refer them to the notes, where Greek type is used in profusion, and humbly remind them that Sophocles himself would not be able to read the Oxford text of his plays.

The book is heavily indebted to all those who have written on Sophocles: adequate acknowledgment is impossible. I make no claim to bibliographical completeness; the literature of the subject is too big to permit that luxury. To balance any debts or anticipations which I have failed to acknowledge I can only hope that the book contributes enough new material to be borrowed by, and to anticipate, others in their turn.

Part of Chapter 2 appeared in the " Classical Journal" in December 1954, and part of Chapter 3 in "Tragic Themes in Western Literature," ed. Cleanth Brooks, New Haven, 1955; my thanks for permission to reprint in a different form are due to the respective editors. I am also indebted to the Morse Fellowship which was granted me in 1952-53 and which made possible the writing of this book.

YALE UNIVERSITY,
SEPTEMBER 1955

POSTSCRIPT

For this re-issue the Press has allowed me to correct the many misprints and mistakes which appeared in the original edition. I have taken full advantage of this generous offer. Apart from these corrections, I have made no changes in the text.

WASHINGTON, D. C.
JANUARY 1965

OEDIPUS AT THEBES

It sometimes happens that a great poet creates a character in whom the essence of an age is distilled, a representative figure who in his action and suffering presents to his own time the image of its victory and defeat. For later centuries this character becomes the central reference point for an understanding of his creator's time; but he is a figure of such symbolic potency that he appears to them not only as a historical but also as a contemporary phenomenon. The poet who created him has penetrated so deeply into the permanent elements of the human situation that his creation transcends time. One such figure is Hamlet, Prince of Denmark, and such another is Oedipus, King of Thebes.

But this double existence of the hero, in time and out of it, creates a critical problem. "Commemoration," says Auden's prize-day orator, "Commemoration. What did it mean to them, there, then? What does it mean to us, here, now?" There is a possibility, if not a probability, that a study of Oedipus as a figure in time, a creation of the human intellect shaped and limited by the ideas and circumstances of the fifth century B. C., may produce an interpretation different from that which emerges from a study of Oedipus out of time, as a figure symbolic of Western man and, most important for us, of Western man in the twentieth century.[1]

This book is essentially a study of the Sophoclean play, *Oedipus Tyrannus*, in terms of the age which produced it, an attempt to answer the question, "What did it mean to them, there, then?" But it suggests also an answer to the question, "What does it mean to us, here, now?" And the answer suggested is: the same thing it meant to them, there, then. For in this case, the attempt to understand the play as a particular phenomenon reveals its universal nature; the rigidly historical method finds itself uncovering the timeless. The materials of which the *Oedipus Tyrannus* is constructed are basic to the human situation; they have not changed since the play was written and probably never will. The play needs only to be seen clearly as what it was, to be understood as what it is.

CHAPTER ONE: HERO

I

An initial obstacle lies square athwart the critical approach to the *Oedipus Tyrannus*: the widely accepted and often repeated judgment that the play is a " tragedy of fate." This judgment is based on a blurred vision of the relation between the hero's predicted destiny and his action in the play, but, although its basis is a misapprehension, its influence has none the less served to pigeonhole the *Oedipus Tyrannus* as the classical example of the " tragedy of fate," the example which is supposed to illustrate the essential distinction between ancient and modern tragedy. The purport of this distinction, expressed or implied with varying degrees of subtlety, is not only that ancient tragedy is less significant for the modern consciousness because it operates in the pre-Christian framework of fate rather than the modern Christian framework of individual free will, but also that ancient tragedy has a lesser inherent dramatic potential than modern, since in ancient tragedy (example, the *Oedipus Tyrannus*) the hero's will is limited by fate, not free, like Hamlet's. But this view of the Sophoclean tragedy conflicts with experience, for every unprejudiced reader and spectator feels that the play has a dramatic power as great as that of *Hamlet*. And this is hard to explain if the play is not dramatically self-sufficient—if the real responsibility for the catastrophe must be attributed to an external factor.

A good example of the fundamental misconception (that the *Oedipus Tyrannus* is a " tragedy of fate "), the problem raised by the misconception, and a brilliant but eccentric attempt to solve the problem is furnished by the comments of Sigmund Freud, whose name, to modern ears, is as closely associated with Oedipus as that of Sophocles—to many, in fact, more so.[2]

> The *Oedipus Rex* is a tragedy of fate: its tragic effect depends on the conflict between the all-powerful will of the gods and the vain efforts of human beings threatened with disaster; resignation to the divine will, and the perception of one's own impotence is the lesson which the deeply moved spectator is supposed to learn from the tragedy. Modern authors have therefore sought to achieve a similar tragic effect by expressing the same conflict in stories of their own invention. But the playgoers have looked on unmoved. . . . The modern tragedies of destiny have failed of their effect. If the *Oedipus Rex* is capable of moving a modern reader or playgoer no less powerfully than it moved the contemporary Greeks, the only possible explanation is that the effect of the Greek tragedy does not depend upon the conflict between fate and human will, but upon the peculiar nature of the material by which this conflict is revealed. There must be a voice within us which is prepared to acknowledge the compelling power of fate in the *Oedipus*, while we are able to condemn the situations occurring in *Die Ahnfrau* or other tragedies of fate as arbitrary inventions . . . this [Oedipus'] fate moves us only because it might have been our own, because the oracle laid upon us before our birth the very curse which rested upon him. It may be that we were all destined to direct our first sexual impulses towards our mothers, and our first impulses of hatred and violence towards our fathers; our dreams convince us that we were.[3]

This famous passage is of course a landmark in the history of modern thought, and it is a token of the vitality of Greek

4

literature that in these sentences one of the most bitterly con-
tested and influential concepts of the modern mind takes the
form of an attempt to solve a critical problem raised by the
Sophoclean play. But quite apart from the value (or lack of
it) of Freud's theory of the Oedipus complex (which he here
announced for the first time), the solution he proposes to the
critical problem raised by calling the play a "tragedy of fate"
cannot be accepted. When he says that Oedipus' fate affects
us because "it might have been our own" he has put his
finger on an essential aspect of the tragedy, the universality
of the theme, which of course extends far beyond the particular
appeal which Freud himself here expounds. But the universal
appeal of the theme, whether understood in psychoanalytical
or other terms, does not explain the dramatic excitement gener-
ated by the tragedy. No amount of symbolic richness—conscious, subconscious, or unconscious—will create dramatic excitement in a play which does not possess the essential pre-
requisites of human free will and responsibility. The tragedy
must be self-sufficient: that is, the catastrophe must be the
result of the free decision and action (or inaction) of the
tragic protagonist.

The problem, stated in Freud's terms, (and he only states
in extreme form what many others imply or assume), is obviously insoluble. If the *Oedipus Tyrannus* is a "tragedy of
fate," the hero's will is not free, and the dramatic efficiency
of the play is limited by that fact. The problem is insoluble;
but luckily the problem does not exist to start with. For in
the play which Sophocles wrote the hero's will is absolutely
free and he is fully responsible for the catastrophe. Sophocles
has very carefully arranged the material of the myth in such
a way as to exclude the external factor in the life of Oedipus
from the action of the tragedy. This action is not Oedipus'
fulfillment of the prophecy, but his discovery that he has

5

already fulfilled it. The catastrophe of Oedipus is that he discovers his own identity; and for this discovery he is first and last responsible. The main events of the play are in fact not even part of the prophecy: Apollo predicted neither the discovery of the truth, the suicide of Jocasta, nor the self-blinding of Oedipus.[4] In the actions of Oedipus in the play "fate" plays no part at all.

This may seem a sweeping assertion, and objections arise at once. For one thing, both the discovery and the blindness (though not the self-blinding) are predicted early in the course of the play by Tiresias, who also informs Oedipus that he is the murderer of Laius, the murderer of his father, and his mother's husband. But this prophecy of Tiresias cannot be considered an external factor operating in the play, since Tiresias delivers it only as a result of Oedipus' action in the first place. Tiresias has made up his mind not to speak a word (343); he delivers the prophecy because Oedipus attacks him so violently and unexpectedly that he forgets his resolution to keep silent. The prophecy is extracted from him by Oedipus, and he says as much himself: "For you impelled me to speak against my will" (358).*

Not only is it not an external factor, it is also without effect. It is pronounced in the course of a violent altercation by a man whom Oedipus suspects of conspiracy against him, and it is attached to the accusation that Oedipus is the murderer of Laius. Oedipus is so furiously angry at this apparently senseless but none the less terrible accusation that the prophecy makes comparatively little impression on him, and in any case

---

* The translations throughout the book are my own and aim merely at a rough equivalence. The same words are sometimes translated differently in different places to bring out the particular connotation, metaphorical suggestion, or emphasis of the original text which is relevant to the discussion.

he does not understand it. "Everything you say is too riddling and obscure," he tells the prophet at the end of their interview (439). It makes no apparent impression on the chorus either, for in the stasimon which immediately follows this scene they discuss the accusation that Oedipus is the murderer but do not even mention the prophecy or any other aspect of Tiresias' statements. When later, Oedipus, after learning from Jocasta the significant detail about Laius' murder, expresses his fear that perhaps the blind prophet can see (747), he is thinking only of the accusation that he is the murderer of Laius. The other, even more terrible, things that Tiresias said he has apparently forgotten; he does not refer to them when he learns that Polybus of Corinth is not, in fact, his father, nor later as he comes swiftly closer to the dreadful truth. For all the effect on Oedipus' action that Tiresias' prophecy has, it might just as well never have been uttered. This prophecy of Tiresias, then, is in the first place produced by the action of Oedipus, and in the second place has no effect on his subsequent action. It can be considered neither external nor causal.

There is, however, one two-line speech of Tiresias which seems to raise an unanswerable objection to this line of argument. "It is not destiny that you should fall at my hands," he says to Oedipus, in all the modern texts and translations,[5] "since Apollo is enough for that, and it is his affair" (376-7). Here the "fall" of Oedipus is specifically attributed to Apollo by Apollo's prophet; the lines are unequivocally phrased in such a way as to emphasize the action of the external factor in the plot of the play.

But the lines, in this form, are a comparatively modern creation; they date from 1786, when Brunck emended the manuscripts in his edition of the play.[6] What the manuscripts say (and they are confirmed by the only papyrus fragment of this passage which has so far been found),[7] is exactly the opposite: "It is not destiny that I should fall at your hands, since Apollo is enough, and it is his affair."[8]

Brunk's emendation has been universally accepted by editors because the preceding speech of Oedipus (374-5), as they understood it, seemed to demand the sense which Brunk's rearrangement affords: "You are maintained in one unbroken night, so that you can never harm either me or any other man who sees the light." If this is the meaning of Oedipus' lines, Brunk's emendation is indeed "imperative," as the editors of the papyrus fragment put it. But the words can also mean: "You are maintained in endless night, so that neither I nor any other man who sees the light would ever harm you." To this statement the reading of the manuscripts is a proper and cogent answer: "You could not harm me in any case," Tiresias replies in effect; "if I am to fall, that is Apollo's business and he can take care of it."[9]

This reading and interpretation make this part of the exchange between Oedipus and Tiresias a logical development: Oedipus dismisses the idea of punitive action against a blind man, and proceeds to find a culprit against whom he *can* retaliate. His answer to Tiresias' defiant speech is "Is this Creon's invention or yours?" (378).[10]

Surely in such an important passage as this the burden of proof is on the corrector and the editors who print the correction; the only possible excuse for Brunk's emendation is that the manuscript text should not make sense, which it does. One cannot quite dismiss the suspicion that the almost universal acceptance of Brunk's version is due, in the last analysis, to the fact that it confirms the preconceived idea that the play is a tragedy of fate by solidly grounding the operation of the external factor in the development of the plot.

It might also be urged that the process of Oedipus' self-discovery starts with his request to the Delphic oracle for advice about the plague, that the plague is therefore the causal factor, and the plague is sent by Apollo, who in this play represents the external factor, "fate." [11] Apollo is, in fact, traditionally the god who sends pestilence; every spectator of the play would in the early scenes think of the opening of the *Iliad*, where Apollo's deadly arrows kill mules, dogs, and men, and "the pyres of the dead burned numerous." [12] The Athenian spectator would also be reminded of the plague at Athens in the early years of the Peloponnesian War, and the current attribution of it to Apollo, on the basis of the god's promise, made oracularly at Delphi at the beginning of the war, that he would collaborate with the Spartans. [13]

If the plague in the *Oedipus Tyrannus* were indeed to be considered as sent by Apollo, this would be a powerful objection, but Sophocles has repeatedly and emphatically indicated that this is not the case. The priest calls on Apollo to rescue Thebes from the plague, and his words contain no suggestion that Apollo is responsible for it in the first place. "May Apollo come as savior and put an end to the sickness" (149-50). He also says that the people are praying to other gods, specifically to Pallas, and at the oracle of Ismenus. The chorus calls on Apollo in similarly neutral terms, praying for rescue (162); it associates him with Athena and Artemis as one of the three defenders from death (163). In this passage it calls him "far-darter" (162), the word that Homer uses to describe him as the plague god, and at the end of the stasimon the chorus mentions his arrows (205). But they call on Apollo not, as we might expect from Homer, to stop shooting them; they call for his arrows to be arrayed on their side as allies, against the plague (206). [14] Nothing could make clearer the fact that Apollo has no connection with the plague, except what the chorus has said a few lines before. They have already identified the plague with a god, not Apollo but Ares; this is the identity of the god whom the priest left unnamed: "The fire-bearing god, hateful pestilence" (27-8). Apollo is called on to help with his arrows, together with Zeus, Artemis, and Dionysus, in the fight against Ares, the god "unhonored among the gods" (215). The plague, whether or not the chorus is right in calling it Ares, is of course, in the last analysis, from a religious point of view, the will of the gods, but Sophocles is clearly insisting, by his unparalleled image of the arrows of Apollo as allies against plague and his equally unparalleled identification of the plague with Ares,[15] that the plague is not to be understood as Apolline interference, that it is not the work of the play's external factor.

The plague, then, is not Apolline interference intended to force the discovery of the truth. It is not the working of "fate." Nevertheless it is an imperative of the initial situation: it calls for action on the part of Oedipus.[16] As ruler of Thebes he must find a way to put an end to the plague or face the possibility that, as the priest tells him, he may be ruler over an empty city.[17] Yet his decision to consult the Delphic oracle is clearly and emphatically presented by Sophocles as an independent decision. The clarity and care with which this essential point is made deserve some notice. The priest, who has come to beg Oedipus to act on the city's behalf, is tactfully vague about what he wants Oedipus to do: he does not come out clearly with advice that Oedipus should consult the oracle. His speech consists of a series of qualified hints that Oedipus might consider some recourse to divine authority: "we consider you first of men in the circumstances of human life . . . and in relationship with the gods" (33-4); "you are said and thought to have set our life straight once before . . . with the assistance of a god" (38); "find some means of rescue for us, whether by hearing the utterance

stop the enquiry or suppress the result later in the course of the action. It is clearly Oedipus' decision and his alone, and just as clearly Creon is made to suggest that the matter would be better discussed in private. Oedipus next decides to undertake the search for the murderer of Laius, and to do so energetically—"I will leave nothing undone" (145). This decision is defined as a free decision by the priest: "What we came here for, he now volunteers" (148).[18] Oedipus implements the decision in the next scene by pronouncing a terrible curse on the murderer if he does not at once come forward, and this of course increases the horror of the catastrophe when he discovers who the murderer is. And the curse is clearly Oedipus' own idea; neither the Oracle nor anyone in Thebes has suggested this step to him. When the chorus proposes that he send for Tiresias the same dramatic device as before is employed to stress the independence of the decision—he tells the chorus that he has already done so. And so with the rest of his actions; the energetic search for the truth is pressed on to the final revelation by the will of Oedipus and by nothing else.[19] The autonomy of his actions is emphasized by the series of attempts made by others to stop the investigation. He is four times advised to drop the matter and be content with ignorance: once at the beginning by Tiresias (320-1), twice in the middle by Jocasta[20] (848 and 1060 ff.), and once at the end by the shepherd (1165). He rejects the advice every time, and goes on his own way. Oedipus' will, in the play, is free. Nothing he does is forced on him by fate, in any of the various senses of that widely ambiguous word.

Oedipus' action is not only the action of a free agent, it is also the cause of the events of the play. The hero is not only free but fully responsible for the events which constitute the plot. The plot, that is to say the process by which Oedipus' identity is revealed, goes far toward meeting Aristotle's ideal requirement of logical development. The recognition and reversal " arise from the internal structure of the plot itself " in such a way that what follows is the " necessary or probable result of the preceding action." The subsequent events are due to the preceding ones, not merely after them—*dia tade* not *meta tade*. (There is only one exception to this, the arrival of the Corinthian messenger.)[21] And the sequence of events is put into motion and kept in motion by Oedipus' action. The actions of Oedipus which cause the final catastrophe begin just before the opening of the play with the sending of Creon to Delphi. Following this he insists on full publication of the oracular response, assumes the responsibility of the search for Laius' murderer, curses the unknown murderer, and sends for Tiresias. He then refuses to accept Tiresias' stubborn insistence that he drop the whole matter, and by his angry accusation stings the prophet into accusing him in his turn. His subsequent attack on Creon brings Jocasta in as peacemaker, and her attempt to comfort him raises the first doubt in his mind. He refuses to accept her proposal that he be content with the situation as it is, and sends for the shepherd who is the witness to Laius' murder. This is already enough to bring about his recognition as the murderer of Laius, if the shepherd can be prevailed upon to speak, and speak the truth.

The situation is changed by an event which happens merely after the others, not because of them: the arrival of the messenger with news of the death of Polybus. From this point on Oedipus is concerned not so much with finding the murderer of Laius as with establishing his own identity. He refuses to accept Jocasta's proposal that he rest content with the confused situation which follows the messenger's revelations, and maintains the decision to talk to the shepherd, who is now the witness to Oedipus' identity as well as to Laius' murder. But when the witness arrives he has no choice but to tell the truth. He is reluctant to a degree, and would clearly have lied or remained silent if he could, but the Corinthian messenger is there to make lies or evasion impossible. The truth is forced out of him by Oedipus, and the *tyrannos* recognizes himself not only as Laius' murderer and son but also as Jocasta's son and husband.

I I

The decisions and actions of Oedipus are the causal factor in the plot of the tragedy, and these decisions and actions are the expression of the character of Oedipus. Oedipus is no ordinary man, he is in fact a very extraordinary one: a man who, starting with nothing but his wits and energy, has become the despotic and beloved ruler of the city to which he came as a homeless exile. This character is many-sided and subtly complicated, yet it has a marvellous consistency. Oedipus is surely the greatest single individual in Greek tragedy.[22]

Oedipus, as one would expect of a *tyrannos*, a self-made ruler,[23] is essentially a man of action. There is nothing passive in his make-up; his natural tendency is always to act, and he scorns inactivity. "I am not a sleeper that you woke from his rest," he tells the priest who speaks for the suppliants of the first scene (65). He imposes himself on people and circumstances: they are the raw material which his will to action forces into a pattern. The words which express action (*dran, prassein*) are typical of his own speech and of the opinions of him expressed by others.[24]

It is characteristic of him to expect the Oracle at Delphi to demand action of him; he waits impatiently to hear "by what action or solemn pronouncement I may save this city" (72).[25] This formulation, an alternative of speech or action, is replaced a few lines later by a more restricted formula which admits only of action. "I would be a coward if I did not *do* everything the god may clearly indicate" (77). He announces his decision to carry out the oracular command in words which show his conception of himself as the active force of the community—"I will do everything" (145).

His confidence in action is based on experience, and it is to Oedipus as an experienced man that the priest appeals at the beginning of the play. "It is men of experience whose decision produces results that are most valid" (45). Oedipus' vigorous action is justified not only in his own mind but also in those of the priest and the chorus, the representatives of Thebes, by his unbroken record of successful action.

His constant will to action is based on a superb courage; one of the aspects of Creon's supposed treachery which most enrages him later is the reflection that Creon must have taken him for a coward. "What cowardice did you see in me . . . ?" he asks Creon indignantly (536). This is no unfounded claim; the courage with which Oedipus assaults the unknown throughout the play is characteristic of the man who risked his life when he answered the riddle of the Sphinx.

His action is lightning swift: once conceived it is not hampered by fear or hesitation; it anticipates advice, approval, or dissent. The characteristic Oedipean action is the *fait accompli*. By the time the priest hesitantly suggests an appeal to the Oracle, Oedipus has already acted several days before.[26] "I have put the idea into action" (69). By the time the chorus suggests recourse to Tiresias, Oedipus has already sent to him, not once but twice: "I did not leave this to wait for tomorrow either" (287). "Swift," *tachys*, is his word. The decision to find Laius' murderer once made, Oedipus sees no point in prolonging a situation which no longer corresponds to the reality. His order to the suppliants to leave the altar is peremptory: "As soon as you can, children, stand up, leave the altar" (*hôs tachista*, 142). Their presence is now inappropriate; for Oedipus' action, which will follow swiftly, he needs not suppliants but the assembly of the people of Thebes to hear his proclamation: "Let someone else summon the people of Cadmus to this place" (144). The chorus, which comes in shortly after, thus represents the people of Thebes, summoned to hear the decision of its ruler. When Oedipus decides to send for the shepherd who is a witness of Laius' murder, he wants him in a hurry: "Get him to me quickly" (*en tachei*, 765), and Jocasta knows her husband well enough to emphasize the speed: "I shall send for him in haste" (*tachynas'*, 861). The most brilliant example of his speed of action is contained in the seventy-five lines in which he examines the shepherd and learns the full truth. The searching questions follow each other in a swift and terrible rhythm, broken only by the increasing reluctance of the witness, a reluctance which provokes Oedipus to angry demands for speed and the application of force to produce it: "Somebody twist his arms back—quickly!" (*hôs tachos*, 1154). The last terrible conclusive questions and answers are framed in the hasty rhythm of the half-lines; the questions, asked now only to confirm the terrible truth Oedipus knows, get shorter until they culminate in the single word *poiôn*: "What oracles?" (1176).

The speed of one of his decisions, his condemnation of Creon, causes the chorus to remonstrate and point out the danger that hasty thought may make a slip: "Those who are quick to think things out are not infallible" (*hoi tacheis*, 617). Oedipus' answer reveals the temper of the man, his insistence on speed as the only guarantee of success, his rejection of passivity: "When the adversary moves fast [*tachys*, 618], plotting in secret, I must be fast [*tachyn*, 619] to make counter-decisions. If I wait for him inactive, his project will be already translated into action, mine a failure."

This speed of his own action is naturally combined with impatience of others' slowness: he can admit no external obstacle to his own swiftness to impose himself on the pattern of events. In the very first scene he is impatient that Creon has not returned. He has presented the priest with a decision that anticipates the cautious hints to consult Delphi, and is already impatient that he cannot present him with the result of the action as well. He counts the days; time is being wasted. The delay is agony for him: " The day measured against the time already pains me . . ." (73-4). So with his repeated summons to Tiresias. He is upset by the prophet's slowness. " I am surprised that he is not here long since " (289).

But this speed is not thoughtless; it is preceded by careful reflection and deliberation. The initial decision to apply to Delphi, swiftly executed though it was, came only after extensive mental ranging over the possibilities and careful considera-tion: " I traveled to the decision over many wandering ways of thought . . ." (67), he says, " carefully considering, I found only one remedy . . ." (68). The decision to reopen the case of Laius' murder is made only after a careful examination of Creon, which elicits the few known facts, and a realistic appraisal of the enormous difficulty of the search. " Where shall it be found, the track of ancient guilt, difficult to find by inference? " (108-9). The decision to excommunicate the murderer, a psychological attack on the unknown criminal combined with an offer of comparative immunity for confession and reward for betrayal, is announced to the people after the singing of a choral ode; the suspension of dramatic time and action creates the impression that while the ode was sung Oedipus, in the palace, has thought his way through to the decision. Even the accusation against Creon, hurled at him from the crest of a wave of tremendous anger, is presented by the same dramatic device as the product of reflection and deliberation. A faint suspicion in the opening scene,[27] then an impulsive reaction in the quarrel with Tiresias, the attack on Creon emerges after the choral ode as a fully accepted conclusion based on political logic. Oedipus sees himself the target of accusations based on past events in Thebes to which he considers himself foreign (220), for they happened before his arrival. His source of information about these events is Creon; Creon urged him to send for Tiresias; Creon's failure to act when Laius was killed seemed to him suspicious from the start. The whole business has the marks of conspiracy, and though Oedipus is wrong, he has already reflected on the situation and arrived at what is, for him, the only possible conclusion.

The swift action is firmly based on reflection, and that reflection is the working of a great intelligence. His bitterest word of condemnation is *môros*, " stupid "; he hurls it at both Tiresias (433) and Creon (540), and it stings him smartly that Creon should have thought him stupid enough not to realize that he was the target of a conspiracy. " Tell me, in the gods' name what kind of a coward or a fool did you take me for . . . ? Did you think I would not recognize your work for what it is, just because it operates by deceit? " (536-8).

Characteristic of his intelligence is his insistence on complete knowledge and clarity. He demands a rational foundation for his existence: he admits no mysteries, no half-truths, no half-measures. He will never rest content with less than the full truth; against this temper both Tiresias' and Jocasta's attempts to stop him from pressing on to the end have no chance of success. A striking example of his insistence on full understanding is the last question he asks the shepherd. He already knows the truth—that Jocasta was his mother and Laius his

18

father—yet there is one detail he does not understand. It is not a detail that offers any hope that the whole story may be false, it is merely a question of the shepherd's motive. "Why did you give the child to this old man?" (1177). Even at the most terrible moment of his existence, he must have the full story, with no trace of obscurity in it anywhere. He must complete the process of inquiry, remove the last ambiguity. His understanding of what has happened to him must be a complete rational structure before he can give way to the tide of emotion which will carry him to self-mutilation.

His is a sharply critical intelligence: it is no accident that Oedipus three times in the play conducts an examination of a witness. In his examination of Creon in the prologue, the swift logical succession of questions reveals the essence of the situation in a few minutes. The questioning of the Corinthian messenger after his announcement that Oedipus is not the son of Polybus gives us an insight into the working of this critical mind. The probability of the story is first attacked from two different angles (1021, 1023), the messenger's connection with Cithaeron established, and then the veracity of the account as a whole tested by the question about Oedipus' maimed foot. But it is in the final examination, that of the shepherd, that the surgical keenness of Oedipus' intelligence is best displayed. Nothing is left to chance in the preliminaries, but there is no waste motion: it is like courtroom procedure in its methodical economy. Oedipus identifies the witness as one of Laius' men by a question to the chorus (1115); as the shepherd of the Corinthian messenger's story by a question to the messenger (1119-20); and then confirms the connection with Laius by a direct question to the shepherd himself. The next step is to have the shepherd recognize the Corinthian messenger and confirm his story, and this is done, after a significant initial hesitation on the shepherd's part, by the vehement intervention of the Corinthian messenger. The witness then becomes recalcitrant, and Oedipus, by threat and physical force, brings him to heel (1161). And from there it is only a few steps to the truth.

But the intelligence of Oedipus is not merely critical, it is creative too. It can not only ask questions: it can answer them. And Oedipus' fame and reputation is based above all on his solution of the riddle of the Sphinx. In this " he was seen to be wise " (*sophos*, 509), sings the chorus: he answered the riddle that no other man could answer, and saved the city. *Gnômêi kyrêsas*, he says of his achievement: " I succeeded by intelligence " (398).

His own account of this intellectual achievement reveals an important aspect of his character: he is the man who by intelligence alone beats the professionals at their own game; he is the intelligent amateur who without special training sees the essential thing the experts could not see. The riddle of the Sphinx was a problem for professionals, for Tiresias, in fact; as Oedipus says, " it called for divination " (*manteias*, 394), and the chorus emphasizes this later when they call the Sphinx " an oracle-chanting maiden " (*chrêsmôidon*, 1200). The priest admits that Oedipus did what should have been done by a Theban, not a foreigner, that it was done without Theban help, and without training (*oud' ekdidachtheis*, 138) but he adds that Oedipus had the aid of a god. Oedipus himself sees it differently. " I came [from outside], I who had no knowledge. I put an end to the Sphinx, finding the answer by intelligence, not learning it from birds " (396-8). It was a triumph of the unprofessional intelligence which had no special skill or even knowledge to buttress it: a sample of the versatility of the Oedipean brain.

The versatility and adaptability of Oedipus is emphasized by the position he has attained in Thebes. He came as a foreigner, a self-constituted exile, but none the less an exile. Now that he is *tyrannos*, far from concealing this fact he glories in it; [28] it is a token of his adaptability, the proof of the superiority of intelligence wherever and in whatever circumstances it may operate. And the situation in the play is like that which faced him then: he must answer another riddle, once again he is an outsider (*ksenos . . . tou logou*, 219), who knows nothing; and he intends to answer it by the same instrument, intelligence, *gnômê*.

This combination of swift decision and action, based on equally swift but unlimited deliberation, springs from and by its success increases an enormous self-confidence. Mistrust of the capacities of others is one of the facets of this self-confidence; Oedipus is not the man to leave action or decision to others. "I came . . . myself" (7). He came himself, not thinking it right to hear through messengers. "I" (*egó*) is a word that is often on his lips: in the first 150 lines Oedipus speaks there are fourteen lines ending with some form of "I" or "my," and fifteen beginning in the same way.[29] His insistence on himself is not mere vanity, it is justified by his whole experience, which presents itself to him as an unbroken record of success due entirely to himself; and this is no subjective impression, it is the conclusion of others too. When he refers to himself as "Oedipus whom all call famous" (8), he utters a boast that is merely a statement of fact: the attitude of the priest and the chorus shows that Oedipus' confidence in himself is no greater than the confidence which his fellow citizens feel in him.[30] "We judge you first of men in the chances of life," the priest says to him at the beginning of the play (33).

The successful record of the past inspires Oedipus with confidence and hope for the future. He loses no whit of his confidence when faced by the plague. It is an unforeseen calamity, but it cannot be counted against him,[31] and his attitude is one of confidence. He expresses the hope, when Creon returns, that he comes with saving fortune, and, through the questioning of Creon about the apparently insoluble riddle of Laius' murder, seeks some basis of hope. There is only one witness, and he said only one thing. " What? " Oedipus asks. " Even one thing might find out the way to learn many, if we could get even the smallest beginning of hope " (*archên bracheian . . . elpidos*, 121). When he decides to undertake the search, it is in full confidence of the outcome: " I shall reveal " (132); " I shall dispel the pollution " (138). It is a promise of success. And it is repeated later when, after reflection, he announces the measures he intends to take. " If you will listen to, and accept what I have to say, you may find some rescue . . ." (217-18). His confidence is revealed again in his reproach to Tiresias, who laments his own knowledge. " What a despondent attitude," Oedipus says (*athymos*, 319); it is a state of mind for which he has no respect. But he comes to it himself before long. Shaken by Tiresias' accusation, he is thrown into despondency (*athymô*, 747) and despair (815 ff.) by the revelations of Jocasta. Yet when the chorus urges him not to abandon hope (*ech' elpida*, 835) he has already found an avenue of escape from what is beginning to seem a terrible certainty, he has established a basis for hope: " Yes, I have this much hope at least " (*tosouton esti moi tês elpidos*, 836). His hope is based on a numerical discrepancy between the account of Laius' death given by Jocasta and his own memory of the events that took place where three roads meet. It seems little enough, " a small beginning of hope," indeed, but it is enough to enable him to face at least the immediate future. And in reaction to the greater revelations which come later, his small beginning of hope grows to enormous dimensions.

22

At the point where Jocasta already knows the terrible truth and Oedipus is only one step from knowing it himself, he reaches the highest point of hope and confidence. "I count myself the son of Fortune, the generous giver . . ." (1080-1). The chorus which sings exultantly of his divine birth soon to be revealed is only making explicit what is implicit in his own declaration. At the very edge of disaster his hopes are at their highest and most fantastic pitch.

This combination of swift action based on intelligent reflection producing success which in its turn gives rise to a justified self-confidence is obviously the mark of a superior individual. But such an individual in society might do either great góod, or, as fifth-century Athens was to find out to its cost, great harm. Such a man might be either a Pericles or an Alcibiades. In Oedipus' case these great gifts are controlled by a deep patriotism and a sense of responsibility to the community: he is presented, in the opening scenes, as the ideal ruler. In his first speech we see clearly his high conception of his duty to the citizens of Thebes. He comes in person to hear his people's wishes, not thinking it just to hear them from messengers (6); he is thus contrasted with the fifth-century idea of the monarch, who holds himself aloof, like Deioces in Herodotus, who established the norms of monarchy, one of which was "that no man should go in to the king, but transact his business with him through messengers, and that the king should be seen by no man." [32] Oedipus feels pity for his suffering people (*katoikteirôn*, 13). And in his second speech he shows a full realization of the obligations which power lays on the ruler. They have each one his individual grief, but he grieves for himself, for them, and for the city as a whole. The collective sorrow increases the burden of his individual sorrow. They are sick, but their sickness cannot equal his (59-64). He feels deeply his responsibility to them, his failure to relieve

23

their distress. It is in this spirit of devotion to the welfare of the citizen-body that he rises to the situation and undertakes the difficult search for the killer of Laius; he will avenge that murder on behalf of the country and the god (136). And in the closing lines of his appeal to Tiresias he states in general terms his conception of the duty to the city incumbent on subject and ruler alike. "The finest activity is for a man to do good for others, with all his resources and capabilities" (ôphelein, 314). It is in terms of this ideal of duty to others that he angrily rebukes Tiresias for his refusal to speak. "Your refusal is an outrage to propriety, and an act unfriendly to the state" (322). From this it is a small step to the accusation of treachery: "You intend to betray us and destroy the city" (330-1). All through the violent quarrel with Tiresias he asserts his pride in his past services to the city, even if, as Tiresias obscurely hints, those services will bring him to destruction now. "It was exactly this good fortune which has destroyed you," says Tiresias, referring to the answer to the riddle of the Sphinx (442), and Oedipus answers proudly: "I don't care, if I saved this city" (443). The high value he places on his past services to the state is not subjective boasting: that value is accepted by the chorus, the people of Thebes. "At the testing time, he was pleasing to the city" (hadypolis, 510), "and therefore never in my mind shall he be convicted of baseness."

This devotion to the welfare of the city and sense of responsibility to his people makes Oedipus a very unusual tyrannos. Not only does he dispense with the formal isolation of the ruler from his subjects but he insists on the full publication of important information which affects them. When Creon returns from Delphi to report to Oedipus he finds the tyrannos outside the palace surrounded by a crowd of suppliants. When Oedipus asks for a report he answers in vague terms, calculated to produce a sense of relief in the minds of the crowd without revealing the nature of the oracular message.[33] This is met by a demand from Oedipus for the exact terms of the message (*toũpos*, 89): the word Oedipus uses can mean either "word" or "hexameter line," the usual medium of Apolline response.[34] Creon must drop hints and speak bluntly: "If you wish to hear it with these people near, I am ready to speak, or, if not, to go inside" (91-2). There is surely a touch of contempt in *tônde plêsiazontôn*, "with these people near"; Creon did not expect to find Oedipus outside the palace with a crowd of suppliants round him, and the words suggest pointedly that Creon would prefer to discuss the matter in private.[35] But Oedipus rejects the suggestion. "Address yourself to all" (*es pantas auda*, 93). And the reason he gives is that the sorrow he feels is more for his people than for himself: "It is for these people" (he pointedly repeats Creon's slightly contemptuous designation) "that I mourn, rather than for my own life" (*tônde*, 93).

Later, at the height of his rage, he yields to the chorus' entreaties to spare Creon, even though he believes this yielding endangers his own life or at least his power. "Let him go then, even if I have to lose my life for it, or be cast out . . ." (669-70). He yields out of respect for the people's pitiful plea not to make an already terrible situation worse.

This is indeed a democratic temper, as the scholiast long ago remarked: "the character of Oedipus is that of a lover of the people and one who takes measures for the common interest."[36] But there is another side, also characteristically democratic, to this strange *tyrannos*: he is quick to suspect a plot. His reaction to the story of Laius' murder is to suspect political intrigue. Ironically, in the light of later developments, he disregards the account that Laius was murdered by a band of brigands, attributes it to one single brigand (*lêistês*, 124)

25

and asserts that the brigand would never have dared assassinate a king unless prompted and paid by someone in Thebes. This comment, as the scholiast points out, is a hit at Creon; [37] Oedipus already suspects that the murder of Laius may turn out to be the work of conspirators at Thebes, and the only answer to the question *cui bono?* is Creon. Oedipus' mind is already prepared for the accusation he is later to fling at Tiresias and Creon. His arrival at Thebes long ago was an unexpected obstacle to their plans then and they are seizing the occasion of the plague and the oracular response to shield themselves and put their original plan into execution. These suspicions, though in fact ill-founded, are not wildly absurd; every Athenian in the audience would from his own political experience have seen their logic and appropriateness. [38] In the same suspicious mood he reacts to Tiresias' refusal to speak; this is the confirmation of his feeling that Creon was at the bottom of the murder of Laius. He is always conscious of the envy which his eminence and his gifts arouse, [39] and quick, when things go wrong, to find a conspiracy against him. By the time Creon comes to defend himself Oedipus has already in his own mind tried Creon, found him guilty, and sentenced him to death. He can even suspect, much later, that Polybus' death is not a natural one; "Did he die by treachery . . . or disease?" he asks the messenger (*doloisin*, 960). He thinks naturally in political terms: his intelligence probes every situation to see in it political causes.

Such a man, fully conscious of his worth as a ruler, secure in his self-confidence and the admiration of his subjects, intelligent, capable of deliberation and used to thinking in political terms, is not easily provoked to anger. But it is to be expected that once he is, his anger will be a terrible thing. Such an expectation is not disappointed in the case of Oedipus; his anger is more terrible than any one could expect. It is an anger that knows no bounds, a force that nothing can arrest or control until it has spent itself. It is not easily provoked, as the scene with Tiresias makes clear, and it arises in the first place from Oedipus' devotion to the city: he is shocked at Tiresias' refusal to give advice. The manner of Tiresias' refusal is provocative enough: he announces that he has knowledge but regrets that he has come, bids Oedipus send him home again, tells Oedipus he is speaking to no purpose, that both he and the people are ignorant, that he will never speak, that Oedipus' questions are a waste of time, that he will learn nothing. And each statement contains a hint that something is wrong with Oedipus. It is enough, as Oedipus says, to make even a stone angry. But his anger is slow to develop. His first answer is to comment on the prophet's lack of spirit; he then reproves him for his impropriety and lack of love for the city. He next associates himself with the chorus as a suppliant in an entreaty to Tiresias to help them, an abject appeal: "We prostrate ourselves before you," he says, *proskynoumen* (327), a hard word for Oedipus to utter.[40] A further refusal provokes a sharp rebuke, intended to bring Tiresias to his senses; his silence can only be interpreted as betrayal of the city. And when this is met with an even more categorical refusal, he at last breaks out into abuse. "You lowest of the low . . ." (334). Tiresias cuts the discussion short: "I shall say no more" (343). But he adds some final words which are a mistake; and they give us a measure of the unpredictable violence of Oedipus' anger. Tiresias challenges him to do his worst: "In answer, if you like, rage in the wildest anger you can muster" (343-4). He is prepared for anything; nothing Oedipus says will wring out of him one word more.

Prophet though he is, he has not foreseen the consequences. Oedipus' furious reply is to accuse Tiresias of responsibility for Laius' death. It is so unexpected that Tiresias forgets his resolution and flings the accusation back in Oedipus' face. As he says later, Oedipus has made him speak against his will (358). This rage of Oedipus, once aroused, flames into a fury that astounds even those who are prepared for the worst. It is not easily extinguished. It rages more and more fiercely, and soon, provoked again,[41] it associates Creon with Tiresias as a plotter against Oedipus' mastery in Thebes.

Tiresias is not an appropriate target for retaliation; Oedipus treats him with contempt (445-6) but disclaims any intention of punishing him (402). Creon, however, has no such immunity as Tiresias; he is neither old, nor blind, nor a prophet, and in the next scene the anger of Oedipus blazes fiercely against him. The intervening time (created by a choral stasimon) has afforded Oedipus time to reflect, to review the case against Creon, to find him guilty and decide on his punishment. The anger, instead of subsiding, finds logical grounds for its existence and determines action. "You are revealed as my murderer" (534), is his greeting to Creon when he comes to justify himself. He will accept no argument from Creon, whose long sophistic defense leaves him unaffected. He must act faster than the conspirators. And he has condemned Creon not to exile but to death (623). This is fast action indeed. It is only avoided by Jocasta's intervention and the appeal of the chorus. And when Oedipus finally yields, he yields sullenly, maintaining his hate for Creon. He accuses the chorus of disloyalty (687-8), and turning to Jocasta, tells her the story, expressing his greater respect for her than for the people in terms that forcibly recall his previous preference of the people to Creon. "I yield in pity not to Creon's appeal but to yours," he had told the chorus then; and now, "I have more respect for you, lady, than for these people" (700).[42] His anger subsides slowly; such natures, as Creon says, are most painful for themselves to bear (674-5). And he has reason to feel bitter. For the first time his independent swift action has met a check: he has found himself isolated, and forced to give up the project on which he had decided. He does not recover his confidence and energy until the great news of the death of Polybus is brought by the Corinthian messenger, and he is able to renew the search, this time not for the murderer of Laius but for the secret of his own birth.

Such is the character of Oedipus: he is a great man, a man of experience and swift courageous action, who yet acts only after careful deliberation, illuminated by an analytic and demanding intelligence. His action by its consistent success generates a great self-confidence, but it is always directed to the common good. He is an absolute ruler who loves and is loved by his people, but is conscious of the jealousy his success arouses and suspicious of conspiracy in high places. He is capable of terrible, apparently ungovernable anger, but only under great provocation, and he can, though grudgingly and with difficulty, subdue his anger when he sees himself isolated from his people.

III

In the relation between this character and the plot, between the nature of the hero and the actions which produce the catastrophe, we shall expect, according to Aristotle's canon, to find the key to the tragic process. From what aspects or aspect of the hero's character do the decisive actions spring? And can that aspect or those aspects be termed a fault (*hamartia*)?

The important initial decisions, those which precede the quarrel with Tiresias, are all traceable to Oedipus' great qualities as a ruler, his sense of responsibility for his people, his energy and intelligence. It is because he possesses these qualities that he sends Creon to Delphi, orders him to report the result of his mission in public, accepts the command of the oracle, pronounces the curse, sends for Tiresias, and refuses to drop the inquiry when Tiresias suggests that he should. In all this there can be no question of *hamartia* in any sense of the word except "mistake," and that, apart from the fact that it certainly is not Aristotle's meaning,[43] is irrelevant here, because from the point of view of avoiding the catastrophe every single action of Oedipus is equally a mistake.

With the Tiresias scene the anger of Oedipus comes into play. It springs, however, from this same sense of public responsibility, in the light of which Tiresias' refusal to speak seems shocking, and, as we have seen, it is not easily provoked. The angry onslaught on Creon stems from the same anger, but the important fact about this outburst is that he does spare Creon, against his own judgment, at the request of Jocasta and the chorus, an action which illustrates the flexibility and democratic temper of his rule.

His refusal to follow Jocasta's advice—that he should not send for the shepherd on whose account of Laius' murder his hope now rests—is recognizably the product of his intelligence, which will accept nothing incomplete, nothing untested, only the full truth. And his second refusal to accept the same advice offered by her at a later and more terrible moment springs not only from his intelligence but from a new and magnificent hope, born of new knowledge which would have terrified any other man. In this decision, as in the other two cases where he refuses to accept the situation as it is and insists on pressing the search for the truth, he is most himself. He has never been satisfied with half-measures and will not now retreat from his own severe standards. The man whose intelligent and courageous action made him the envy of his fellow men will not accept a life based on willed ignorance; he cannot inhabit a world of uncertainties but must re-establish the intellectual clarity in which he has always existed. He will be himself still, or nothing.

From this analysis of the relation between the hero's character and the plot it results clearly that though the hero's character is causal, its operation in the plot does not fit the Aristotelian formula. For the actions of Oedipus which produce the catastrophe stem from all sides of his character; no one particular action is more essential than any other; they are all equally essential, and they involve not any one trait of character which might be designated a *hamartia* but the character of Oedipus as a whole. The catastrophe of Oedipus is a product not of any one quality of Oedipus but of the total man. And the total man is, to use Aristotle's phrase, more good than bad. The decisive actions are the product of an admirable character; with the possible exception of his anger (and even that springs initially from his devotion to the city), their source is the greatness and nobility of the man and the ruler. Which makes the play correspond fairly closely to Aristotle's description of what tragedy should avoid: " the spectacle of a virtuous man brought from prosperity to adversity —this moves neither pity nor fear: it merely shocks us." [44]

It shocks us especially in the case of Oedipus because the catastrophe is one of such tremendous proportions. The catastrophe consists of Oedipus' recognition of his true identity, but this constitutes in itself a reversal of the most fearful kind. The catastrophe of the play is an example of what Aristotle defined as the best type, reversal combined with recognition; perhaps it would be truer to say that the catastrophe of the *Oedipus Tyrannus* is the basis of the definition. *Peripeteia,* " reversal," Aristotle defines as *eis to enantion tôn prattomenôn metabolê,*[45] a phrase which, because of the ambiguity of the word *prattomenôn*, has been taken to mean either "a change of the [hero's] situation into its opposite," that is, a complete reversal of fortune, or "a change of the action into its opposite," that is, the result of the action appearing as the opposite of the actor's intention. Surely the phrase has both meanings, for Aristotle proceeds to explain it by giving two examples, which aptly illustrate each one a different meaning of the phrase but cannot both be made consistent with either one or the other.

In the case of Oedipus the *peripeteia* is both a reversal of situation and a result of action contrary to the actor's intention. It is a reversal of situation as complete as may be imagined: from *tyrannos* whose phrase is *arkteon* (628), "I must rule," to subject whose phrase is *peisteon* (1516), "I must obey"; from wealth to beggary, as Tiresias puts it (455); from "best of men," *brotôn arist'* (46), to "worst of men," *kakiston andr' eme* (1433); from sight to blindness (454); from fame (*kleinos*, 8) and highest honor (*megist' etimathês*, 1203) to utter uncleanliness—he is an *agos* (1426), a source of pollution which must be covered up (1427).[46] And the production of a contrary result is the essence of Oedipus' action in the play: he undertakes the search for the murderer to protect himself, to benefit himself (*emauton ôphelô*, 141), to cleanse himself from the general pollution in which, as a Theban, he is involved (138), with the result that he destroys himself; he curses and excommunicates the unknown murderer, with the result that he is himself cursed (*araios hôs êrasato*, 1291) and excommunicated (*apesterês' emauton*, 1381). After the *peripeteia* the farseeing rich autocrat is a blind powerless beggar, the most honored man in Thebes an exile and polluted outcast. He has brought it about himself, and the actions which produced these results proceed from a character which is in almost all respects admirable. It is shocking, because it seems to suggest that what he does and suffers is meaningless. And tragedy is, among other things, an attempt to penetrate the mystery of human suffering.

I V

If the meaning does not lie in the action of the tragedy, it must be in the initial situation. And in this there *is* an element outside the character and action of Oedipus which plays an important part. The actions of which Oedipus at last discovers the true nature were predicted. What he discovers in the play is not only that he is his father's murderer and his mother's husband, but that he has long ago fulfilled to the letter the prediction which he thought he had so far dodged, and which, at the height of his hope, he thought he had escaped forever. The prediction was made twice: once to his father Laius [47] (and of this he at first knows nothing, and when he does know he cannot connect it with himself), and once to him in person, when as a young man he consulted Delphi about his birth. The problem of fate does enter here, not as a factor detracting from the dramatic autonomy of the play, for Sophocles has carefully excluded it from the action, but as a fundamental problem posed by Oedipus' life as a whole. In the solution of this problem must lie the tragic meaning of the play.

The problem needs to be sharply defined, for the English word *fate* covers a multitude of different conceptions. It does not correspond exactly to any particular Greek word; [48] it is in fact a word which is for the modern consciousness a con· venient way to summarize, and often to dismiss, a complex of subtly differentiated Greek conceptions of the nature of divine guidance of, and interference in, human life.

For Sophocles and the fifth century the problems of human destiny, of divine will and prediction, presented themselves in a bewildering variety of subtly different forms. The shaping of human destiny by divine power might be presented in different ways, with different resulting ideologies, or it might be rejected altogether. Even if we omit the philosophers (who present a rich variety of discussion),[49] and limit ourselves to the presentation of the problem in Sophocles' fellow tragedians and his friend Herodotus, we are confronted with a bewildering variety of irreconcilably different views.

The effect of divine will on human action might be presented, to take an extreme case first, as determining, that is, fully causal. The human beings act as they do *because* a god has so willed it. In the *Hippolytus* of Euripides,[50] for example, the goddess Cypris determines the outcome of the extremely complicated action of the human characters; not only does she determine the outcome but she creates the initial situation too. This is an extreme case (and in that typical of Euripides), for the possibility of dramatic excitement seems to have been excluded from the start; but the excitement of the action exists nevertheless, because Aphrodite does not inform the human beings involved of her intentions for the future nor her responsibility for the past. The drama is thus played out by characters who are under the illusion that their will is free; the audience sees the apparent unpredictability of their frequent changes of mind in the framework of Aphrodite's predetermination of the outcome.

In this instance the determining power has nothing to do but wait for the human beings to create, without realizing what they are doing, the pattern of its own will; there is no need for specific interference, for the result is predetermined as a whole. But there are also cases in which the human being falls short of or exceeds the divine intention, so that the deity must interfere to correct the course of the action. Xerxes in Herodotus,[51] for example, after deciding to invade Greece, yields to the influence of Artabanus and announces the cancellation of the expedition. He is then threatened by an apparently divine figure which appears to him in a dream, and this persistent visitation manifests itself to Artabanus, too, when at Xerxes' request he puts on the royal robes and lies on the royal bed. Although Xerxes and Artabanus interpret the dream as a favorable injunction to invade Greece, this is clearly a case of intervention to keep the human beings involved on the path of the divine will—which is that the Persians shall suffer defeat in Greece. In this case the human beings fall short of the divine intention and must be spurred on; [52] but the process may work also in reverse fashion, as in the *Ajax* of Sophocles where Athena intervenes to prevent an overfulfilment of the divine will. She makes Ajax temporarily mad, so that instead of killing the Achaean chieftains, which was his intention when sane, he kills and tortures captured cattle, thus ruining himself (which was the divine intention) without killing Agamemnon, Menelaus, and Odysseus.

The external power might predetermine, with or without direct interference; it might also merely predict. This is, it is true, a form of intervention, for the human being to whom the prediction is imparted may be affected in his decisions by the prediction (though in Herodotus there is at least one case where the god makes the prediction not to the person concerned but to others: Herodotus vi. 19). Yet this is an entirely different way of presenting the problem, for it leaves the individual concerned a large measure of free will; the prediction is not fully causal, as the predetermination, with or without incidental interference, is.

Prediction might take the form of oracular utterance, portent, or dream. These last two are clearly dependent on interpretation. That is to say, the human being has freedom to understand or misunderstand the prophecy. So Croesus misunderstood the Delphic oracle and crossed the Halys; [53] Apollo's rebuke—that he should have enquired a second time for clarification of the oracle [54]—implies that he was free to understand it. So the Magi of Xerxes misinterpreted the eclipse of the sun as a portent of Greek defeat,[55] and Cyrus misunderstood the dream about Darius that came to him in the country of the Massagetae.[56] It is possible that an oracle may be both understood and misunderstood at the same time; different people interpret it different ways, as happened to the famous oracle about the wooden walls of Athens.[57] The person concerned may not trouble himself to interpret the divine sign at all, as Xerxes disregarded the portent of the mare that gave birth to a hare: "although it was easy to guess the meaning of this," says Herodotus, "Xerxes ignored it." [58] Or the sign may be clearly and correctly interpreted, as in the case of the portent seen by Hippocrates, father of Pisistratus, and deliberately disregarded.[59]

In the case of oracular responses which are clear enough to need no interpreters (a category which Herodotus singles out as especially worthy of respect),[60] a similar variety of effect and human reaction may be observed. For one thing the oracle may offer alternatives, thus specifically leaving the responsibility of choice to the human being concerned.[61] Such was the oracle given to the Spartans at the beginning of the Persian War: either Sparta would be razed by the barbarians or the Spartan king should perish.[62] This oracle is mentioned by Herodotus as the main factor in Leonidas' decision to fight to the death at Thermopylae.[63]

But if the oracle was a clear prophecy and offered no alternatives it still did not operate as a determining factor, for if it were unacceptable to the human consultant it could be disregarded, and even forgotten. So the Lydian kings, particularly Croesus, the one most concerned, paid no attention to

36

the Delphic prophecy that vengeance would come for the Heraclid dynasty in the fifth generation from Gyges,[64] and the Euboeans neglected the oracle of Bakis which warned them to remove their cattle when a foreign-speaking man threw a rope yoke over the sea.[65] The prophecy of the Athenian Lysistratus was forgotten by all the Greeks, but was fulfilled, Herodotus says, after the battle of Salamis.[66]

A prophecy unqualified by alternatives, even if taken seriously, might mistakenly be regarded as fulfilled by circumstances which are not the real fulfilment at all, as in the case of Astyages in Herodotus,[67] who is wrongly advised by the Magi that his dream has been fulfilled by the symbolic kingship assumed by the young Cyrus in play, and accepts their advice. Similarly Oedipus in Sophocles' tragedy suggests, but without taking it too seriously, that the prophecy that he would kill his father has been fulfilled by the death of Polybus his supposed father, through yearning for his self-exiled son. " He is dead and buried . . . and I here in Thebes did not put my hand to the sword, unless he died through longing for me. In that sense you could call me responsible for his death " (967-70).

The prophecy might mistakenly be considered fulfilled " in some indirect and figurative sense ";[68] or it might actually be so symbolically fulfilled, contrary to the recipient's grandiose expectations. So Hippias' dream of sexual union with his mother was fulfilled, not, as he expected, by his recapture of Athens, but by the loss of a tooth which fell on Attic soil,[69] and similarly the oracle to Cleomenes that he would take Argos was fulfilled by his destruction of the grove named Argos, not the city.[70]

Finally the recipient of the oracle might understand the prophecy perfectly and, instead of disregarding it, might attempt to defy it and prove it false. Mycerinus of Egypt received a prophecy from Boutopolis that he would live only six years. He turned the nights into days, lighting lamps and feasting every night, so that his six years should be actually twelve, and he did this, says Herodotus, " to prove the oracle false." [71] In a sense he may be said to have succeeded, and it is remarkable that Herodotus makes no comment except to state his aim and describe his method.

Not only does prediction assume many forms and produce many different reactions in human beings, it also varies greatly in its relation to the divine will. Apollo may prophesy something imposed on him by destiny against his will, as in the case of Croesus; he tries to change it and does actually succeed in postponing Croesus' disaster for three years.[72] Usually Apollo predicts events which represent not his own will but the will of his father Zeus, and in the *Oresteia* of Aeschylus he demonstrates that in this particular case he himself does not fully understand the will of Zeus, for his own action is a contributing factor to a solution which he himself did not clearly envisage.[73] Often the relation of the prophecy to the divine will is simply left undefined; it is a mystery which can only be guessed at from the particular circumstances of its delivery and fulfilment.

This summary exploration of the many different ways in which the working of the external factor could be viewed is enough to show that the particular frame chosen by the dramatist is highly significant for the meaning of his work. And in the *Oedipus Tyrannus* Sophocles has chosen to present the terrible actions of Oedipus not as determined but only as predicted, and he has made no reference to the relation between the predicted destiny and the divine will. The divine will is represented in the play by the prophecy and by the prophecy alone.

The foreknowledge of Oedipus' actions possessed by the gods does not detract from the independence of Oedipus' actions in the play, since it does not affect the decisions which produce the catastrophe. But this foreknowledge, made objective in the form of a prophecy, does affect the actions of Oedipus before the play begins. It does not however, entirely negate the independence of those actions. For, as is clear from the examples quoted above, prophecy, in the Greek view, far from excluding free human action actually requires it. The prophecy allows for the independent action of the recipient; the fulfilment of the prophecy results from the combination of the prophecy with the recipient's free action.

Logically, divine foreknowledge and human free will cannot exist together, yet the Greek view of prophecy admits the existence of these two mutually exclusive factors, and of course the Christian view has to embrace this same illogicality. It is indeed, by the admission of no less an authority than St. Augustine, " the question which torments the greater part of mankind, how these two things can fail to be contrary and opposed, that God should have foreknowledge of all things to come and that we should sin, not by necessity, but by our own will." [75]

The problem faced by Christian thought is, it is true, different; it is to reconcile human free will with divine prescience rather than prediction, for God, as Christians understand Him, does not predict the future to mankind. But there was a time when He did. In the New Testament, in all four Gospels, there is a story of a prophecy made by God to a man and its fulfilment. In the account given by St. Matthew are to be found the classic elements of a Greek oracular story: it contains the prophecy of Jesus given directly to the man concerned, his refusal to accept the prophecy, his unconscious fulfilment of it, and his terrible dramatic awakening to the fact that the prophecy has come true. The man is the Apostle Peter, and here is the story:

Jesus said unto him, Verily I say unto thee, that this night, before the cock crow, thou shalt deny me thrice. Peter said unto him. Though I should die with thee, yet will I not deny thee. . . .

Now Peter sat without in the palace: and a damsel came unto him saying, Thou also wast with Jesus of Galilee. But he denied before them all, saying, I know not what thou sayest. And when he was gone out into the porch, another maid saw him, and said unto them that were there, This fellow was also with Jesus of Nazareth. And again he denied with an oath, I do not know the man. And after a while came unto him they that stood by, and said to Peter, Surely thou also art one of them, for thy speech bewrayeth thee. Then began he to curse and to swear, saying, I know not the man.

And immediately the cock crew. And Peter remembered the word of Jesus, which said unto him, Before the cock crow, thou shalt deny me thrice. And he went out, and wept bitterly.[76]

No one, so far as I know, has ever suggested that Peter's will was not free, that he was " fated " to deny his Master.

But the case of Oedipus is not strictly comparable. The god's predictions do have an important influence on the suffering and action of Oedipus. The first prediction, made to Laius,[77] influences him to expose his three-day-old son on the mountain in order to avoid his own predicted death at the child's hands. The second prediction, made to the son, influences him to turn away from Corinth towards Thebes and inspires in him a fear which he carries always with him, which he must constantly dominate if he is to live as other men do. Yet the effect of the prophecies is only part of the process. The prophecies, through the reaction of Laius and Oedipus against them, produce the situation which makes Oedipus' later actions and suffering possible; but what makes them certain is the character of Oedipus himself. The external factor and the independent human being work together to fulfil the prophecy.

The character of Oedipus in action in the present time of the play makes plausible and explains his actions in the past; it does this with especial force since one of the purposes of Oedipus' present action is precisely to reconstruct and understand his past. The discovery of the past in the present action of the play explores the area of the given situation, which Sophocles has excluded as a causal factor in the action itself; the character of Oedipus is shown to be a consistent whole—he was the same man then as he is now and will be later. The actions which fulfilled the prophecy are clearly seen as springing from the same traits of character which lie behind the action that reveals the prophecy's fulfilment. He was always the man of decisive action: the priest addresses him as " savior " because of his energy (*prothymias*, 48) in former time, and refers to his liberation of the city from the Sphinx: " you who came and liberated the city." In Oedipus' acceptance of the challenge of the Sphinx the great qualities of the hero of the play were all displayed. It took courage, for the price of failure was death; it required intelligence: *gnômêi kurêsas*, says Oedipus, " I found the answer by intelligence "; and it needed also a tremendous self-confidence. It was an action which saved the city—" in the hour of testing he was the city's delight," (*hadypolis*, 510)—so the chorus celebrates his claim to the mastery in Thebes. The intelligence that will not be satisfied with half-measures or politic ignorance is seen in his refusal to accept his supposed parents' attempt to smooth down his anger at the indiscreet revelation of the drunken guest; even then he demanded clarity, he had to know the truth, and went to Delphi to find it. His killing of Laius and his followers

in any terms outside themselves would be a spectacle too terrible to contemplate. He would be simply a hideous product of erratic circumstances, comparable to a biological sport, a freak of nature, a monster. His incest and parricide would be as meaningless as the indiscriminate mating and killing of the birds and beasts; [79] his cry of agony an echoless sound in an indifferent universe. Fortunately for his sanity, and ours, there *is* an echo; what he has done can be referred to something outside himself, indeed outside all human understanding —the prophecy. The existence of the prophecy is the only thing that makes the discovery of the truth bearable, not only for us but for Oedipus himself. In fact the prophecy, which as the expression of fate is often supposed to detract from the play's tragic impact, is the only thing that makes it possible to consider the *Oedipus Tyrannus* tragedy in any sense of the word. The hero's discovery of his own unspeakable pollution is made tolerable only because it is somehow connected with the gods. The man who was the archetype of human magnificence self-sufficient in its intelligence and action has now only one consolation in his lonely shame—the fact of divine prescience demonstrated by the existence of the original prophecy.

The play is a terrifying affirmation of the truth of prophecy. Oedipus at the beginning of the play is a man who has apparently defied the most dreadful prophecy ever made to and about a human being; the man who was promised intolerable pollution sufficient in itself to make him an outcast is the splendid and beloved *tyrannos* of a great city. Oedipus at the beginning of the play is a Mycerinus who has attempted to prove the oracle a liar, apparently with complete success; the catastrophe consists of the revelation that the prediction has been fulfilled long since. The play takes a clear stand on one

43

of the intellectual battlegrounds of the fifth century—the question of the truth or falsehood of prophecy.

This was at the time the play was first performed a very live question indeed. Sophocles' friend Herodotus, critical and open-minded as he was, held firm to the belief that prophecy was a revelation of the divine will, and always fulfilled. "I cannot say that there is no truth in prophecies, or feel inclined to call in question those prophecies that speak clearly when I think of the following," he says, referring to the prophecy of Bakis about Salamis, and after quoting the prophecy he continues, "I neither venture myself to say anything against prophecies, nor do I approve of others impugning them." [80]

But the emphasis of the statement reveals that the speaker is making a polemical claim. The validity of prophecy was no longer taken for granted in Periclean Athens. In Thucydides we can see the opposite point of view. Thucydides does not even argue the point—he assumes that prophecies are worthless; the keen sarcasm of his comments on the old oracle about the Dorian War and the plague or famine that was to accompany it,[81] like the comment on Nicias (that he was too much influenced by "inspired prophecy and that kind of thing"),[82] reflect a tired cynicism that takes prophecy to be what Alcibiades at Sparta called democracy, "an acknowledged folly." [83] Against Herodotus' defense of prophecy must be placed Thucydides' general statement about the many oracles that were current in the Athens of the Peloponnesian War [84]— that only one of them was fulfilled, a prophecy that the war would last twenty-seven years. "This was the only one that in the event justified those who rely on prophecies." [85]

Thucydides is not alone in this attitude. The plays of Euripides are full of fierce attacks on human prophets who set themselves up as divine mouthpieces,[86] and, though his Tiresias in the *Phoenissae* draws a distinction between human and divine prophecy,[87] asserting that Apollo alone should prophesy, his *Ion* is a remarkably irreverent treatment of Apollo the prophet himself.[88] The philosophical attack on prophecy is more radical; the critical rationalism of Protagoras, with his appeal to human intelligence as the criterion of reality, abolishes prophecy as an incidental feature of the abolition of the supernatural as a whole. "Man is the measure of all things: a measure of the existence of the existent, and the nonexistence of the nonexistent." [89] Antiphon the sophist could reply to the question, "What is prophecy?" with the answer, "the guess of an intelligent man"; [90] and this is not very different from the conclusion of the Euripidean messenger in the *Helena*— "the best prophet is intelligence and good counsel." [91]

The attack on individual professional prophets found an echo even in the minds of the most devout, for, as is clear from Euripides and Aristophanes alone,[92] Athens during the Peloponnesian War was plagued with degenerate exponents of the prophetic art, men who were in the business for money and who carefully shaped their prophecies to fit the desires of their customers. In fact it is this contemporary situation which makes thoroughly understandable Oedipus' furious reaction against Tiresias; the use of prophets in political intrigue was perfectly familiar to the Athenian audience,[93] and the Athenians themselves in 413 B. C. turned in fury upon the prophets who had foretold the conquest of Sicily.[94] Most sensible men, even if they fully accepted the religious view of human life as subject to divine control, must have been disgusted by the cynical excesses of professional prophets. But to deduce from the demonstrable bad faith of charlatans the falsity of prophecy as a whole was a further step which few were willing to take, for the truth of divine prophecy was a fundamental assumption of that combination of ritual cult and heroic literature which served the Greeks as religion. Any attack on this sector of the religious belief was an offensive against the whole front. And this was in any case the decisive sector. "The real clash," says Nilsson, "took place between that part of religion which interfered most in practical life and with which everyone came in contact every day, namely, the art of foretelling the future, and the attempts of natural philosophy to give physical explanations of celestial and atmospheric phenomena, of portents, and of other events." [95] The question at issue in the debate was not just the truth or falsehood of prophecy, but the validity of the whole traditional religious view.

The Sophoclean play presents the issue in precisely these terms. After Jocasta, to her satisfaction and that of Oedipus, proves that the prophecy about Laius' son has not been and can now never be fulfilled, and on this basis urges him to reject Tiresias' accusation in spite of the terrible indications that Tiresias may have been right, the chorus, which previously backed Oedipus against Tiresias, abandons the *tyrannos* and his wife, presenting the issue in terms of the truth or falsehood of the religious view as a whole. "If these things [i. e. the prophecy of Apollo and the actions of Laius' son] do not turn out to correspond exactly [*harmosei*] so that all mankind can point to it, I shall no longer go in reverence to the inviolable center of the world [Delphi] nor to the shrine at Abae, nor to that of Olympia" (897-903). "The old prophecies given to Laius are dying, they [Jocasta and Oedipus] are now excluding them. Apollo is not made manifest by worship, divinity disappears" (906-10). This last phrase, *errei ta theia*, is untranslatable, but clearly implies the ruin and disappearance of divine order. [96]

This is a clear statement. If the prophecy given to Laius does not correspond with reality, then all prophecy is false, Apollo dishonored, the gods a lost cause, religion meaningless. The chorus takes this so seriously that it actually calls on Zeus to fulfil the oracles (904-5), to make it come true, impossible as that now seems to them, that Laius' son kill his father and marry his mother. Terrible as this would be, it is better, they feel, than the alternative—the demonstration of the falsehood of oracular utterance and the corollary impotence or even nonexistence of the divine. For the chorus, the issue has become a test of divine power: "If irreverent action is to be respected and profitable," they sing, "why should I dance?" (895).

With this phrase the situation is brought out of the past and the myth into the present moment in the theater of Dionysus. For these words of the chorus were accompanied not only by music but, as the chorus' very name reminds us, by dancing: this is the choral dance and song from which tragedy developed, and which is still what it was in the beginning, an act of religious worship.[97] If the oracles and the truth do not coincide the very performance of the tragedy has no meaning, for tragedy is itself a form of worship of the gods. This phrase, "why should I dance?" is a *tour de force* which makes the validity of the performance itself depend on the *dénouement* of the play.[98]

V I

The play, in the simplest analysis, is a reassertion of the religious view of a divinely ordered universe, a view which depends on the concept of divine omniscience, represented in the play by Apollo's prophecy. It is a statement which rejects the new concepts of the fifth-century philosophers and sophists, the new visions of a universe ordered by the laws of physics, the human intelligence, the law of the jungle, or the lawlessness of blind chance. Indeed, the intellectual progress of Oedipus and Jocasta in the play is a sort of symbolic history of fifth-century rationalism.[99] The formal, shallow piety of Oedipus in the opening scenes is followed by the attack on the human representative of the god (Tiresias) and then by Jocasta's attack on the prophecies of the god himself. This culminates in a triumphant and contemptuous rejection of prophecy of all kinds by both Jocasta and Oedipus. The next stage is Jocasta's rejection of order of any kind, the statement that chance governs human life, that man must live haphazardly. This statement Oedipus rejects, for he is still seeking full understanding; he cannot abandon the intellectual search as Jocasta has done. But at the very moment that Jocasta knows the truth and her own ignorance Oedipus is impelled by his discoveries to the same view which she has just abandoned; what he has found out seems to confirm the truth of her belief in the dominance of chance. He proclaims himself the "son of Chance," a further development of her doctrine; the personification of chance as a goddess foreshadows the desperate creeds of later centuries. This picture of the intellectual progress of the fifth century Sophocles has ironically placed in a dramatic framework which shows it to be wrong from the start. It is as if the gods are mocking Oedipus; they watch the critical intelligence work its way through to the absolutely clear vision, to find out that the prophecy has been fulfilled all the time. The man who rejected prophecy is the living demonstration of its truth: the rationalist at his most intelligent and courageous the unconscious proof of divine prescience.

For that is what Oedipus is, a proof, a demonstration, a paradigm (*paradeigma*, 1193), as the chorus calls him in the great ode which it sings after he has made the discovery. He is an example to all mankind of the existence and authority of divine prescience and of the fundamental ignorance of man. This function of Oedipus helps to explain the character which Sophocles has given him. The demonstration of the proposition through the person of a bad man would be clearly untragic, even uninteresting; and the demonstration of it through the person of an Aristotelian hero, the good man who wrecks himself through a "fault," would obscure the issue by suggesting an explanation of Oedipus' fall in terms of human ethics. The divine demonstration needs a protagonist whose character does not obscure the meaning of his fall: the affirmation of the existence of divine prescience and the ignorance of man must not be confused by any crosscurrent of feeling that Oedipus' catastrophe can be attributed to a moral fault.

To emphasize this point Sophocles has done something very remarkable in the second half of the play. He has presented us with a ruined, blind, polluted Oedipus whose character is no different from that of the magnificent *tyrannos* of the scenes before the catastrophe. This is not due, as some intellectual historians might suggest, to the fifth century's incapacity to conceive or present change of character; it is rather an emphatic way of showing that it is not Oedipus' character which was at fault in the first place. The blind Oedipus thinks and acts still like Oedipus *tyrannos*, the elements of his character are unchanged. His character does not change, because Oedipus is not a man guilty of a moral fault. Such a man can learn from his fall, eliminate the fault, and change his character. But all that Oedipus learns—and all that he had to learn—is that he was ignorant. And that demands not a change of character but the acquisition of knowledge.

That knowledge he now possesses. It is Oedipus, not Creon, who insists on immediate obedience to the Delphic oracle which demanded the exile or death of the murderer of Laius. "You would trust the word of the god now," Creon says to him reproachfully (1445), but the ironic turn of events presents us with a Creon who wishes to consult the oracle again and an Oedipus who without demur accepts literally the original oracular utterance.[100] Oedipus has learned well what his own tortured mind and body bear witness to, the existence of divine prescience and of an order beyond human understanding.

The reversal of Oedipus is not then a meaningless calamity, but seen as a demonstration of the validity of divine prescience it runs dangerously close to the opposite extreme: it may be a calamity which has too much meaning to be tragic. Such a demonstration seems a subject more apt for tract than tragedy; it seems to call for homily or philosophic discourse as its medium rather than the drama. The dramatist who presents such a theme must avoid creating the impression that his tragic hero is a puppet manipulated by the strings of the author's intention or the god's purpose to point a moral.

No such impression is created by Sophocles' play, and this is due to two things: the greatness of the hero and the dramatic independence of his action.

Oedipus is clearly a very great man. The hero is worthy of the great purpose with which he unknowingly cooperates to produce the demonstration; his action, which must complement the prophecy in order to fulfil it and which is solely responsible for the discovery of that fulfilment, is magnificent action. The play is concerned not only with the greatness of the gods but also with the greatness of man. "The god is great," sings the chorus (872), but Oedipus can use the same word of himself, and justly. "Reproach me," he says to Tiresias, "reproach me with those things in which you will find my greatness lies" (441). He is referring to his victorious action in the past (his solution of the riddle of the Sphinx), but the adjective can be applied to his present actions too: he is if anything greater in the play than he has been in the actions which preceded it. Oedipus represents all that is intelligent, vigorous, courageous, and creative in man. In his relentless pursuit of the truth he shows his true greatness: all the powers of intellect and energy which make him a hero are exhibited in his lonely, stubborn progress to knowledge. Faced with the spectacle of this heroic action, even the most profoundly religious spectator must recoil in horror from the catastrophe to which Oedipus so energetically forces his way. The greatness of the man sets up a counteraction to the play's tremendous demonstration of the greatness of the divine. We do not want him to discover the truth. It is clear that he will, and it seems right that he should, but we do not want to see it. So deeply do we desire to see him escape that we are momentarily caught up in the mad enthusiasm of his most confident declaration: "I count myself the son of Chance, the giver of good." Sophocles composed the choral ode which follows this speech with a sure dramatic instinct and knowledge of the human heart; the chorus with its wild speculation that Oedipus may be revealed as of divine birth, perhaps even the son of Apollo (1102),[101] is hoping for a miracle that will save Oedipus from destruction, and that is how we feel too. What Sophocles has done is to make the proof of divine omniscience so hard to accept that we are emotionally involved in the hero's rejection of that omniscience. No man, no matter how deeply religious, can look on Oedipus, even when he is most ignorant and blind, without sympathy. For Oedipus represents man's greatness.

The hero's greatness is a partial counterpoise to the awful weight of the divine omniscience which he denies and tries to escape; the balance is made perfect by the dramatic autonomy of his action. Sophocles' careful exclusion of the external factor from the plot of the play is more than a device to preserve dramatic excitement: it is essential to the play's meaning. For the autonomy of Oedipus' action allows Sophocles to present us not with a hero who is destroyed, but with one who destroys himself. Not only that, but the process of self-destruction is

CHAPTER TWO: ATHENS

I

Sophocles' Oedipus is more than an individual tragic hero. It is characteristic of the Greek attitude towards man to see him not only as an individual but also as an individual in society, a political being as well as a private person. When Aristotle began his *Politics* with the famous sentence " Man is by nature a political animal," he was saying nothing new; the formula expresses an assumption so basic to Greek feeling of the fifth and earlier centuries that only the analytical spirit of a later time saw the need to state it explicitly. The action and reversal of Oedipus is presented in terms not only of the individual man but also of the society, or as Sophocles would have said, the *polis*, the city, which he represents. This aspect of Oedipus is in fact forced on our attention from the very first line of the play; Oedipus is the supreme power in the state, and, as we have seen, the motivation of many of his decisive actions is to be found precisely in his attitude towards his political responsibility. He is *tyrannos*. The attempt to understand Oedipus as man in society must begin with the difficult question raised by that title. Why does Sophocles so insistently and emphatically call him *tyrannos?* [1]

This is not the same question as that asked by one of the ancient *hypotheses*—" Why is it entitled *Tyrannos?* "—for the title by which the play is known is clearly post-Aristotelian.[2] But the title owes its origin, as Jebb points out, to the frequent occurrence of the word *tyrannos* in the text of the play.

It is of course true that this word *tyrannos* (partly perhaps because of its greater convenience for iambic meter) is often used in tragedy (especially in Euripides) as a neutral substitute for *basileus*, " king." [3] But in the Sophoclean play it is used in at least one passage with the full import of its historical and political meaning: an unconstitutional ruler, who has seized power, and generally abuses it. Jebb, who translates the word *tyrannos* and its cognates as "king," "prince," "royalty," "empire," "crown," and "throne" elsewhere in the play, comments on 873 (*hybris phyteuei tyrannon*: "Violence and pride engender the *tyrannos*") as follows: "Here not a prince, nor even, in the normal Greek sense, an unconstitutionally absolute ruler (good or bad), but in our sense a 'tyrant.'" Other passages, too, insist on the historical figure of the *tyrannos*, a despot who has won power through "friends . . . masses and money," as Oedipus himself puts it (541-2).[4] The word cannot then be considered neutral in any of its appearances in the play; it is colored by the reflections of these clear references to the traditional Athenian estimate of the *tyrannos*.

In what sense is Oedipus a *tyrannos*? There is one aspect of his position in Thebes which fully justifies the term: he is not (as far as is known at the beginning of the action) the hereditary successor to the throne of Thebes but an outsider (*ksenos*, as he says himself),[5] who, not belonging to the royal line, for that matter not even a native Theban, has come to supreme power. This is one of the fundamental differences between the historical *tyrannos* and the "king," *basileus*. Thucydides, for example, makes this distinction in his reconstruction of early Greek history: "Tyrannies were established in the cities as the revenues increased . . . previously there was kingship with fixed prerogatives handed down from father to son."[6]

This sense of the word *tyrannos* is exactly appropriate for Oedipus (as far as he understands his own situation at the beginning of the play): he is an intruder, one whose warrant for power is individual achievement, not birth. But though exact, it is not a flattering word, and Creon, whose sophistic defense later marks him as the subtle politician of the play, seems to be aware of its implications, for in the opening scene he refers to Laius, who was king, not *tyrannos*, in terms which avoid pointing the contrast between Oedipus' title to power and the hereditary title of his predecessor. "We once, my lord, had a leader [*hêgemôn*] called Laius," is his formula which avoids what might have seemed an odious comparison (103).[7]

Oedipus, in his reply, carries on this diplomatic misnomer of Laius: he refers to the power of his predecessor by a word which equates it with his own, *tyrannis* (128). Later in the play he twice calls Laius himself *tyrannos* (799, 1043), and the reason why he calls him *tyrannos* instead of *basileus* in these lines is all too clear. By this time he suspects that Laius may have been the man he killed so many years ago where the three roads meet, and it is only natural that in these circumstances he should avoid the use of a word which would invest his violent action with a darker guilt. The psychological nuance of his use of the word *tyrannos* here emerges clearly from the comparison of this situation with that in which, for the only time in the play, he gives Laius his proper title. "It was not right," he tells the chorus, "that you left this matter unpurified, the death of a good man—and a king" (*basileôs*, 257). The context explains his choice of terms. For in these lines, which follow the pronouncement of the curse on the unknown murderer, Oedipus, with terrible unconscious irony, is dwelling on the close connection between himself and Laius. "Since now it is I that am in authority, holding the powers which he formerly held . . . married to his wife . . . and if his line had not met with disaster we would have been connected by children born in common to us both . . . for all these reasons I shall fight on his behalf as if he were my father . . . seeking the murderer . . . on behalf of the son of

55

Labdacus, whose father was Polydorus son of Cadmus before him, whose father in ancient time was Agenor " (258-68). The involved irony of these lines has earned much admiring comment; their motivation also deserves attention. The resounding, half-envious recital of Laius' royal genealogy emphasizes Oedipus' deep-seated feeling of inadequacy in the matter of birth; though he claims the royal line of Corinth as his own, he cannot, in his inmost heart, be sure of his parentage.[8] And he tries, in this speech, to insert himself into the honorable line of Theban kings. "Having his powers"—his successor then; "married to his wife"—Oedipus feels himself almost legitimized by this connection,[9] and his children completely so; " we would have been connected by children "—the presence of an heir of Laius would have drawn attention to the royal blood in the veins of his own children, born of the same mother; and then, inconsistently (the typical inconsistency of deep unconscious desires thrusting themselves up violently on to the surface of rational speech)—"as if he were my father." In this context, where Oedipus' misgivings about his birth express themselves as a fantasy that he is in one sense or another of the line of Laius, Labdacus, Polydorus, Cadmus, and Agenor, it is only natural that he should give Laius his proper title, *basileus*, " king." It is what he would dearly like to be himself.

The terrible truth is that he *is* king; no man more legitimately. He is the son of Laius, direct descendant of Cadmus and Agenor. But it is only when he and all Thebes know the truth that he is finally addressed by this title. "You rose up like a fortified wall against death for my city," sings the chorus in the tremendous ode which follows the recognition; "since then you are called my king" (1202).[10] Once he was called "Oedipus, famous among all men" (8), and now "you are called my king." But this transformation from *tyrannos* to king is his reversal; the revelation that he is king is the overthrow of the *tyrannos*. The proof of his legitimacy is at the same time the exposure of his unspeakable pollution.

The title *tyrannos* has then a magnificent ironic function, but if it makes a great contribution to the complexity of the dramatic texture, it raises some problems as well. For the word meant more to the fifth-century audience than a usurper who replaced the hereditary king: the *tyrannos* was an adventurer who, however brilliant and prosperous his régime, had gained power by violence and maintained it by violence. This aspect of the *tyrannos* is emphasized when the chorus sings: "Violence and pride engender the *tyrannos*." And the succeeding sentences of this choral ode are an estimate of the origin, nature, and end of the *tyrannos* in terms of the current moral and political tradition of the last half of the fifth century.

What is the reason for the chorus' attack on Oedipus? And why does it take this particular form? According to Jebb, "the strain of warning rebuke" is suggested by "the tone of Oedipus towards Creon," but this does not seem an adequate explanation. The chorus' last word on the subject of Creon was a declaration of complete loyalty to Oedipus: "I should be clearly insane, incapable of intelligence, if I turned my back on you" (690-1). The change from this attitude to "Violence and pride engender the *tyrannos*," is clearly a decisive change; it must be due to something that has happened since the quarrel with Creon.

Not much has happened, but much has been revealed. Oedipus came to Thebes with blood on his hands, and one of the men he had just killed was a person of some importance, who rode in a carriage and was accompanied by a herald. True, Oedipus struck in self-defense, but none the less the chorus has come to know an Oedipus they had not suspected, a man of violence who can say, not without a touch of pride, "I killed the whole lot of them " (813). "Violence and pride engender the *tyrannos*." The elevation of Oedipus to the throne of Thebes was preceded by the bloody slaughter on the highway.

But this is not all. Oedipus has good reason to suspect that the man in the carriage was Laius, the hereditary king of Thebes, and the chorus is afraid that he is right.[11] If he is, then Oedipus won his power by killing the hereditary king and taking his place both on his throne and in his marriage bed—like Gyges of Lydia, one of the classic types of the *tyrannos*; Gyges is in fact the first man to whom the title is applied in extant Greek literature.[12] "Violence and pride engender the *tyrannos*"; in the case of Oedipus violence was the instrument of his accession to power.

These aspects of Oedipus' present title to power and his past actions, together with the choral ode on the *tyrannos*, clearly raise the whole issue of *tyrannis* in terms of contemporary political ideas. Why? The play cannot have been intended as an attack on *tyrannis* as an institution, for not only was *tyrannis* universally detested, it was also, by the beginning of the Peloponnesian War, a dead issue. Though he was to be a typical phenomenon of the next century, in the last half of the fifth century the *tyrannos* was a bitter memory of the past rather than a fear of the future. The Athenian assembly still opened its proceedings with the recital of prayers which included curses on those who aimed to restore the *tyrannos*, but the acknowledged irrelevancy of this antiquarian survival is emphasized by the Aristophanic parodies of the formulas employed. "If anyone kill any of the dead tyrants, he shall receive a talent as a reward," sings the chorus of *The Birds* (1074), and the herald in the *Thesmophoriazusae*, reciting the prayer for the " women in assembly," [13] proclaims a curse on " anyone who makes evil plots against the female people, or enters into negotiations with Euripides or the Persians to the detriment of the women, or plans to become *tyrannos* or to cooperate in restoring a *tyrannos*, or denounces a woman who passes off a substitute child as her own, or any slave girl who, acting as a procuress for her mistress, tells tales to her master" (334-41). In *The Wasps*, when the choleric chorus of jurymen accuses Bdelycleon of attempting to establish "tyranny" because he has prevented his father from attending court, Bdelycleon bursts out into a famous tirade. "Everything with you is tyranny and conspiracy, whether the indictment is great or small. Tyranny! For fifty years I haven't heard the word mentioned—and now it has become cheaper than salted fish. The name of tyranny rolls around the marketplace. If somebody wants perch and doesn't happen to be in the mood for sprats, the sprat-seller at the next stand says right away, 'Here's a man who does his shopping with tyranny in mind'" (488-95). The example which follows is even more ridiculous, and the final one (contributed by the slave Xanthias) grotesquely obscene. This passage (and others in the same play) shows that aggrieved and ignorant people as well as unscrupulous prosecutors made free with accusations of tyrannical ambitions, but it surely suggests at the same time that no honest or intelligent man took such accusations seriously. It also suggests that the whole subject was unsuited to the dignity of the tragic stage.

And in any case Oedipus is a figure who does not conform to the classic pattern of the *tyrannos* of the Greek tradition. The typical *tyrannos* might begin as one who shared power with others, but would soon banish or kill his coregents.[14] But Oedipus, by the admission of Creon, has for many years been ruling on terms of equality with Creon and Jocasta. Nor can the other characteristics of the *tyrannos* be found in the actions of Oedipus in the play. He does not defy ancestral laws, outrage women, or put men to death without trial.[15]

He does not plunder his subjects,[16] distrust the good and delight in the bad,[17] or live in fear of his people.[18] He is not equipped with that armed bodyguard which is the hallmark of the *tyrannos* in real life [19] and of Aegisthus, for example, on the tragic stage.[20] Oedipus has attendants,[21] but he is not a ruler who walks in fear of his people; he comes directly to them—"not through messengers," as he says (6)—he is loved, not feared. His political acts in the play are the reverse of tyrannical. He deliberately ignores Creon's hint that the oracular message should be discussed in private,[22] calls an assembly of the people of Thebes,[23] and later, on a matter which he considers vital to his own safety, the condemnation of Creon, he gives way to Jocasta and the chorus, which represents the people of Thebes. Thebes under Oedipus may be a *tyrannis*, but what it most resembles is a democracy ruled by its first citizen. What are we to make of this combination of democracy and *tyrannis*?

It must have been familiar to the Athenian audience, who were themselves citizens of just such a state. The situation calls to mind a similar contradiction which is one of the central themes of Thucydides' history of his own times. "We are called a democracy," says Pericles in the Funeral Speech (ii. 37), but he also tells the Athenians, "You hold your empire as a *tyrannis*." [24] He is repeating the phrase which, according to Plutarch, was used by his political opponents to characterize his direction of Athenian imperial policy: they claimed that "Hellas thinks herself subjected to terrible insult and violence, openly tyrannized over, when she sees that with the forced contributions she makes to the war, we Athenians gild and beautify our own city." [25] Cleon too calls the Athenian empire a *tyrannis* (Th. iii. 37), and the Athenian envoy Euphemus, addressing the people of Camarina in Sicily, speaks of Athenian imperial policy in the same terms—"for a man who is *tyrannos* or a city which has an empire, nothing is unreasonable which is expedient." [26] But this description of Athenian power is not restricted to Athenian speakers; it is also the word used by Athens' bitterest enemies. "We are allowing the establishment of a city [Athens] as *tyrannos*," the Corinthians complain at Sparta, and later in the same speech they repeat the phrase —"the city which has been set up as *tyrannos* in Greece." [27]

It is clear from these passages that the idea of Athens as the *polis tyrannos* was a commonplace both at Athens and elsewhere in the second half of the fifth century. The individual *tyrannos* had receded into the past to become a bitter memory, but he had been succeeded by the *polis tyrannos*, Athens, which had the resources and the skill, as it undoubtedly had the ambition, to become supreme master of the Greek world. In these circumstances, and the climate of feeling which they produced, the title which Sophocles has so repeatedly conferred on his hero served to provide not a historical framework, nor even a moral criterion, but a vital contemporary reference which enabled him to appeal directly to the hopes and fears of his audience not only as individuals but also as Athenians.

This suggestion, that Oedipus' peculiar *tyrannis* is a reference to Athens itself, rests on the assumption that the tragedy was conceived in terms of contemporary situations and attitudes. Such an assumption is justified not only by many incidental details in this play,[28] but also by the regular practice of Athenian tragic poets. The contemporary reference in all Attic tragedy is so obvious and insistent that the term "anachronism," often applied to details of the tragic presentation of the mythical material,[29] is completely misleading; in Attic tragedy of the fifth century anachronism is not the exception but the rule.

The majestic theological atmosphere of the Aeschylean *Eumenides*, for example, in which Olympian and pre-Olympian deities, contesting the case of the legendary hero Orestes, bring

61

to fulfilment Zeus's will that man should progress from the primitive anarchy of tribal vengeance to civilized institutions of justice—this august and ancient atmosphere is filled with political sermons on the proper internal balance of mid-fifth-century democracy and with legal procedures which are those of the fifth-century courts; the final speech of Orestes is a patent reference to the alliance between Athens and Argos which had been concluded just before the play was produced. Even the *Prometheus Bound*, with its dramatic date fixed at thirteen generations before the birth of Heracles (*P. V.* 774), and its extraordinary *dramatis personae* of whom only one is human (and she "provided with four hoofs, two horns, one tail"), is presented throughout in terms of fifth-century politics; [30] and, towards the end of the play, Prometheus is abused by Hermes as a "sophist."

This is typical of all Attic tragedy; the Athenian tragedians wrote not historical but contemporary drama. The "anachronistic" details are not careless slips, nor are they necessarily evidence of the absence of a historical viewpoint; [31] they are incidental but natural results of a fully and deliberately contemporary presentation of the mythical material. Euripides can make his Amphitryon and Lycus in the *Heracles* discuss the burning contemporary issue of the comparative value of light-armed infantry and archers [32] with the same freedom which permits Shakespeare to make a Roman tribune talk of "chimney-tops" and an eleventh-century Scottish porter refer jocularly to the execution of Father Garnet, which took place in 1606. [33] The basis of this freedom from historical verisimilitude is the same in both cases: Euripides, like Shakespeare, is thinking and writing for and about his time.

In the *Oedipus Tyrannus* this local and contemporary reference is visible at every turn. A typical example is a jarring inconsistency of speech and setting which occurs in the priest's lines early in the play. It is a geographical rather than an historical inconsistency, not an anachronism but a "metatopism." The priest of Zeus appeals to Oedipus to stop the plague before Thebes is depopulated—"for a fortification or a ship is nothing if deserted, without men to live together inside it" (56-7). Thebes had fortifications, of course, but why should the priest mention ships? Plautus could talk about the "harbor" of Thebes without shocking his Roman audience,[34] most of whom knew no more about Thebes than he did, but to an Athenian poet and audience who took the Theban setting of the play seriously the phrase would surely have a disturbing sound.[35] But it is perfectly appropriate in an Athenian rather than a Theban context: Athenian power depended on two things, fortifications (the Long Walls) and ships, and this phrase is a cliché of Attic oratory which recurs in almost any discussion of the nature and history of Athenian imperial policy and power.[36]

This is a minor but highly indicative detail; the topical and contemporary reference is unmistakable also in larger aspects of the dramatic situation which the play presents. Athens, like Thebes in the play, had suffered the ravages of plague; the terrible conditions described by the chorus in the opening stasimon must have reminded the audience not of the mythic past but the immediate present.[37] And the resemblances between Oedipus and Pericles, though it is true that they have often been exaggerated and overinterpreted, are still striking and not to be lightly dismissed. Pericles was under a hereditary curse because of the sacrilegious murder of Cylon by his ancestors, and although Pericles himself does not appear to have taken this seriously, his political opponents no doubt made good use of it: this hereditary guilt had been invoked, before Pericles' time, as an excuse for armed Spartan intervention in Athenian politics.[38] The dominance of Oedipus in Thebes, a combination of unquestioned authority and readiness to yield to public opinion, resembles that of Pericles in Athens: " first of men " the priest calls Oedipus (33), and Thucydides describes the Athenian government as " technically a democracy but in fact rule by the first man." [39] And the enemies of Pericles called him *tyrannos*. " Civil Strife *[stasis]* and old Cronos joined in union," says the comic poet Cratinus, speaking of the birth of Pericles, " and gave birth to the greatest *tyrannos*." [40] ". . . that power of his," says Plutarch, " which aroused such envy, and which had been spoken of as monarchy and *tyrannis*." [41] " His opponents," says Plutarch, " called his associates young Pisistratids, and challenged him to swear an oath that he would never become *tyrannos*, alleging that his superiority was too imposing, and disproportionate to democratic institutions." [42]

But the fact that the situation of Oedipus, and more especially his title, might well have suggested a comparison with Pericles should not be overemphasized.[43] Sophocles is not a comic poet attacking a contemporary politician as Aristophanes did Cleon in *The Knights*; these similarities are only incidental details of a basic pattern which suggests a comparison of Oedipus not to any individual Athenian but to Athens itself.

Oedipus talks about his power (*archê*, 383) in terms which vividly recall the contemporary estimates, both hostile and friendly, of the power of Periclean Athens. " O wealth and *tyrannis*," he exclaims, when he first decides that Tiresias and Creon are conspiring against him, " and skill surpassing skill in the competition of life, how much envy and hatred [*phthonos*] is stored up in you " (380-3). Wealth and skill were the two most conspicuous assets of Athens *tyrannos*. " They are provided," says Archidamus the Spartan king, warning the Peloponnesian League that Athens is a dangerous enemy, "with wealth, public and private, ships and horses and arms, and a population larger than is to be found in any other one Hellenic territory." "The memory will live," says Pericles to the Athenians, "that we are inhabitants of a city endowed with every sort of wealth and greatness." [44]

If Athenian wealth was the boast of her statesmen and the terror of her enemies, Athenian skill was the source of her commercial and naval supremacy. The Athenians were skilled in naval warfare, in siegecraft, in manufacture—in everything which required the ingenuity and adaptability of an urban population rather than the simple qualities of the predominantly rural population of her enemies. [45] It is against the dynamic of Athenian skill that the Corinthians warn Sparta at the congress of the Peloponnesian allies: "Your attitude to them is old-fashioned. As in technical and artistic matters [technês], it is always the newest development that prevails. For a community which can live in peace, unchangeable institutions are best, but when varied situations have to be met, much skilful contrivance is required." [46] Above all it is Athens' technical superiority in naval warfare which is recognized and feared by her enemies; enemy commanders cannot deny it and, to encourage their own sailors, must try to minimize its importance. "Without courage," says the Spartan admiral to his men before one of the naval battles in the Gulf of Naupactus, "no technical proficiency avails against danger . . . skill without bravery is no advantage." [47] In the discussion at the Peloponnesian congress there is a different emphasis. "As soon as we have brought our skill to the level of theirs," say the Corinthians, "our courage will give us the victory. Courage is a natural gift which cannot be learned, but their superior skill is something acquired, which we must attain by practice." [48] But Pericles has no fear that the Athenians will lose the long lead they have established in the race for technical naval supremacy. "Our enemies," he says, "will not easily acquire naval skill; even you, practicing it ever since the Persian War, are not yet masters of it . . . Naval power, like anything else, is a matter of skill; it does not allow itself to be exercised casually or as a secondary occupation, but rather itself excludes secondary occupations." [49]

The "wealth, *tyrannis,* and skill" of Athens, like those of Oedipus, arouse *phthonos,* "hatred" and "envy." "When you consider the energy and intelligence which we displayed then," say the Athenian envoys at Sparta, "do we deserve the excessive hatred and envy the Greeks feel for us because of the empire we hold?" [50] "Any one," says Pericles, "who does not possess [an empire such as ours] will envy us. To be hated and considered offensive has always been temporarily the lot of those who have felt themselves worthy to rule others. The correct decision is to accept this envy when the power involved is great." [51]

The Athenian *archê,* like that of Oedipus, is not an inherited power but something comparatively new in the Greek world, and it was won by self-exertion. Pericles proudly refers to the fathers of the Athenians whom he is addressing as men "who by their own efforts and not by inheritance gained this power and maintained it." [52] And, like the power of Oedipus, it was originally offered, not sought. "This power," says Oedipus, "which the city put into my hands, as a free gift, not something I asked for . . ." (303-4). "We did not take power by force," the Athenian envoys remind the Spartans, ". . . the allies themselves came to us and asked us to be their leaders . . . an empire was offered to us, and we accepted it." [53]

These resemblances between the Athenian supremacy in Greece and Oedipus' peculiar power in Thebes suggest that the word *tyrannos* as applied to Oedipus is part of a larger pattern, a comparison of Oedipus to Athens itself. The character of Oedipus is the character of the Athenian people. Oedipus, in his capacities and failings, his virtues and his defects, is a microcosm of the people of Periclean Athens. That such a generalized concept, the "Athenian character," was current in the late fifth century is clear from the speeches in Thucydides alone (especially the brilliant contrast between Athenian and Spartan character made by the Corinthians in the first book); and for an example of a national character portrayed on the tragic stage we have only to look at Euripides' *Andromache*, where Menelaus is clearly a hostile portrait, verging on caricature, of the worst aspects of the Spartan character as seen by the Athenians in wartime.[54] The character of Oedipus, one of the most many-sided and fully developed in all of Greek tragedy, bears a striking resemblance to the Athenian character as we find it portrayed in the historians, dramatists, and orators of the last years of the fifth century.

Oedipus' magnificent vigor and his faith in action are markedly Athenian characteristics. "Athens," says Pericles, "will be the envy of the man who has a will to action,"[55] and the boast is fully supported by Thucydides' breath-taking summary of the activity of the "fifty years." And in the same speech Pericles gives the highest praise to the kind of swift resolute action which is typical of Oedipus: "those who in the face of hostile circumstance are least adversely affected in judgment and react most resolutely with action are the most effective citizens and states."[56] The enemies of Athens, while recognizing the existence of Athenian vigor, naturally take a less favorable view of it. "Their idea of a holiday," say the

Corinthians, "is to do what is necessary," [57] and this hostile but admiring assessment of the Athenian genius ends with the famous epigram: "They were born never to live in peace themselves, and to prevent the rest of mankind from doing so." [58] This is an apt description of Oedipus in the play: his will to action never falters, and it forces Tiresias, Jocasta, and the shepherd, in spite of their reluctance, to play their parts in the dynamic movement towards the discovery of the truth and the hero's fall.

This constant activity of the Athenians makes them, like Oedipus, rich in experience, which is a source of pride to them, of comfort to their friends and fear to their enemies. "Any among you who are Athenians," says Nicias to his troops before the final battle at Syracuse, "have already behind you the experience of many wars." [59] It is to the well-known Athenian experience in naval warfare that Phormio appeals in his speech to his sailors before the brilliant naval victory in the Gulf of Naupactus. [60] Pausanias, at Plataea, called on the Athenians to take the place opposite the Persian contingent, reminding them that they alone among the Greeks had already faced Persian infantry at Marathon: "you understand them . . . we are inexperienced." [61] And the Corinthians, in their appeal to Sparta to attack Athens, call for new attitudes, pointing to the changes made by the Athenians "as a result of their great experience." [62]

Oedipus has magnificent courage, and Athenian courage was the admiration, as well as the terror, of Greece. Every Athenian speaker appeals to the tradition of Athenian bravery at Marathon, Salamis, Plataea, and a score of other engagements. The Athenians at Plataea, Herodotus tells us, claimed the left-wing position from the Tegeans on the basis of this reputation for courage: "it is our hereditary right to be always in the first place." [63] The courage Athens displayed in the Persian war was in fact the cause of the general Greek fear of Athens; the allies of Sparta, according to Thucydides, "feared the audacity which they had displayed in the Persian war." [64] The Spartans feared it too; to this fear Thucydides attributes the Spartan dismissal of the Athenian forces which they had called in to besiege the helots on Mount Ithome—"fearing the audacity and originality of the Athenians . . . they sent them away." [65] The Athenians of Pericles' time had not fallen short of this tradition of courage. The Athenian sailors, says Thucydides in his account of Phormio's naval victories, "had for a long time held this estimate of themselves, that being Athenians, they should not retreat before any superior number of Peloponnesian ships." [66] "We have forced every sea and land to open up a path to our courage," Pericles tells the Athenians in the Funeral Speech, and, according to Thucydides, the courage which after seventeen exhausting years of war inspired the Athenian attack on Sicily was the wonder of her contemporaries. [67] It was a constant feature of this courage that it seemed to be out of proportion to Athenian strength. "Our ancestors," says Pericles, "repelled the Persian with a courage greater than their resources," and his proud phrase finds a hostile echo in the Corinthian assessment of Athenian capabilities—"they have courage out of proportion to their resources." [68] Like Oedipus, they are most courageous when the situation seems worst. "We displayed the most courageous energy," say the Athenian envoys at Sparta (they are speaking of Salamis), "based on a nonexistent city and running risks for a future city which rested only on a slim hope." [69]

The speed of decision and action which distinguishes Oedipus is another well-known Athenian quality. "They are quick to form a plan and to put their decision into practice," say the Corinthians: "they are the only people who simultaneously hope for and have what they plan, because of their quick

fulfilment of decisions." [70] Like Oedipus, they prefer to anticipate rather than react: "When the Athenians realized [that
Perdiccas was about to stir up a revolt in the North] they
resolved to forestall it," says Thucydides. Their action when
the revolt of Mitylene seemed imminent was similar—"they
wished to forestall them." [71] The speed of Athenian action
was time after time an unpleasant surprise for their enemies:
two famous examples are the building of the walls after the
Persian invasion and the building of the siege wall at Syracuse
which "astonished the Syracusans, so quickly was it built." [72]
"So swiftly did they deal with the danger," says the author
of the *Funeral Speech* attributed to Lysias (he is speaking of
Marathon), "that the same messengers announced to the rest
of Greece both the arrival of the Persians and the victory of
our forefathers." [73]

Like Oedipus, the Athenians, precisely because of their own
speed of decision and action, are impatient at the slowness of
others or events. "If they do not carry out a plan they have
formed, they consider themselves deprived of something they
actually had," say the Corinthians (Th. i. 70). Herodotus
tells the story of the oracle that came to the Athenians from
Delphi, bidding them set aside a precinct for Aeacus and wait
thirty years before beginning the war against Aegina about
which they had consulted the oracle. They set aside the
precinct for Aeacus, "but," says Herodotus, "they could not
bear to hear of waiting thirty years . . . They began preparations
for retaliation." [74]

Oedipus' combination of swift action with careful reflection
is mirrored in the Athenian confidence in discussion as a
preparation for action, not, as happens with some people, a
deterrent to it. "We do not believe," says Pericles, "that
discussion is an impediment to action. We are unique in our
combination of most courageous action with rational discussion

of our projects, whereas others are either overcourageous from ignorance or made cautious by reasoning." [75]

The intelligence in which Oedipus takes such pride is another recognized Athenian characteristic. Herodotus, commenting on Pisistratus' return to power by means of a "silly trick," professes astonishment that such things could have happened in Athens, "among the Athenians, who are said to be the first of the Greeks in wisdom." [76] The Athenian orators refer to the Athenian role in the Persian wars in terms not only of courage but also of intelligence. The Athenian envoys at Sparta speak of "the energy and intelligence which we displayed then," [77] and Pericles claims that the Persian defeat was due to "intelligence rather than chance." [78] Of his own generation he makes the famous boast that "we cultivate the mind without loss of manliness," [79] and in his last speech he tells the Athenians to rely on their intellectual superiority to the enemy. "Meet your enemies not just with confidence but with contempt. Confidence may spring simply from ignorance which has been lucky, and may exist in a coward; contempt is reserved for him who has faith in his intellectual superiority to the enemy, and this is the case with us. Intelligence strengthens the courage which is based on the evenness of the chances, by adding contempt, and this intelligence trusts not in hope, which is a source of strength in desperation, but in a reasoned judgment of circumstances, which provides more reliable foresight." [80]

The magnificent self-confidence so typical of Oedipus is the dominant note of the speeches which Thucydides attributes to Pericles in the first two books of his history. The estimate of Athenian and Spartan war potentials which Pericles presents in his speech urging the rejection of the Spartan demands, as well as the panegyric of the Athenian temper and institutions in the Funeral Speech, are eloquent testimony to Athens'

unlimited confidence in its capacity to overcome all opposition
and all obstacles. Even in an Athens chastened by the plague
and the Peloponnesian invasions, Pericles can talk of Athenian
potentialities as unlimited: "The land and the sea are the two
elements which are useful to man, and of the sea you are
absolute masters, both as far as your empire extends and as
far as you wish to extend it." [81] And of the Athenians who
fell in the first year of the war Pericles says: "they assigned
to hope the invisible chance of success, but in action, where
the issue was clearly seen, they thought it right to rely on
themselves." [82] This confidence can lead the Athenians, as
it does Oedipus, to extravagant hopes. "When they profit
from an enterprise," say the Corinthians, "they think they have
gained little, compared to what is to come." [83] And, like those
of Oedipus, their hopes are strongest in the face of danger
and even of impending disaster. "In such a crisis as this,"
says Demosthenes on Sphacteria, addressing men who are about
to attack Spartan infantry on Spartan soil, "let none of you
try to get a reputation for intelligence by calculating the full
extent of the danger which surrounds us. Rather close with
the enemy in reckless hopefulness." [84] And Nicias, in even
more dangerous circumstances, before the last battle at Syracuse, tells his troops: "Even in our present situation, we must
hope. Men have been saved before this from even more
terrible straits . . . My hope of the future remains confident." [85]
"In terrible circumstances," say the Corinthians, "they are full
of good hope "; [86] it reads like a comment on the hopeful outburst with which Oedipus follows Jocasta's agonized farewell.

Oedipus, speaking of the solution of the riddle of the Sphinx,
claims that he was the amateur ("the know-nothing Oedipus,"
397) who put the professional, Tiresias, to shame on his own
ground. This resembles one of the proud claims which Pericles
makes for the citizens of the Athenian democracy. "In military

training our enemies pursue the goal of manliness by laborious exercises begun in extreme youth, while we live a life free of restraint and yet face just the same dangers as they do . . . We prefer to face danger taking things easily rather than with laborious training, with a courage which comes more from character than institutions." [87] This prized superiority of the intelligent amateur was most highly developed in Themistocles, the Thucydidean archetype of the Athenian democratic character at its best. "He was competent to form an adequate judgment even in matters of which he had no experience. . . . By native intelligence, without learning anything either before or after the event, he was the most effective judge of the immediate issue with the least deliberation." One is reminded of the estimates of Oedipus' solution of the riddle, both that of the priest—" knowing no more than us, not taught "—and that of Oedipus himself—" finding the answer by intelligence, not learning it from birds." [88]

The adaptability and versatility of Oedipus, his success in imposing himself on unfamiliar surroundings even in disastrous circumstances, all this is typically Athenian. "I sum it all up," says Pericles, "by stating that the whole city is the school of Hellas, and that the individual Athenian citizen addresses himself to the most varied types of action as a self-sufficient personality with the utmost versatility and charm." [89] The classic example of this adaptability is again Themistocles, who, exiled from Athens and driven from Greece, took refuge at Sardis. Like Oedipus at Thebes he was a foreigner (and a hated one at that), but within a year he was in a position of power. "He got as good a grasp of the Persian language as he could," says Thucydides, "and also of the customs of the country. He became a greater power with the king than any Greek before him." [90]

Oedipus' devotion to the city is another Athenian trait. " I

am a lover of the city," says Pericles,[91] and in the Funeral
Speech he calls on his fellow citizens to be lovers of the city
in stronger terms, using the word *erastae*, which suggests the
violent passion of the lover for the beloved.[92] " In their city's
cause," say the Corinthians, " they use their bodies as if they
did not belong to them." [93]

Oedipus' keen nose for a plot is so thoroughly Athenian that
the audience which saw the play may well have enjoyed the
development of his subtle suspicions.[94] An attitude such as his
was justified in the light of Athenian political experience. The
democracy was menaced from the very first days of its existence
by oligarchical plotters who did not stop short of intelligence
with foreign or even enemy powers. The shield signal to the
Persian fleet after the Battle of Marathon (whoever was responsible for it) was only the first of a long series of treacherous
maneuvers. A similar intrigue was being carried on before
the battle of Tanagra in 457 B. C. " Certain Athenians," says
Thucydides, " were secretly inviting the Spartans in, hoping
that they would put an end to the democratic régime. . . . The
Athenians had their suspicions that the democracy was to be
destroyed." [95] At the time of the Sicilian expedition the mutilation of the Hermae was immediately taken as an indication of
conspiratorial action against the democracy; the Athenians
" reacted to everything with suspicion," their mood was " savage
and suspicious." [96] Pericles was well aware of the suspicious
nature of his fellow countrymen, and at the beginning of the
war he was afraid that if his own property was spared in the
Spartan devastation of Attica he would fall under suspicion
of collusion with the enemy; he therefore announced publicly
that if his lands were spared, he would give them to the state.[97]
Under the strain of war and the plague this all too ready
suspicion became an unhealthy obsession. " The man who
offers excellent advice is suspected of doing so for private

74

profit," Diodotus complains in his speech against Cleon in the debate over Mitylene; ". . . when a man makes what is clearly a good contribution to public policy, his reward is a suspicion that in some obscure way he is going to benefit from it personally." [98]

The particular type of plotting which Oedipus suspects—a political conspiracy which uses religious pretexts and machinery —can in fact be paralleled from Athenian history. "Isagoras," says Herodotus in his account of the early struggles of the Athenian democracy, "defeated in his turn, replied with the following device. He called in Cleomenes the Spartan. . . . Cleomenes, at the suggestion of Isagoras, sent a herald to require that Cleisthenes [the opponent of Isagoras] and a large number of Athenians as well, whom he declared were under a curse, should be expelled from Athens." [99] The word which Herodotus uses to characterize Cleomenes' "expulsion of the accursed" is *agêlatein*, "to drive out the defilement," the same word exactly that Oedipus uses to describe what he thinks is the intention of Tiresias and Creon. [100] And this "device" was used again by the Spartans. Before the beginning of the Peloponnesian War they demanded the expulsion of Pericles from Athens on the same grounds. [101]

Oedipus' initial suspicion, which is the basis of the subsequent explicit and circumstantial accusations against Tiresias and Creon, springs from the belief that the murder of Laius would never have been undertaken by a single man unless he had the backing of conspirators in Thebes. "How could the brigand have shown such audacity, unless there had been some negotiations, and some money passed from here in Thebes?" (124-5). So the chorus of Aristophanes' *Wasps*, keen-scented detectors of plots, cannot believe that Bdelycleon, without some conspiratorial backing, would have kept his father from attending court: "Never would the man have had the audacity to say what he has said, unless there were some fellow conspirator." [102]

The anger of Oedipus is easily recognizable as the terrible swift anger of the Athenian people which Athenian politicians had learned to fear. Herodotus' account of the stoning of Lycidas (who proposed acceptance of the Persian overtures to Athens before the battle of Plataea), and the murder of his wife and children by the Athenian women, is a specimen of the monstrous potentialities of Athenian anger.[103] Pericles knew this temper well. "I was expecting this angry reaction," he says to an assembly exasperated by the invasion and the plague; "he wished," says Thucydides, "to reduce their angry temper to a gentler frame of mind." [104] "Pericles was afraid," says the chorus of Aristophanes' *Peace* to the Athenian audience, "fearing your nature and your habit of biting once and once only." [105] This anger raged against the suspected mutilators of the Hermae, and after the Sicilian disaster against the oracle-mongers who had predicted success.[106] Aristophanes is never tired of ringing the changes on this theme; his Dêmos (the Athenian people) in *The Knights* is described as "an old man . . . with a rude anger . . . irritable," [107] and Aristophanes refers often to an aspect of this Athenian anger which directly concerns him, that of the theatrical audience, from which, for example, the comic poet Crates suffered.[108] The Athenian jurors in *The Wasps* set off to the law court as if to war "with three days' ration of vicious anger," [109] and throughout the comedy they emphasize, as does Philocleon, this characteristic of the Athenian jury. It was well known in the law courts as well as in comedy, and there it was no joke. The defendant in the case of the murder of Herodes begs the jury to decide "without anger or prejudice." [110] "It is impossible for an angry man to make a good decision. For anger destroys man's judgment, the instrument of his deliberation." This warning is no mere rhetorical commonplace, for he has just reminded the court of the fate of the treasurers of the Hellenic League, falsely accused of emblezzlement but all (except one) condemned and summarily executed in a blaze of anger. "Their death was due to your anger rather than your judgment." [111]

But the anger of the Athenians, like that of Oedipus, could subside—sometimes, as in the case of the Mityleneans, in time to avoid violent action which they would later have regretted,[112] sometimes, as in the case of the victorious generals who failed to pick up their shipwrecked sailors at Arginusae, too late to do anything except punish those who had taken advantage of their angry mood to push them to extremes.[113]

A constant will to action, grounded in experience, inspired by courage, expressing itself in speed and impatience but informed by intelligent reflection, endowed with the self-confidence, optimism, and versatility of the brilliant amateur, and marred by oversuspicion and occasional outbursts of demonic anger—this is the character of Athens and Oedipus alike. Both the virtues and the faults of Oedipus are those of Athenian democracy. Oedipus son of Laius, a Theban mythical hero, has been transformed into an Athenian and contemporary figure. Not, however, a specific individual; the resemblances that have been pointed out to Themistocles, to Pericles, to Cleon are all minor facets of his resemblance to Athens itself, in all its greatness, its power, its intelligence, and also its serious defects. The audience which watched Oedipus in the theater of Dionysus was watching itself.

The character of the protagonist is, however, only one of the factors which combine to create the contemporary, Athenian atmosphere of the play. Another is the nature of one of the principal modes of the action. The action of the play is a characteristically Athenian process: it is a legal investigation, the identification of a murderer. Oedipus himself is comparable to Athens, the *polis tyrannos*, in all its political dynamism, its intelligence, its will to power; his action is presented in terms of the legal process, an aspect of civilized social organization in which Athens was an example to all Greece and to succeeding generations.

The proud Aeschylean claim that the civilized administration of justice began on the Areopagus in Athens, under the patronage of Athena,[114] is echoed by other voices, among them Aristotle,[115] and Attic legal procedure had developed by the end of the fifth century into the most advanced and progressive code of law and procedure, the admiration of other cities, and, for many of them, a *paradeigma*, a model and example.[116] The name of Athens, for the Greeks of the fifth century, was inseparably associated with the legal institutions, and the litigiousness, for which Athens was famous. "That's not Athens," says Strepsiades in *The Clouds* of Aristophanes, when shown his native city on a map; "I don't see any courts in session." [117] "The Athenians," says the critical author of *The Constitution of Athens*, a fifth-century antidemocratic pamphlet, "sit in judgment on more legal actions, public and private, more investigations, than all the rest of the human race put together." [118] Athenian preoccupation with legal forms, as the sarcastic tone of this comment indicates, was often carried to excessive lengths, and the Aristophanic comedies show that the Athenians were conscious of this failing, and, among themselves, always willing to listen to a joke on the subject. But they were none the less convinced of the superiority of their institutions and the principles underlying them. The statement made by the Athenian envoys at the first Peloponnesian congress before the war makes no concession to criticism on this point. "We are supposed to be lovers of litigation," they say, "because in cases involving contractual relationships with the allied cities of our empire we reduce ourselves to their level and bring the case to judgment at Athens under laws before which both parties are equal." [119] As they go on to point out, the complaint that such cases are tried at Athens admits the superior justice of Athenian rule, in that they are tried at all: "this is not a reproach that is made against other imperial powers, which are less moderate in their attitude to their subjects." There may be abuses of law in the Athenian system of imperial administration, but there is at least law to abuse.

To the outsider Athens was a city of law courts; to the Athenian citizen himself the legal process was a familiar part of his daily life to an extent which we can hardly imagine. The large juries and the long sessions, the frequency and multiplicity of public and private legal action in every imaginable sphere, and above all the absence of a professional class of lawyers and the consequent obligation to plead one's own case in person made the Athenian citizen familiar with legal procedure as a normal part of his existence as a citizen. Legal technicalities were as familiar in his mouth as household words. Almost every Athenian citizen would sooner or later serve on a jury, and, very likely, plead before one; the legal context was as native to the Athenian citizen as the political, and in both he acted not through representatives but in person.

It is in this thoroughly and typically contemporary Athenian atmosphere that Sophocles has set the action of the *Oedipus Tyrannus*. The hunt for the murderer of Laius is presented in terms of Attic private and public law. Once again the language of the poet suggests that Oedipus is a contemporary rather than a mythical figure.

The task which Oedipus undertakes at the suggestion of the oracle—to find the murderer of Laius—is one which, in the legal framework of Athenian democracy, would have involved both private legal action (for in Attic law it was the individual, not the state, which prosecuted for murder) and public, politico-legal action (for the murdered man was king of Thebes, and the oracular response makes clear not only that his murderers were Thebans [120] but also that the preservation of the city depends on their identification and punishment). Accordingly the investigation of the murder of Laius is invested by Sophocles with the current forms and formulas of both the politico-legal and the private process.

When Creon tells Oedipus (100-1) that Apollo demands action, in the form of banishment or death, against the murderers to requite the "blood which brings storm and winter on the city," Oedipus characterizes Apollo's statement and the resultant situation with a word which transfers the action out of the mythical and supernatural atmosphere springing from the Apolline response into the contemporary and practical context of Athenian politics and law. "Whose blood?" he asks. "Whose mischance does he inform us of?" [121] "Inform" (*mênyei*) is a basic technicality of fifth-century law, and its technical significance is strictly applicable to the situation presented in the opening scene of the play. An "information" (*mênysis*) was the name given to a denunciation made to the Athenian assembly of past crimes which the informant considered worthy of investigation, but could not himself prosecute, since he was not a citizen.[122] On receipt of the "information" the assembly would assess its validity, and if it was not dismissed as patently false would elect investigators (*zêtêtai*).

These investigators would offer rewards for further information, promise immunity to persons involved who were willing to denounce their accomplices, and examine witnesses. If their investigation produced a strong case against definite persons, they would hand it over to the assembly or the courts of law for further action.

In the Sophoclean play Apollo, a noncitizen, lays information [123] against the murderers of Laius (that they are to be found in Thebes) and demands their punishment, stating that the unavenged murder of Laius is the cause of the plague. Oedipus replies that the crime was committed so long ago that no trace of the criminals can possibly be found, but Creon, quoting Apollo, refutes this objection: "They are in this land, he said. What is investigated can bring capture and conviction [haloton]; what is neglected allows escape and acquittal [ekpheugei]." [124] The word translated "investigated" (zêtoumenon) suggests the investigators (zêtêtai) of Athenian procedure. Oedipus assumes their functions, and by further questioning assesses the possibility of a successful outcome. He learns that one eyewitness of the murder survived to report it to the Thebans, and he leaps to the conclusion that the murder was the fruit of a political intrigue which had its roots in Thebes itself. This conclusion confirms the information of Apollo that Thebes is the proper place to enquire and also involves Oedipus personally in the search, for his own power may be at stake. He assumes full responsibility. The investigation is launched. "I shall start over again from the beginning, and bring this matter to light" (132).

His first step is that of the Athenian investigating commission—he tries to gather new evidence by offering a reward, and, to anyone who may himself be involved, comparative immunity.[125] With the rewards he couples punishments, pronouncing a sentence of excommunication from all normal civic and domestic functions on any Theban who withholds information (236-40), a solemn curse on the actual murderer (246-8),[126] the same curse on himself if he should knowingly give the murderer shelter and on all who refuse to cooperate with his efforts to find the guilty man (269-72).

The situation, the measures taken, and the formulas used are exactly paralleled in the investigation of the sacrilegious actions of 415 B. C., as it is described in Thucydides, Andocides, and Plutarch. "No one knew who had done it," says Thucydides of the mutilation of the Hermae, "but the perpetrators were searched for by means of public rewards for information, and the assembly decreed that if anyone had knowledge of any other act of impiety, he should volunteer information about it without fear, whether he was a citizen, an alien, or a slave." [127] Oedipus' activity and authority is like that of an Athenian investigator; [128] and the first step in the search for new evidence is the calling of a witness, Tiresias the prophet.

The situation and action of the protagonist recalls the politico-legal process of denunciation and investigation, but the language of Sophocles also suggests a parallel to a purely legal process, the prosecution for murder, *dikê phonou*. Such proceedings, in fifth-century Athens, could be set on foot only by a relative (or by the owner) of the murdered person.[129] This fact gives an additional dimension to the passage (258-64) in which Oedipus emphasizes his close connection with Laius: "as if he were my father," he concludes, "I shall fight on his behalf, and go to every length in the investigation to catch the man whose hand did the deed." It is as if Oedipus were trying to establish a basis in relationship to ground his right and duty to search for and prosecute the murderer of Laius.

The curse pronounced on the murderer and the proclamation aimed at getting information correspond to the normal initial measures against "a person or persons unknown" as far as we can reconstruct them from Athenian juridical literature.[130] The next of kin made a proclamation by means of a herald, announcing the circumstances of the murder and asking for information. Such a procedure is described in detail in Plato's *Laws*, and, although that work is not a safe authority for fifth-century Attic legal procedure, the account given there is not inconsistent with the scattered references to the fifth-century process which are to be found in earlier literature. " If anyone be found dead," says the Platonic law, "and the slayer be unknown, and remain undiscoverable after careful search, there shall be the same proclamations made as in other cases, and the same interdict on the murderer. They shall proceed against him, and announce by the agency of a herald in the market place that the slayer of so-and-so has been convicted of murder and shall not set foot in the temples nor anywhere in the country of the murdered man." This is exactly the procedure (except that Oedipus is his own herald) and these are exactly the formulas of the opening scenes of the play.[131] Oedipus' curse on the murderer would remind the Athenian audience also of the normal procedure in a prosecution for murder in which the defendant was named; the accused was formally interdicted by the magistrate presiding over the preliminary trial from access to temples, sacrifices, prayers, and public places.[132]

The chorus of Thebans feels confident that the terrible imprecations of Oedipus will frighten the unknown criminal into surrender or flight (294-5), though Oedipus does not share their confidence. The arrival of Tiresias, the first witness, is greeted by the chorus with enthusiasm—" here is the one who will convict the criminal." [133] But when Oedipus' appeal to the prophet is followed by Tiresias' disturbing regrets that he has come, we find ourselves suddenly in a familiar ambience, the examination of a reluctant witness. " How dispiritedly you have come in," says Oedipus (319), and this word "come in" (*eiselêlythas*) is the technical term for "coming in to court." [134] Tiresias replies in similar language: "Send me home" (*aphes m'*, 320); the word he uses is the normal law-court term for release, acquittal, and dismissal. [135] Oedipus' answer draws on the same source: "Your proposal is illegal" (*out' ennom' eipas*, 322). [136] Tiresias' repeated refusal to speak provokes a veiled accusation of complicity—"You know, and will not denounce?" [137] "Your questioning," Tiresias replies, "is useless" (*allôs elencheis*, 333). Oedipus, as his anger mounts, now makes explicit the accusation he hinted at before: he charges Tiresias with complicity in and responsibility for the murder of Laius. The accusation is hurled back at him at once, a common phenomenon in the Attic law court where it was clearly a time-honored maxim that the best means of defense is attack. [138] But Oedipus sees more in it than a defensive reaction. The pieces are beginning to fit together in his swift and suspicious mind, and he now denounces Creon as the real inspiration of Tiresias' charges. This is followed by a passage typical of Athenian courtroom pleading. Oedipus contrasts the record of his own services to the city with that of his adversary: at the moment of supreme crisis for Thebes, the appearance of the Sphinx, Tiresias was silent; it was Oedipus who saved the city. [139]

Tiresias' terrible reply (408-28) begins with a forensic claim to an equal right to free speech: "you must make me your equal in this at least, the chance to make an equal reply. [140] For I too have power, in this respect." [141] He is no slave, he asserts, nor an alien who must be registered as a dependent of a free citizen—"I shall not be inscribed on the rolls as a protégé of Creon" (*Kreontos prostatou*, 411)—but a citizen who has the right to conduct his own defense. His defense, as so often in Attic courts, is an attack. It is a prophecy of

Oedipus' future blindness and fall, containing a series of hints at the terrible truth of his identity. Yet even in the mantic invective of the outraged seer the forensic tone can be heard. When Tiresias asks Oedipus if he knows who his parents are (415), we are reminded of the vituperation of the law court, where one of the commonest weapons of both prosecution and defense was a suggestion that the adversary was of low, illegitimate, foreign, or even servile birth.[142] The mysterious questions of 420-1—"What shall not be a haven of your cries, what Cithaeron not ring in echo?"[143]—recall the indignant rhetorical questions which are a recurrent formula of the forensic orator. "What suit would they not bring to judgment, what court would they not deceive . . . ?" asks Antiphon in the speech *For the Choreutes*; "What opinion do you think they would have of him, or what kind of a vote would they give . . . ?" asks Lysias in the speech against Agoratus.[144] Tiresias concludes by qualifying his opponent's speech as vulgar abuse (*propêlakizein*, 427), a regular device of the courtroom orator.[145] It provokes the standard reply: "Am I supposed to tolerate this kind of thing from this man?"[146] Oedipus angrily and insultingly orders Tiresias out, and the prophet's reply contains a word that defines the relationship of the two men and their situation: "I would not have come if you had not *called* me." The word he uses (*'kaleis*) is the normal legal term for "calling" a witness.[147]

When the chorus, in the second half of the following stasimon, discuss the prophet's accusations, the legal process advances to a further stage of development. Their deliberations are phrased in terms appropriate for a board of judges weighing the charge and countercharge of prosecutor and defendant.[148] They cannot decide between them—"I neither affirm nor deny" (485). But a significant development has taken place. Oedipus was the first accuser, yet the chorus considers him, not Tiresias, as the accused: they do not mention Oedipus' charges against Tiresias, but are concerned only to examine Tiresias' accusations against Oedipus. The action is moving towards a reversal; in terms of the legal mode of the action, the investigator and accuser has become the defendant.

The chorus searches for, and fails to find, a motive that would makes accusation against Oedipus plausible. "What quarrel was there between the son of Labdacus [Laius] and the son of Polybus [Oedipus]? I never learned of one in time past, nor do I know of one now" (489-93). This is of course the stuff of which murder trials are made; the prosecutor seeks to prove and the defendant to deny enmity between the victim and the accused. "What, according to them, was my motive for killing Herodes?" asks the defendant in Antiphon's famous speech. "There was not a trace of enmity between us." [149]

The chorus can find no motive to buttress the charge; its authority must rest solely on Tiresias' credibility as a prophet. They are willing to believe that Zeus and Apollo know the truth (498-500), but Tiresias, though a prophet, is only a man, and between his word and another man's there is "no true judgment" (501).[150] Against Tiresias' word must be set Oedipus' record; he was tested, and seen to be wise, and the city's delight (509-10).[151] "Therefore he shall never in my mind incur the charge of baseness." The chorus speaks like a board of Athenian judges; it reviews the evidence so far presented and rejects the case against Oedipus. But it is significant that they consider Oedipus the defendant; the accuser is now the accused.

But Oedipus has directed his accusations against a fresh target; Tiresias, he claims, is only the mouthpiece of Creon. And Creon comes on stage ready to deny the charge. "Fellow citizens, I hear that Oedipus makes dreadful accusations against me . . . [152] I am here to refute them. If he believes that I have injured him in word or deed . . . I have no desire to live out the rest of my life, subject to such a reputation " (513-19). This is the familiar tone of indignation, the introductory cliché of the Athenian defendant in all his injured innocence. " If anyone," says Aeschines," either of the spectators here . . . or of the judges, is convinced that I have done anything of the sort, I consider the rest of my life not worth living." [153]

Creon's exploratory dialogue with the chorus is interrupted by the entry of Oedipus, who savagely denounces Creon as a traitor and attempted murderer. " Have you so bold a face as to come here . . . you who are so plainly proved my murderer? " (532-4). Both the indignant protest against the opponent's boldness in appearing to argue his case and the illogical use of the word " murderer" are commonplaces of the Athenian courtroom. " I am astonished at my brother's boldness," says the prosecutor in Antiphon's speech *Against the Stepmother for Poisoning*.[154] " By these actions," says Demosthenes in the speech against Meidias, " he has become, in my opinion, my murderer." " They are planning my death by unjust means, upsetting the laws, and becoming my murderers," says the defendant in one of the forensic tetralogies of Antiphon, and his opponent replies with a hit at the rhetorical exaggeration of the cliché—" Alive and with his eyes open he calls us his murderers." [155]

In the heated exchange which follows this outburst, Oedipus questions Creon, and uses the answers to the questions to attack Tiresias on a new ground—that he did not accuse Oedipus when the initial investigation was made. Such a delay in prosecuting was always used to good advantage by the defense in an Athenian court; [156] in this case the inference is clear—it is a trumped-up charge and Creon is behind it. Creon in his turn asks permission to question Oedipus, and is told to go ahead. " Find out what you want. For I shall never be convicted as the murderer." [157] Creon's questions lead up to his famous speech in his own defense, a masterpiece of the new sophistic rhetoric; it employs the argument from motive (probability), or rather, in this case, from lack of motive. This was the most widely used forensic weapon of the period. Antiphon's *Tetralogies*, a sort of textbook for aspiring legal speakers, is a collection of ingenious arguments for and against hypothetical accusations, all based on the canon of probability. It is a remarkable coincidence that the only surviving fragment of Antiphon's great (though unsuccessful) speech in his own defense against the charge of treason [158] presents an argument exactly parallel to Creon's in the play. After dismissing many motives that might be thought to make plausible the charge of antidemocratic activity, Antiphon proceeds as follows:

> My accusers state that my profession was the writing of speeches for persons involved in lawsuits, and that the Four Hundred profited from my activities. But is it not true that under an oligarchic régime I could not exercise my profession, while under the democracy I am a power in the city, even as a private individual? That under an oligarchy my powers as a speaker would be as worthless as they are valuable under a democracy? Tell me, what probability is there in the idea that I would long for oligarchy? Do you think I could not figure this out for myself? Am I the only man in Athens who cannot see what is profitable for him? [159]

This is exactly the tone and import of Creon's argument: the down-to-earth sensible appeal of one man of the world to another—"I am not so deceived as to want anything but what is proper—and profitable" (*ta syn kerdei kala*, 595); the emphasis on the speaker's material reasons for satisfaction with

88

the existing régime—" Now I am hailed by everyone, everyone salutes me, the men who need something from you flatter me " (596-7); and on the disadvantages he would experience if the régime were changed—" If I were ruler I would have to do many things against my will " (591).

After rejecting Oedipus' accusation as unreasonable because of its psychological improbability, Creon offers something more substantial. " As a test of my statements [*tônd' elenchon*, 603] go to Pytho and enquire what the oracle said, to see if I delivered an exact account." [160] This appeal to objective evidence corresponds to the calling of witnesses in an Attic law case; Creon is in a sense calling on Apollo as a witness to his honesty. The conclusion of his speech is a miniature anthology of the clichés with which the Athenian defendant customarily padded his final appeal to the judges. " If you prove me guilty of conspiracy with the seer, kill me, and not by a single vote, but a double one, yours and mine "—so runs the beginning of Creon's appeal; " if I have acted impiously, kill me," says Andocides in his speech *On the Mysteries.*[161] " You will know the truth in time without fail, for time alone shows who is the just man," is Creon's last sentence; " Make a concession to time, with the help of which those who seek the truth of the event most successfully find it," says Antiphon in the speech on the murder of Herodes.[162]

Though the chorus approves Creon's speech and advises caution, Oedipus replies with vigorous counteraction. In a blaze of anger characteristic of Athenian assembly and law court alike he passes sentence—death. Jocasta's arrival interrupts the passionate argument which follows, and she and the chorus now combine in urging Oedipus to absolve Creon. It is to her that both parties in the argument address their pleas, as if she were a judge. " Sister, your husband Oedipus thinks it just [*dikaioi*, 640] to take terrible action against me . . ."

89

says Creon, and Oedipus explains his reason: "I have caught him acting evilly against my person, with evil skill" (*sun technêi kakêi*, 643). This phrase is a legal technicality of the fourth-century courtroom, and its use as a technical term almost certainly dates back to the fifth century.[163] As a legal term (*kakotechnia*) it means "to suborn perjury," and this is precisely the nature of Oedipus' accusation against Creon, that he is using Tiresias to bear false witness.[164]

Creon swears a solemn oath protesting his innocence and placing himself under a curse if he is lying. Jocasta and the chorus both urge Oedipus to respect the oath. "Do not," says the chorus, "subject to accusation and dishonor on the basis of obscure hearsay evidence [*aphanei logôi*, 657] a friend who has put himself on oath." "You seek to destroy me," says the defendant in the case of the murder of Herodes to his accusers, "by means of obscure hearsay evidence" (*aphanei logôi*).[165]

Oedipus yields and reprieves Creon, not, as he says, because of any pity for Creon himself, but because he is moved to compassion by the pleas of the chorus. "It is your words, not his, that move me to pity and compassion . . ." (671). This is the atmosphere of the law court again: it is a weary commonplace of Attic forensic oratory to appeal to the mercy of the judges, or, in the case of the prosecutor, to attempt to undermine their pity for the defendant. "If they start lamenting," says Demosthenes, for the prosecution, "just consider the victim more to be pitied than those who are going to be punished."[166] The defendant, with the famous exception of Socrates, never omits this appeal, no matter how strong his case, and the appeal is often couched in maudlin terms that explain why Socrates refused to demean himself by making it —"take pity on my misfortunes," "have pity on my child."[167]

The trial of Creon ends, if not with an acquittal at least with a reprieve, but Oedipus is still the accused. "He says I am the murderer of Laius," he tells Jocasta (703). When Jocasta discovers that the basis of the accusation is a declaration by Tiresias, she dismisses the charge. For she can prove the general unreliability of all prophets. "Acquit yourself of this charge you mention" (*apheis seauton*, 707), is the opening line of her speech, which is intended to release Oedipus from anxiety. Before she reaches the end of it, Oedipus is a frightened man. She has mentioned, almost casually, a detail full of terrible significance, the fact that Laius was killed at place where three roads meet. In a series of swift questions Oedipus establishes, with legal precision, the place and time of Laius' murder, the age and description of the victim, and the number in his party.[168] Jocasta's answers tally exactly with the circumstances of his own bloody encounter at the crossroads. "O Zeus, what have you planned to do to me?"

"What is this matter that so haunts you?" (*enthymion*, 739), asks Jocasta. This word is pregnant with sinister meaning. It is a word characteristic of the fifth-century murder trial, and describes the mental disturbance which the revengeful spirit of the murdered man is supposed to produce in his murderer. "If you unjustly acquit the defendant," says the prosecution in the first tetralogy of Antiphon, to the judges, "it is not on us that the wrath of the murderer will fall, it is rather you who will be haunted." And in the second tetralogy the defense uses the same argument in reverse: "if my son, who is innocent, is put to death, those who have condemned him will be haunted."[169] The word which Sophocles puts into Jocasta's mouth is a fine example of poetic economy; it is appropriate in the sense in which she intends it, but points ironically to the real situation of Oedipus, of which she is ignorant.

The intervention of Jocasta shifts the emphasis from Tiresias to a new witness whose veracity cannot be impugned by attacks on prophecy, for he is no prophet but a servant of Jocasta's household and, at the moment, a shepherd. He is an eye-witness of the murder of Laius. Oedipus insists that he be sent for at once, and then, at Jocasta's prompting, gives his account of the affair at the crossroads and of the events which had brought him there. He begins at the beginning: "My father was Polybus of Corinth, my mother Merope, a Dorian" (774-5). The fullness of his account has often been censured as dramatically implausible, for Jocasta, though it is conceivable that she does not know of Oedipus' fight at the crossroads or the oracular response (one can well imagine that Oedipus suppressed and even tried to forget these uncomfortable facts), surely knows the identity of Oedipus' supposed parents. This implausibility is to some extent relieved by the fact that the formality and abruptness of this beginning recall the court-room speech, especially that section of it which comes after the introduction and aims to present the relevant facts, tracing them from the beginning. Thus Lysias, in the great speech against Eratosthenes, makes his introduction and then goes right back to the beginning of the affair, his father's decision to emigrate from Syracuse to Athens. "My father Cephalus was persuaded by Pericles to come to this country, and lived here thirty years." [170] "Diodotus and Diogeiton, gentlemen of the jury, were brothers, born of the same father and mother," says the prosecutor of Diogeiton in the speech Lysias wrote for him (xxxii. 4). And Demosthenes' client, Euxitheus, who is pleading to retain his citizenship, goes even further back: "My grandfather, men of Athens, the father of my mother, was Demostratus of Melite." [171]

The opening of Oedipus' narrative, after his preliminary address to Jocasta, reminds us once again of the atmosphere of the court of law. But in ironic circumstances, for Oedipus' speech is a self-indictment. He presents the killing of the man he now fears was Laius as self-defense, but nevertheless, if it was in fact Laius, Oedipus is excommunicated by his own curse and banished from Thebes by his own sentence. And he cannot return to Corinth, for fear of the oracle: "Nor can I set foot in my fatherland" (825); the word he uses (*embateusai*) is another legal term, its technical significance in Attic law is "to enter into possession of a father's estate." [172]

Oedipus cannot take up his inheritance in Corinth, and now stands to lose what he has won by his own efforts in Thebes. "Would not one who judged that this is inflicted on me by some cruel power be right in his estimate?" he asks bitterly (828-9). Even here there is an echo of the court of law, for *ômos* (cruel) is the word customarily used by the defense to describe a demanding and savage prosecutor. Demosthenes, for example, in the speech against Aristogeiton, refers to the prosecutor's "cruel and bitter attitude," "his bitterness, blood-thirstiness, and cruelty." [173]

The prosecutor is cruel, but the evidence is contradictory, or at least incomplete. There is a discrepancy between Jocasta's account of the murder of Laius by brigands, and Oedipus' knowledge that at the crossroads he was alone. The testimony of the eyewitness is now vital. Jocasta does not see the need to question him. "Let me assure you that this was the public version of his story, and he cannot retract it now." [174] But Oedipus insists, and Jocasta finally agrees to summon the witness.

The famous choral stasimon which follows is a commentary on the situation and conduct of Oedipus and Jocasta in political, ethical, and religious terms. But also in terms of the law. The chorus appeals from the laws of man to higher laws "whose father is Olympus alone—no mortal man gave them birth, nor does forgetfulness lull them to sleep. In these laws the god is great, and he does not grow old" (867-72). This appeal to

93

a higher law is dictated by the revelations of the preceding scene. Jocasta has been revealed as privy to, if not responsible for, the death of a royal infant, her son by Laius, and Oedipus is now seen to be responsible for the deaths of four (or as he thinks, five) men, one of whom was very likely his predecessor Laius. Whatever may be the extenuating circumstances in either case, according to the normal fifth-century conception of responsibility for the taking of life Oedipus is certainly (and Jocasta possibly) polluted, impure. That is why the chorus prays for *hagneia* (864), "purity, holiness," in word and deed. This word occurs frequently in the speeches of Antiphon which deal with murder cases; not only is the killer impure (whatever his motive and the circumstances may have been) but he makes the whole community which shelters him as impure as he is. "It is contrary to your interests," runs a typical variation on this theme, "that this despicable and impure wretch should pollute the purity of the divine precincts by entering them." [175]

The appeal to divine law is prompted also by the fact that human law seems to have failed. Both the exposure of Laius' child and the killing at the crossroads happened long ago, but no human authority has intervened or punished. The laws of man have grown old and powerless, they have been deceived and are forgetful. But the divine law cannot be put to sleep or deceived, and the god does not grow old. Oedipus and Jocasta "walk proudly in word and deed, with no fear of Justice" (*dikês*, 885)—the word means also judgment, trial, and penalty. They scorn prophecy and therefore Apollo. The chorus appeals to a higher authority, to Zeus, as supreme judge. "You who are in power, if you are rightly so addressed, Zeus, let not these things escape the notice of your everlasting rule" (*mê lathoi*, 904). This word *lathoi* is a commonplace of the prosecutor's appeal to the judges. "Let it not escape your notice," say Demosthenes in a typical passage, "that he is lying." [176]

This stasimon marks a further development in the attitude of the chorus. After the argument between Oedipus and Tiresias the chorus spoke like a judge, but it speaks now like a prosecutor before a supreme tribunal, appealing for a condemnation as the only possible vindication of that tribunal's authority. "Unless these oracles are reconciled with fact, so that all mortal men point the finger at them,[177] I shall no longer go in reverence to the untouchable center of the earth." [178]

Before the eyewitness can be brought into court, the whole direction of the enquiry, and with it the bearing of his testimony, is changed. The Corinthian messenger reveals that Oedipus is not the son of Polybus and Merope; he is of Theban origin. Jocasta realizes what this means, and rushes off to hang herself, but Oedipus, full of an irrational hope (which the chorus shares), determines to question the shepherd, who is now a witness to Oedipus' identity as well as Laius' murder.

The examination of this witness is conducted in unmistakably legal forms.[179] The witness' identity is established by an appeal to the chorus and to the Corinthian messenger (1115-20). He is then invited to confirm it. "You, old man, look here at me, and answer my questions" (1121-2). So Socrates crossquestions Meletus: "Look at me, Meletus, and tell me . . ." [180] The question and the answer resemble the semiformal steps of the *erôtêsis*, the questioning of witnesses,[181] as it is preserved in a few passages of the Attic orators. "Were you one of Laius' household?" "I was." So Andocides in his speech *On the Mysteries*: "Were you one of the board of investigators?" "I was." And Lysias questions Eratosthenes: "Were you in the council chamber?" "I was." [182]

But the witness' memory is at fault, and he has to be

prompted. "I will remind him," says the Corinthian messenger (1133).[183] The shepherd is reluctant to admit his former acquaintance with the Corinthian, and when he is asked about a child which he once gave to his insistent questioner, he professes complete bewilderment. The Corinthian condescendingly points out to the apparently stupid old man the importance of the evidence he is withholding. "This man here, my dear sir [ô tan], is the child who was then so young" (1145). This complacent ô tan—"my dear sir, my good man"—is a characteristic colloquial phrase of the Athenian orator. In Demosthenes it is often put in the mouth of an imaginary objector to the speaker's argument, who is himself ignorant, and is confuted by the speaker's reply—a straw man, in fact. In the first speech against Aristogeiton, for example, Demosthenes, after building up the case against his target, deals with the grounds on which he can be expected to plead for clemency, putting these grounds into the mouth of an imaginary friend of the accused.

> "What can he say that is true?" "He can cite some action of his father's, by Zeus." "But, gentlemen of the jury, you condemned his father to death in this very courtroom." . . . "Well, by Zeus, if this matter of his father is difficult for him, he will have recourse to his own life, so self-controlled and moderate." "What? Where did he lead that kind of life? You have all seen him; he is not that kind of man." "But, my dear sir [ô tan] he will turn to his services to the state." [And now follows the body blow.] "Services? When and where? His father's? Nonexistent. His own? You will find denunciations, arrests, informing—but no services."[184]

The use of this condescending phrase by the Corinthian messenger suggests an ironic effect. He, not the shepherd, is the ignorant man, and his condescension could be knocked out of him with a single word—but it is a word the shepherd would prefer not to pronounce. "Damn you," he bursts out instead, "will you keep your mouth shut?" (1146). Oedipus quickly reproves this recalcitrant and offensive witness. "Do not correct him; your words need a corrector more than his" (1147-8). But the word which Oedipus uses (*kolazein*) is stronger than the context warrants; it is in fact the legal term for punishment. "It is possible to punish [*kolazein*] by means of fines, imprisonment, and death," says the accuser of Alcibiades, and Plato, speaking of incorrigible criminals, says, "In such cases we are forced to assign to the lawgiver, as a corrector [*kolastên*] of their misdeeds, death."[185] This threat of punishment is made more explicit a few lines later. "If you will not speak to please me, you will do it in tears" says Odeipus (1152), and the shepherd understands the import of these words. "Do not torture me, I am an old man" (1153). But tortured he is. "Somebody twist his arms behind him. Quick" (1154). And the old man at last answers Oedipus' questions under the imminent threat and the physical preliminaries of torture.

But this is Attic legal procedure too. The evidence of a slave (and the shepherd so identifies himself at the beginning of the scene, 1123) was admissible in the Attic courts only if given under torture.[186] In most cases, our evidence seems to show, this torture was not administered but was rather a measure which allowed complicated maneuvering—demands and counterdemands for the torture of slaves which served simply as preliminary points that prosecution and defense might score off each other. But sometimes it was administered: the evidence in the case of the murder of Herodes, for example, was mainly extracted by the prosecution before the trial began from slaves under torture.

It was a commonplace of the defense against such evidence that the tortured slave naturally made the confession which his torturers wanted to hear. "I need not remind you," says the defendant accused of the murder of Herodes, "that generally, in the case of evidence given under torture, the evidence is in favor of the torturers." "He knew what his own interest was," says the same defendant, speaking of a slave tortured by the prosecution; "he knew that he would cease to be racked as soon as he said what they wanted to hear." [187] But in the case of Oedipus the normal situation appears in reverse. Oedipus forces the slave, reluctant even under torture, to confess the truth that will reveal the torturer as the criminal. "I am faced with the dreadful thing itself, I must say it," says the old man (1169). "And I," replies Oedipus, "must hear it." The final revelation is extracted from the shepherd by the last extremity of the the legal process, but the torturer suffers more than his victim. "I am exposed [*pephasmai*—another legal term], born of the wrong parents, married to the wrong wife, killer of the man I must not kill."

The choral stasimon sums up the case of Oedipus. "Time which sees all things has found you out—it gives judgment on the unnatural marriage which is both begetter and begot." [188] The investigator has found the criminal, the prosecutor obtained a conviction, and the judge passed sentence, but, like the marriage, the legal process is both begetter and begot. Oedipus finds himself, convicts himself, and, in his last words before he rushes into the palace, passes sentence on himself. "Light, let this be the last time I look on you." His conviction is, as the chorus says, an example, *paradeigma*, the example which the Athenian prosecutor calls for in speech after speech; [189] Oedipus is an example to all men.

Oedipus *tyrannos*, then, is more than an individual tragic hero. In his title, *tyrannos*, in the nature and basis of his power, in his character, and in the mode of his dramatic action, he resembles Athens, the city which aimed to become (and was already far along the road to becoming) the *tyrannos* of Greece, the rich and splendid autocrat of the whole Hellenic world. Such a resemblance, whether consciously recognized or not, must have won him the sympathy of the Athenian audience and firmly engaged the emotions of that audience in the hero's action and suffering. But it does something more. It adds an extra dimension of significance not only to his career but also to his fall, which suggests, in symbolic, prophetic, riddling terms, the fall of Athens itself. Like Oedipus, Athens justifies unceasing and ever more vigorous action by an appeal to previous success; like Oedipus, Athens refuses to halt, to compromise, to turn back; like Oedipus, Athens follows the dictates of her energy and intelligence with supreme confidence in the future; and like Oedipus, the tragedy seems to suggest, Athens will come to know defeat, learn to say " I must obey " as she now says " I must rule." Athens, in the words of her greatest statesman, claimed that she was an example to others, *paradeigma*; Oedipus is called an example too, but in his fall. " Taking your fortune as my example [*paradeigma*]," sings the chorus, " I call no mortal happy." [190]

This resemblance between Oedipus and Athens suggests a solution of the chief problem of interpretation presented by the play—the meaning and application of the magnificent central stasimon (863-911). The problem lies in the fact that this stasimon, which for over half its length deals, in general terms, with the origin, nature, and fall of the *tyrannos*, contains some phrases which can be made applicable to Oedipus only with great ingenuity (which has of course not been lacking), and others which, to quote Bruhn, "no technique of interpretation in the world can make applicable to Oedipus and Jocasta." These lines constitute for the editor or critic of the play a problem which is central, for his solution either determines or is determined by his interpretation of the play as a whole.

Many solutions have been proposed. For those who consider Oedipus an ethical example whose fall is due to a fault, these condemnatory phrases, though perhaps verging on the irrelevant, are confirmatory evidence of the rightness of their assumption of Oedipus' guilt. Those who consider that Oedipus is not, in ethical terms, paying the penalty of his own misdeeds or wrong attitude, have a more difficult task before them. Sir John Sheppard, whose edition of the play is a pioneering attempt to understand the play in fifth-century terms, explains these awkward phrases as part of the general moral and literary estimate of the *tyrannos*. Oedipus may not have done what the chorus implies, but the stereotype of the *tyrannos* as the completely lawless ruler is so influential in the fifth-century mind that these reflections are, in the circumstances, almost inevitable. This explanation, maintained with a wealth of illuminating citation and judicial comment, is, however, fundamentally a desperate one; it is precisely the mark of a great poet that he is the master, not the slave, of the tradition in which he works. More recently a brilliant and at first sight convincing explanation has been offered by the Spanish scholar Ignacio Errandonea in his monograph "El estasimo segundo del Edipo Rey." [191] He suggests that the person referred to in the central section of the stasimon is not Oedipus at all, but his father Laius. The language employed by Sophocles (especially the phrases "make profit" and "touch the untouchable") is shown to be exactly appropriate for the unsavory story of

Laius and Chrysippus. This explanation has the great merit of giving clear and relevant point to the lines in question, but it does so at a disastrous cost. For if the stasimon refers to Laius, the effect is to suggest strongly that Oedipus is paying for the sins of his father.[192] This was the standard version of the story, the version used by Aeschylus; but Sophocles, in the *Oedipus Tyrannus*, resolutely ignores this traditional burden of the myth. In the Aeschylean trilogy Laius is ordered three times by Apollo not to beget children, and disobeys; in the Sophoclean play " an oracle came to Laius once . . . that he should die at the hands of his son." At point after point Sophocles remains silent on the question of Laius' responsibility, a silence all the more noticeable and emphatic because he was addressing an audience familiar with the Aeschylean handling of the material. If this central stasimon is interpreted as a reference to the sins of Laius, all that has been achieved by the explanation is the replacement of a coherent play which contains a few puzzling choral lines by a coherent choral ode which is set in the center of an utterly baffling play.

The solution of the problem which has been generally accepted is that these lines are in fact extraneous and refer to Athens, not Oedipus. It is generally assumed that Sophocles, in these two lines at least (889-90), if not in the whole of the stasimon, is speaking directly to the Athenians, in a sort of tragic *parabasis*, about Athens, and that Oedipus is, for the moment, ignored. The rent in the dramatic texture is accepted as a deplorable but undeniable fact, and discussion is confined (if that be the proper word in view of the voluminous literature on the subject) to a dispute about the aspects of Athenian policy which are here referred to—a dispute all the more heated because for most critics these lines constitute the main evidence for dating the play.

But if Oedipus is throughout the play, by one detail after

another, built up into a figure which suggests Athens, the rent in the dramatic texture, though it may still be felt to leave a scar, is effectively healed. The stasimon is an estimate of the origin, nature, and inevitable fall of the *tyrannos*; by the time the chorus sings its solemn opening lines the resemblance between Oedipus and Athens is clearly and firmly enough established for the poet to speak of them as one and the same. As the chorus appeals over the laws of man to the justice of a supreme tribunal, Oedipus *tyrannos* and the Athenian *tyrannis* are so closely associated in the poet's mind and language that he can attribute to Oedipus faults which are not to be found in the hero of the play but in the actions of the city of which he is the dramatic symbol.

Just as Oedipus, who pursues a murderer according to the processes of law, is himself a murderer, but goes unpunished, so Athens, the original home and the most advanced center of the law, rules with a power based on injustice and is beyond the reach of human law. As the fury and passion of the war spirit mounted, the actions of Athens became more overtly violent and unjust; the contradiction between the laws of the city and a higher law beyond the one man has made, a contradiction already explored in the Sophoclean *Antigone*, became more open, insistent, and oppressive. The appeal of the chorus of the *Oedipus Tyrannus* to laws " whose father is Olympus alone " which cannot " be deceived, forget, or sleep " is, like the *Antigone*, a reminder that there are standards beyond those of the *polis*, that Athens, righteous in its own eyes and vindicated in its own courts, may yet have to face a higher, and impartial, judge.

" *Hybris phyteuei tyrannon.* Violence and pride engender the *tyrannos*." That the Athenian *tyrannis* was based on violence no one could deny; Sophocles himself had taken part in a war against Samos, an allied city which had tried to secede from the Athenian empire. The language which follows is highly metaphorical and the text, unfortunately, corrupt; it seems however to present the fate of this violence and pride in the figure of a wrestler, who, recklessly gorging himself on improper food, goes to the decisive contest and is defeated. " *Hybris*, if it wantonly gorges itself [193] on many things that are neither suitable nor to its advantage, goes up to the highest ramparts, and leaps into sheer necessity, where it finds the use of its foot of no avail. But that wrestling hold which is good for the city I pray the god never to loose. The god I shall not cease ever to hold as my champion " (873-82).

This is a figurative discussion of the dynamics of Athenian imperial policy. It does not reject action entirely; the god is asked to acquiesce in, not to loose, " the wrestling hold which is good for the city." But it predicts defeat for action inspired by drunken pride, and, faced with such action, the chorus turns from human to divine guidance; *prostatên* (" champion ") is a word which describes the unofficial position of leadership occupied by the statesman who in Athens directed policy, and was applied to Pericles and Cleon alike.[194]

In the next strophe the misdeeds of *hybris* are defined, and it is in this passage that the language can apply fully to Oedipus only in the light of his comparison to the *polis tyrannos*. "But if one goes on his way [195] contemptuous in action and speech, unterrified of Justice, without reverence for the statues of the gods, may an evil destiny seize him, in return for his ill-fated pride and luxury" (883-8). The word translated " pride and luxury" (*chlidas*) calls to mind the wealth and comparatively high standard of living made possible by the Athenian commercial supremacy, as well as the wealth which Oedipus associates with *tyrannis* (380); the reference to the " statues of the gods" may in a strained sense be appropriate for the irreligious sentiments expressed by Oedipus and Jocasta, but it is exactly applicable in a more literal fashion to a *cause célèbre* of the immediate prewar years—the impeachment of Phidias for dishonesty and sacrilegious conduct in connection with his famous statue of Athena. The action against Phidias was aimed at Pericles, the leader of the Athenian imperial party; he was the man whose portrait Phidias was alleged to have carved on the goddess' shield. The contemporary reference of these phrases is made clearer as the stasimon proceeds. "If he will not gain his profit justly, and refrain from impious actions, or if he recklessly lay hands on the untouchable, what man in such circumstances will be able to ward off the god's missiles and defend his life?" (889-95). There is nothing in the play which makes the remark about profit fit Oedipus, but Athens maintained its power on the forced tribute of the members of what had once been the Delian League and was now the Athenian empire. The money collected was used for the embellishment of Athens and the maintenance of the fleet which guaranteed continued collection; a large sum had been converted into gold to adorn the Phidian statue of Athena in the Parthenon. It was an openly avowed intention of Pericles to use this gold on the goddess' statue for war purposes in case of emergency. The money which was in the first place unjust profit had been devoted to the adornment of the statue of the goddess; to take it from the temple might well be regarded by many religious Athenians as an impious act which would "lay hold on the untouchable." This is a detail (though it is one which seems to fit the terms of the chorus' formulation); the truth is that imperial Athens, both Periclean and post-Periclean, had in more ways than one shown an overriding contempt for religious scruples of all kinds.

In these lines the terrible implications of the resemblance between Oedipus and Athens are made clear; the words of the chorus are a warning and a prophecy of Athenian defeat.

That Sophocles at an early stage in the war could contemplate the possibility of defeat should not seem surprising; the elaboration and energy of the Periclean arguments for confidence in victory suggest that there was an important section of the Athenian population which was far from taking it for granted that Athens was bound to win. Even Pericles, the architect of the war policy and the constant prophet of eventual victory, could admit, in the speech after the plague, the possibility that Athens might lose. "Even if we should ever in the present struggle be forced to give in (for all things are born to be diminished) yet the memory will live that being Greeks we ruled over the greater part of the Greek nation, that we sustained the burden of wars against our enemies both as individuals and as members of a united league, and that we inhabited a city that was in all respects the greatest and richest of its time." [196] The words which Thucydides puts into the mouth of Athens' most farseeing statesman contemplate the possibility of defeat in the language of the tragic vision: "all things are born to be diminished," the heroic city no less than the tragic hero.

All this does not mean that the *Oedipus Tyrannus* is defeatist propaganda, nor that it is an appeal for a negotiated peace, as the *Acharnians* and the *Peace* of Aristophanes, in some sense, are. The *Oedipus Tyrannus* is tragedy, and tragedy deals with "the irremediable," *to anêkeston*; the play is a tragic vision of Athens' splendor, vigor, and inevitable defeat which contemplates no possibility of escape—the defeat is immanent in the splendor. The mantic vision of the poet penetrates through the appearances of Athenian power to the reality of the tragic reversal, the fall towards which Athens is forcing its way with all the fierce creative energy, the uncompromising logic, the initiative and daring which have brought her to the pinnacle of worldly power. All the Athenians had to do to win the war, as Pericles told them, was to refrain from activity (*hêsuchazein*); [197] but the future was to show, and the Athenian character in any case made sure, that Athens could no more refrain from action than Oedipus could. Athens and Oedipus alike push on to the logical consequences of their energy and initiative. Both come to disaster though the valiant exercise of the very qualities which have made them great; their ruin is the result of a stubborn and heroic insistence on being themselves. "What man," sings the chorus, after Oedipus knows the truth, "what man attains more prosperity than just so much as will make an appearance and no sooner appear than decline?" These words are not only a comment on the ruin of Oedipus; they are also a tragic epitaph of the Athenian golden age, a brief period of intellectual, artistic, and imperial splendor which at its supreme moment was pregnant with its own destruction, which, like the prosperity of Oedipus, was based on a calamitously unsound and unjust foundation, and like him was to shatter itself by the heroic exercise of those great talents and powers which had brought it into being.

CHAPTER THREE: MAN

I

Oedipus, in his character and his mode of action, is a symbolic representation of Periclean Athens. But that Athens was not only the magnificent *polis tyrannos* and the source of law, it was also the center of the intellectual revolution of the fifth century. "Athens," says the sophist Hippias in Plato's *Protagoras* (337d), "is the *prytaneion*, the council chamber, of the wisdom of Greece." This is a compliment paid to his hosts by a visiting rhetorician (and put into his mouth by a subtle master of irony), but it is none the less the truth. The rich metropolis attracted to itself the discoverers, scientists, and teachers of the whole Hellenic world. With the practical innovating spirit of the democratic Athenian in politics, commerce, and warfare were now combined the intellectual innovations of philosophers and teachers who explored and explained a revolutionary view of man's stature and importance. It was in Athens that the new anthropological and anthropocentric attitude reached its high point of confidence and assumed its most authoritative tone. The idea that man was capable of full understanding and eventual domination of his environment found its appropriate home in the city which could see no limits to its own unprecedented expansion.[1] The splendor and power of the *polis tyrannos* encouraged a bold conception of *anthrôpos tyrannos*, man the master of the universe, a self-taught and self-made ruler who has the capacity, to use the words the chorus applies to Oedipus, to "conquer complete happiness and prosperity."[2]

The essence of the new optimistic spirit is distilled in the poetry of the famous chorus in the *Antigone* (332-75). The first two thirds of that choral ode might well be entitled " A

Hymn to Man," for it is a catalogue of man's triumphs in his unaided struggle to civilize himself and assert his mastery.

> Many are the wonders and terrors, and nothing more wonderful and terrible than man. This creature crosses the white sea with the stormy south wind, forward through the swell that crashes about him. And earth, oldest of the gods, indestructible, inexhaustible, he wears down as his ploughs move back and forth year after year, turning the soil with the breed of horses. He snares the tribe of light-witted birds, the nations of wild beasts, the salt life of the sea, takes them in his net-woven meshes, man the intelligent. He masters by technique the mountain-roaming beast that beds in the wilderness, he puts under the yoke the neck of the shaggy-maned horse and the tireless mountain bull. Speech, and thought swift as the wind, and a temper that enables him to live in communities, all these he has taught himself, and also means of escape from the frost when man cannot sleep under the clear sky, and from the hostile shafts of the rain—he is resourceful in every situation, nothing in the future toward which he moves shall find him without resource. From death alone he will not procure escape. But from desperate diseases he has contrived release. He possesses knowledge, ingenuity, and technique beyond anything that could have been foreseen.

These famous lines trace the progress of man from primitive ignorance to civilized power. He conquers the elements, sea and land; masters animate nature, the birds, beasts, and fishes; communicates and combines with his fellows to found society; protects himself against the elements; begins to conquer disease —there seems to be no limit to his advance except his own death. This proud view of man's history is a fifth-century invention. It is particularly associated with the name of Protagoras, who wrote a famous book called *Primitive Conditions*,[3] and who, in the Platonic dialogue which bears his name, is made to tell the story of man's development through stages similar to those described in the Sophoclean ode. Plato's Protagoras was influenced by the account of the same historical process given by Prometheus in the Aeschylean play. But there is one marked difference between the Sophoclean version and the one found in Aeschylus and Plato. Both of these accounts emphasize strongly the role played by divine beings who are responsible for man's advance. In Aeschylus, Prometheus, single-handed, gives to a passive mankind all the arts and techniques of civilization; " all arts came to mortals from Prometheus," the divine champion proclaims (506). In the myth told by Protagoras in Plato's dialogue, the gods create men, Prometheus saves them by stealing fire (and so technical proficiency) for them, man is distinguished from the other animals by his belief in the gods, and the first thing he is supposed to have done is to set up altars and statues in their honor. (So Prometheus, in the Aeschylean version, teaches man to pray, to sacrifice, to interpret dreams and omens.) Finally Zeus, in the Platonic account, gives man " a sense of shame, and justice," which makes possible civilized communal life. But in the Sophoclean version this is a human invention, and there is no mention whatever of the gods except that earth, " oldest of the gods," is worn away by man's ploughs. The whole process of human development to technical mastery and civilization is presented as man's achievement, and his alone: to use a modern and fashionable term, this is a fully " secular " view of human progress.[4] " Man," says the Sophoclean chorus, " taught himself."

This is not of course what Sophocles himself believed. The concluding words of the stasimon raise doubts which undermine the proud confidence of the opening, and the subsequent events of the play completely shatter the possibility of a "secular" view of the human condition. But the chorus' hymn certainly represents a point of view current, and in intellectual circles probably dominant, in the poet's time. It is found, for example, in the oration of Gorgias, the *Palamedes*, where the speaker details his inventions which have made "the life of man full of resources instead of resourceless, and ordered instead of disordered,"[5] without mentioning divine intervention, help, or inspiration; and in the Hippocratic treatise *On Ancient Medicine* there is a similarly "secular" account of human progress in medicine and nutrition (*V. M.* 3). Such a conception of human progress is very likely closer to Protagoras' real ideas than that attributed to him by Plato, for Protagoras is the man who above all the other sophists defined the new anthropocentric outlook in the famous phrase "man is the measure of all things" and who also dismissed the gods as irrelevant. "As to the gods," he said, "I have no means of knowing either that they exist or that they do not exist."

These lines of the *Antigone* describe the rise to power of *anthrôpos tyrannos*: self-taught, unaided, he seizes control of his environment; by intelligence and technique he wins mastery over the elements and the animals. The language of the *Oedipus Tyrannus* associates the hero of the play with this triumphant progress of man. Oedipus is compared not only to the city which man has created with his "attitudes that enable him to live in communities" but also to man the conqueror and inventor, with all the achievements which have raised him to the level of civilization and made him *tyrannos* of the world. Three of the most striking images of the play, for example, are drawn from the first three items of the catalogue of human conquests in the *Antigone* stasimon.

Oedipus is metaphorically presented as helmsman, conqueror of the sea, ploughman, conqueror of the land, and hunter, pursuer and tamer of wild nature. These images extend the symbolic significance of the tragic hero beyond the limits of the comparison to Athens, the center of civilization, to include the most impressive and revolutionary achievements of the whole human race.

Oedipus as hunter is an image which stems naturally, almost inevitably, from the nature of the plot—a search. It is a difficult search for the murderer of a man now long dead; the scent has faded. It is in these terms that Oedipus first characterizes the task which the Apolline response lays on him: "Where shall it be found, this track of an ancient guilt, difficult to trace?"[6] "If you search for it," runs Creon's answer, "you can catch it, but if you neglect it, it escapes."[7] Oedipus announces his decision to search for the murderer in terms of the same figure: "I shall make an announcement —for I could not track him far alone, without some clue."[8]

But at the very beginning of the chase, the interview with Tiresias, he finds himself faced with an unexpected turn of events: Tiresias identifies the hunted murderer as Oedipus himself. Oedipus' angry reply describes this accusation by means of a technical term drawn from the vocabulary of hunting. "So shameless?" he says. "To flush such a word from cover!" (*exekinêsas*, 354).[9] The hunt for the murderer of Laius, which he at first thought impossible because the track was faded, is turning out to be too rich in clues, too complicated and full of surprises.

Oedipus is the hunter, and the chorus, appropriately, sings of the hunted murderer as a wild animal: "It is time for him to move in flight a foot swifter than wind-swift mares . . . the divine command has flashed from Parnassus to track down by all means in our power the man who has left no trace.[10]

For he ranges under the shade of the wild forest, among caves and rocks, like a bull, solitary in misery, with miserable foot." These words of the chorus, with their unconscious punning on Oedipus' name,[11] emphasize for us the terrible and so far unsuspected truth that hunter and hunted are the same, that Oedipus is both the tracker and the wild bull. But Oedipus confidently applies the metaphor to a different set of circumstances, Creon's supposed attempt to win power: "Is your enterprise not stupid—to hunt, without masses and friends, supreme power [*tyrannis*]—a thing which is caught only with masses and money?"[12] He sees Creon as the foolish hunter who is not equipped for the chase, a contrast to himself who has long ago captured the prey. But he is now engaged on another hunt, and the capture of the prey will bring the downfall of his power. The tracks lead to a terrible discovery: the hunter is the prey. In the messenger's account of the catastrophe there are two touches which recall the chorus' comparison of the unknown criminal to a wild bull. "He ranged about," says the messenger, using the same word which in the previous passage described the movements of the hunted bull,[13] and he adds that when Oedipus saw Jocasta hanging he "loosened the noose . . . with a dreadful, *bellowing* cry."[14] And Oedipus' own words, towards the end of the play, suggest that he sees himself as a fit inhabitant of the wild: "Let me live on the mountains."[15]

Oedipus as helmsman is also of course an appropriate image, for as *tyrannos* he is naturally thought of as guiding the ship of state. The city is inferentially compared to a ship in the opening lines of the play, a ship "with a cargo of burning incense, prayers for healing, and laments for the dead" (4-5),[16] and a few lines later the metaphor is fully developed. "The city . . . is already pitching excessively and cannot lift its head up out of the trough of the bloody swell."[17] Creon, bringing the news from Delphi, speaks of the blood of Laius "which brings this storm on the city" and connects Oedipus with his predecessor at the helm of the state through this same metaphor: "we once had . . . a captain, Laius, before you steered the city on a straight course" (103-4).[18] And the chorus, after the quarrel between Oedipus and Creon, asserts its loyalty to Oedipus as the successful pilot of the ship of state: "You set my beloved land on a fair straight course when it was storm-tossed in troubles, and now may you be its fortunate guide" (694-6).[19] It soon becomes clear that this wish is in vain; "He is a stricken man," says Jocasta, "and we tremble to look at him, as passengers would a stricken pilot" (922-3). Oedipus can no longer steer the ship of state, for he has reason to fear that he has steered the ship of his own fortune with terrible results. And he has not yet discovered the full extent of the frightful truth. When he does, he will understand Tiresias' riddling questions at last. "What harbor," the prophet had asked him, "will not ring in concert with your cries . . . when you know the truth about the fatal anchorage into which you sailed, your marriage in this house, after so fortunate a voyage?" (420 ff.). Oedipus had plotted his course with care "measuring the distance from Corinth by the stars" (794-5), but it brought him to an unspeakable harbor. "O famous Oedipus," the chorus sings when the truth is known, "the same harbor sufficed to contain you both as child and bridegroom" (1207-10).[20]

The imagery of the play presents Oedipus also as ploughman and sower. This agricultural metaphor is connected always with his birth and begetting. Such a transference of agricultural terms to the process of human procreation is commonplace in Greek poetry,[21] as it was in seventeenth-century English ("the seed of Abraham," "the fruit of the womb," etc.) and indeed in the figurative language of any people which lives in close contact with the work of the fields. But in this play the metaphor is pushed to the limits of its capacity. "The images which Sophocles employs in describing the situation of Jocasta by her new relation with her son," says an eminent Victorian editor,[22] "will not always bear a minute explanation"; by which he means, of course, that they are hideously exact. It is true enough that these metaphors are used to adumbrate physical enormities that would have been intolerable in plain speech,[23] but they draw part of their force from the striking appropriateness of this type of imagery to the dramatic situation. Thebes is afflicted by a blight on the crops and herds as well as a plague which affects the population. The normal cycle of ploughing, sowing, and increase has broken down—"the fruit of our famous land does not increase" (171-2)—and this is accompanied by an interruption of the cycle of human procreation and birth—"the land is dying . . . in the birthless labor pangs of the women" (25-7). This sympathetic relationship between the fruits of the soil and the fruit of the womb is reflected in the transference of agricultural terms to the involved pollution of the marriage of Oedipus and Jocasta, and what the reflection suggests is the responsibility of that unholy marriage for the stunted crops.[24] This was an idea which needed no heavy emphasis for a Greek audience; the magical connection between the king and the fertility of his domains was an old belief in Greece. A famous example is the "blameless king" described by Odysseus, who "upholds justice, and the black earth bears wheat and barley, the trees are heavy with fruit, the flocks breed unceasingly, and the sea provides fish, all because of his good rule . . ."[25] And the ceremony of a sacred marriage which had almost certainly begun as a magical guarantee of the renewal of the crops was widespread in Greece in historical times.[26] Such a ceremony in fact regularly took place in Athens in Sophocles' time;

the sacred marriage between Dionysus and his Athenian bride
had been celebrated just a few weeks before the tragic festival
at which the *Oedipus Tyrannus* was performed.[27] The marriage of Oedipus is a blasphemous antitype of this "holy
marriage." "O marriage, marriage," he cries in his agony,
"you gave me birth, and then you who begot me raised my
own seed . . ." (1403-5).[28]

Oedipus' first statement about his relationship with Laius
is made in terms of this metaphor. "I possess the powers he
once held, his marriage bed, and his wife *homosporon*" (259-
60)—a word which in this sentence can only mean "who is
sown with seed by both of us," for Oedipus adds the qualifica-
tion that the seed of Laius, at any rate, had borne no fruit.
This use of the word distorts its usual meaning, which is "sown
together, of the same seed," hence "brother" or "sister." The
unusual meaning forced on the word by the context revives
a metaphor that was probably moribund, if not dead, through
overuse, and the revived metaphor is kept alive when Tiresias
uses the same word in a different, but still unusual, sense.
He prophesies that the murderer will be revealed as "his
father's cosower [*homosporon*] and murderer" (460). But it
is after the fulfilment of this prophecy that the metaphor
reaches the ghastly stages of its full development. "How,"
sings the chorus, "how could the furrows which your father
ploughed bear you in silence for so long?" (1210-12). Oedipus
burst in, the messenger tells us, asking where he could find
"the maternal ploughland which had borne a double crop,
himself and his children" (1256-7). Oedipus himself explains
his own polluted state to his daughters in terms of this same
image: "your father, by the mother in whom I myself was
planted" (1485). And in similar terms he sums up the
reproach all mankind will level at him: "he ploughed the field
where he himself was sown" (1497-8).[29]

The imagery thus links Oedipus with the three basic steps in the progress of humanity described in the *Antigone* stasimon, the conquest of the sea, the soil, and the animals. Oedipus is figuratively presented as helmsman, ploughman, and hunter. All three images add to the stature of Oedipus, who begins to appear as a symbolic representative not only of the tyrannic energy and legal creativity of Athens but also of mankind as a whole in its difficult progress towards mastery over nature. And the reversal of the tragic hero, of the *tyrannos*, and of the prosecutor is paralleled in the development of these metaphors which extend his significance. Oedipus the helmsman has steered the ship of state into a storm which threatens to destroy it, and his own destiny into a unspeakable harbor. The hunter has tracked down the prey only to find that it is himself. And the sower is not only the sower but also the seed.

II

These images of Oedipus as hunter, helmsman, and cultivator function as an ironic commentary on the proud and optimistic conception of man's history and supremacy current in the fifth century. That conception was itself one of the greatest achievements of several generations of critical and creative activity unparalleled in the story of the ancient world. And the language of the play identifies Oedipus as the symbolic representative of the new critical and inventive spirit. At every turn it associates Oedipus with the scientific, questioning, and at the same time confident attitude of the fifth-century Greek, especially the Athenian, whose city was " the council chamber of Greek wisdom."

The action of the tragedy, a search for truth pursued without fear of the consequences to the bitter end, mirrors the intellectual scientific quest of the age. The fame of Oedipus is based on his solution of a riddle; when he accuses Tiresias of speaking in riddles he is scornfully reminded of his reputation: "Are you not the best man born at finding answers to them?" (440). Gorgias the sophist, in his speech to the Greeks assembled at Olympia, spoke of riddles too. "Our struggle demands two virtues, courage and wisdom; courage to withstand the danger, wisdom to solve the riddle." [30] The solution to the riddle of the Sphinx was "man," [31] and in the fifth century the same answer had been proposed to an even greater riddle: "Man," said Protagoras the sophist, "is the measure of all things." Oedipus is made to speak time and again in words that typify the scientific spirit and its dedication to truth, whatever the cost. "Nothing could persuade me not to learn this fully and clearly" (1065). "Burst forth what will. Mean though it may be, I intend to see the seed that gave me birth" (1076-7). And in a more somber key he answers the shepherd's agonized cry, "I am on the verge of saying the dreadful truth," with the words, "And I of hearing it. But all the same, hear it I must" (1169-70).

The attitude and activity of Oedipus are images of the critical spirit and the great intellectual achievements of a generation of sophists, scientists, and philosophers. Oedipus investigates, examines, questions, infers; he uses intelligence, mind, thought; he knows, finds, reveals, makes clear, demonstrates; he learns and teaches; and his relationship to his fellow men is that of liberator and savior. The Greek words to which the items of this list correspond bulk large in the vocabulary of the play; they are the words which sum up the spirit and serve the purposes of the new scientific attitude and activity.

The word *zētein*—to "search for, investigate"—is one which naturally finds a prominent place in the vocabulary of the play,[32] both in its literal and (as we have seen) in its legal sense, for Oedipus is investigating a murder and searching for a murderer. But this word does not come from the traditional poetic vocabulary,[33] and in the fifth century it was one of the distinctive words of the new scientific outlook. "Investigating things under the earth and in the sky," runs Socrates' paraphrase of the accusation against him,[34] and in Aristophanes' parodic presentation of the scientists at work, *The Clouds*, this word plays a prominent role. Socrates is described as "investigating the paths and circuits of the moon," and his pupils, their backsides in the air, "investigate the subterrestrial."[35]

The scientific connotations of the word are emphasized in the *Oedipus Tyrannus* by the use of two forms of it which draw attention to the technical associations which the word acquired in the late fifth century. "What is searched for," says Creon, reporting Apollo's reply, "can be caught; what is neglected, escapes" (110-11). The legal connotations of this formula have already been discussed; the initial word, *to zêtoumenon*, "the thing searched for," is a term associated with the new investigative processes of philosophy and science. "The object of our present investigation," *to nyn zêtoumenon*, is a phrase used by the Eleatic in Plato's *Sophist* (223c). "It might cast light on the object of our investigation," *to zêtoumenon*, says Socrates in Plato's *Theaetetus* (201a).[36] Apart from the scientific flavor of the initial word, Creon's statement as a whole is an eloquent expression of the scientific attitude, with its insistence on search and effort and its promise that they will be rewarded.[37] "To discover without searching is difficult and rare," says Archytas of Tarentum in his work on mathematics, "but if one searches, discovery is frequent and easy." This sentence, couched in the broad Doric of South Italy, was written long after Sophocles wrote the *Oedipus Tyrannus*, but the sentiment (and the key word) is the same as that of Creon's speech in the play.[38]

Another form of this word *zêtein* occurs in the *Oedipus Tyrannus*, *zêtêma*, "enquiry," an abstract noun which is even more clearly a term of scientific and philosophical discussion. "As to the enquiry," says the chorus, "it was the responsibility of Apollo who sent the oracle to say who committed the crime" (278-9). This word *zêtêma* occurs only here in Sophocles, and not at all in Aeschylus; it does not seem to be used in Greek before the fifth century. But it is common in Plato [39] and also in the fifth-century Hippocratic treatise *On Ancient Medicine*, where it is used to describe the whole of the long process of trial and error which has led to the development of medical science. "To this discovery and research [*zêtêmati*] what juster or more appropriate name could be given than medicine?" the author asks at the end of his account.[40]

Oedipus is challenged to "search," and after sizing up the problem he accepts the challenge. "I shall go to any length in the search" (*zêtôn*, 266). He will not "neglect" anything in the search for truth. He is an example of that scientific spirit which Thucydides claims is so rare among men: "so little labor do most people undertake in their search for the truth—they turn rather to what lies ready to hand." [41] But nothing can turn Oedipus from his chosen path; Jocasta may be content with explanations that lie ready to hand untested, but Oedipus will "go to every length." It is a terrible truth which he discovers. He is not only the searcher but also the thing searched for, the object of enquiry as well as the enquirer. He is *to zêtoumenon*, the thing he was looking for. "Oedipus," says Plutarch in his essay *On Curiosity*, "searching for himself (for he believed that he was not a Corinthian but a foreigner), met Laius, killed him, received, in addition to a kingdom, his own mother to wife, and, thinking that he was a happy man, again began to search for himself." [42] The *peripeteia* of the tragic hero is reflected in the *peripeteia* of one of his characteristic words.[43]

Oedipus' methods of investigation are those of the critical spirit of the age which he represents: *skopein*, " to contemplate, examine "; *historein*, " to question, inquire "; *tekmairesthai*, " to judge from evidence, to infer." The first of these words, *skopein*, has a special importance in the new scientific vocabulary. It describes a critical, calculating scrutiny, which assesses and draws conclusions. It is a word much favored by Thucydides. " From evidence which, after the most extensive scrutiny [*epi makrotaton skopounti*] turns out to be trustworthy . . . ," he says in the opening sentences of his *History* (i. 1. 3), and the element of calculation in the word emerges clearly from his use of it in his attempt to estimate the size of the Greek army at Troy. " In any case, if you examine the mean [*to meson skopounti*] between [the crews of] the largest and the smallest ships, the number of men who went on the expedition does not seem large " (i. 10. 5). So later he uses this word to distinguish between emotional judgments and the scientific historical view: " Although men judge the war in which they happen to be fighting the greatest always, but when it is over are more impressed by former events, this war will nevertheless, to those who examine it on the basis of the facts themselves [*ap' autôn tôn ergôn skopousi*], prove to have been greater than its predecessors." [44]

Oedipus uses this word in precisely this critical sense. He applies it both to examination of a situation with a view to action (" the only remedy I found after careful consideration," *eu skopôn*, 68), and to critical examination of statements about the death of Laius (" I examine every word," *panta . . . skopô logon*, 291). It is with this word that the chorus reproachfully tries to divert him from his angry assault on Tiresias to his proper task: " This is not what we need. How to find the best solution for the oracle of the god, there is what you should examine" (*tode skopein*, 407). But the critical overtones of *skopein* (one remembers that the Skeptic philosophers took their name from a closely allied word) come out most clearly when Jocasta announces her proof that the oracle was wrong. "Listen to this man, and as you listen, examine what the hallowed oracles of the gods come to" (*skopei*, 952). And Oedipus goes further. "Why should one scrutinize the prophetic hearth of Pytho or the birds screaming overhead?" (*skopoito*, 964). For him they are not worth the trouble of a critical examination. They are worth, as he says a few lines later, "nothing" (972).[45]

Historein, "to ask questions," is a word particularly associated with the Ionian investigative spirit, and most of all with Herodotus, whose *historiai* (researches, questions and answers) are the beginning of what we know as "history." In Herodotus this word usually means "to question," though in two cases it shades off into the meaning "to know as a result of questioning."[46] In the *Oedipus Tyrannus* the first of these two meanings is the dominant one. The characteristic tone of Oedipus in the first two-thirds of the play is that of an impatient, demanding questioner.[47] The tragedy opens with a question which Oedipus puts to the priest. When Creon arrives he is met with a rapid barrage of questions (eleven of them in 89-129) which exhaust his information about the oracle and the murder of Laius. In the quarrel with Tiresias, Oedipus hurls a series of questions at the blind prophet, some real questions, some imperative, some rhetorical: five in the initial brush between them (319-40), six more before Oedipus makes his long speech (380-403), which itself contains two questions. Tiresias' reply to it is followed by an outburst of four violent questions (429-31) which are really imprecations, and his reference to Oedipus' parents (435-6) by two genuine and heartfelt questions (437) which the prophet answers with riddles. Creon's second appearance is greeted by an angry explosion of eleven lines which consists entirely of rhetorical questions, and this is followed by a rapid examination of Creon's knowledge of the previous attitude of Tiresias, phrased in six questions (555-68). Jocasta's account of the oracle that failed is followed by a series of swift precise questions (732-65), seven of them; the answers are enough to make him fear the worst. The next subject for interrogation is the Corinthian messenger, whose examination is introduced by the typically businesslike question, " Who is this, and what does he have to say to me? " [48] One is reminded of Strepsiades in Aristophanes' *Clouds*, who welcomes his son back from his studies at the " thinking-shop " with the gleeful comment, " That local ' what-do-you-say? ' look is positively blooming on him." [49]

The Corinthian messenger gives his news, but his real interrogation does not begin until he tells Oedipus that Polybus was not his father. This revelation is followed by no less than fourteen searching questions (1017-45), which prepare the way for the examination of the last witness, the shepherd. In the course of this last interrogation the shepherd refuses to answer in plain terms, and Oedipus backs his questions with threats and physical force.[50] It is at this point that the shepherd makes a final attempt to stop the relentless questioning. " No, by the gods, master, do not ask any more questions." [51] The answer is another threat, and more questions, culminating in the rapid half-line questions which extract the dreadful truth (1173-6). " If you are the one of whom he speaks, know that you were born unlucky," is the shepherd's last answer. Oedipus is not only the questioner but also the answer to the question.[52]

Tekmairesthai is a word which (though it is used in Homer in a different sense) sums up, in its fifth-century meaning

and the scientific process of inference. "I shall not prophesy," says the medical author; "I simply record the symptoms from which inferences must be made" (*hoisi chrê tekmairesthai*).[58]

The instrument of these scientific procedures—investigation, enquiry, deduction—is the human intelligence, *gnômê*. Prometheus, in the Aeschylean play, describes the primitive stage of human history in terms of the absence of this faculty: "they did everything without intelligence" (*ater gnômês*, 456). The great reputation of Oedipus is based on his answer to the riddle of the Sphinx and, though the priest suggests that he was helped in this achievement by a god, Oedipus proudly defines it as the work of his unaided intelligence. "I found the answer by intelligence [*gnômêi*, 398]—I did not learn it from birds." The human intelligence is here posed in opposition to the inspired, unscientific apprehension of the prophet,[59] a contrast fundamental not only for the play but for an understanding of the age in which it was written.

This intelligence, *gnomê*, is the capacity to distinguish, recognize, *gignôskein* [60] (just as the English, or rather Latin word "intelligence" means etymologically "choosing between"). *Gignôskein* is a significant word in the dramatic context, for Oedipus is eventually to recognize himself. "May you never recognize your identity" (*gnoiês*, 1068),[61] says Jocasta just before she rushes off stage, and Oedipus, in the speech which accompanies his self-blinding (a speech reported by the messenger), consigns to darkness those eyes which "failed to distinguish those whom he sought" (1273-4).[62] But before the failure of Oedipus' intelligence is revealed, the chorus, in a supremely ironic phrase, joins in unity the intelligence of man and the religious apprehension of the prophet which Oedipus had put asunder. They celebrate the imminent revelation of Oedipus' birth, which they claim will prove to be of divine origin. "If I am a prophet, and have knowledge based on intelligence" (*kata gnôman idris*, 1087)[63]—these are the opening words of the stasimon which precedes the great discovery of the truth of prophecy and the inadequacy of that human intelligence which Oedipus represents.

This *gnômê*, the active intelligence which distinguishes and recognizes, is a function of *nous*, the mind. This word *nous* was in Periclean Athens pregnant with scientific and philosophical significance, if only because of the widely discussed theories of Anaxagoras, who made *nous* the moving force of the universe in his philosophical system and was himself nicknamed *Nous* by his contemporaries.

The mind of Oedipus is the driving force behind the action of the Sophoclean drama, and just as he opposes his *gnômê* to the divine inspiration of the prophet, so he taunts Tiresias with the failure of his *nous*. " You are blind, in ears and mind and eyes" (371). This extraordinary phrase echoes many formulas of the philosophical and religious traditions. " Mind sees and Mind hears," said Epicharmus; " everything else is dumb and blind." [64] " The divinity," says Xenophanes, " is all seeing, and mind, and hearing." [65] Oedipus' savage taunt denies Tiresias religious insight as well as human reasoning power. The prophet's reply is a warning that before long the same taunts will be flung at Oedipus himself—and before the play is over he blinds himself, and wishes that he could have deafened himself and so cut off his mind from the cognizance of his disasters. Meanwhile, under the impact of Jocasta's revelations the mind of Oedipus begins to lose control. " He does not," says Jocasta, " like a man in control of his mind [*ennous*] judge the present on the basis of the past " (915-16). This word *ennous* indicates a person whose mind is in full control of his faculties: it is used by Agave in the *Bacchae* of Euripides to describe her return to sanity from Dionysiac ecstasy, and by Plato to describe the rational, controlled mind which is incapable of inspired prophesy.[66] The word occurs nowhere else in Sophocles; in Aeschylus it occurs only once, and that once in a significant context. It is the word Prometheus uses to describe the state of the human race after his intervention had brought about the transition from savagery to civilization: "before, they were childish; I made them into rational beings" (*ennous*, 444).[67]

But when Jocasta speaks of Oedipus he is no longer a rational creature; he is a prey to pain and fear. The next reference to his mind comes after the revelation of the truth and his violent reaction to it. When he tries to justify on rational grounds the impulse which led him to put out his eyes, the chorus says to him: "I feel pity for you—for your mind and your disasters equally" (1347).[68]

The intelligence, the mind of Oedipus are always active; their activity is *phrontis*, "thought." "I came wandering over many roads of thought" (*phrontidos*, 67), he tells the priest early in the play.[69] This word was closely associated in the popular mind with the new scientific developments, as is plain from Aristophanes' satirical offensive against the new outlook, *The Clouds*. In this comedy the "school" of Socrates is called the *phrontistêrion*, "thought-shop." "Quiet!" says one of the students to Strepsiades as he hammers at the door. "You have just aborted a thought [*phrontid'*, 137] which I had discovered."[70] And Socrates in the same play, describes himself as "suspending the operation of his mind and thought" (*phrontida*, 229).[71]

Oedipus has wandered over many roads of thought in his attempt to find a remedy for the plague, but the chorus, which has not heard this statement of his, provides an ironic echo of his words as it enters the orchestra. "The whole of my people is sick, and there is no sword of thought [*phrontidos*, 170] with which one can defend oneself."[72] The thought of

Oedipus does finally reach its objective, the truth, but his reaction to the discovery is to blind himself. He would have deafened himself too, he says, if there had been any way to block the sense of hearing—" so that I could be blind and totally deaf. That my thought [*phrontid'*, 1390] should dwell outside my miseries—that would be sweet." [73] He wishes, for a moment, to isolate his thought from all contact with the world of his senses, and be what he called Tiresias, " blind in ears and mind and eyes."

The search for truth, guided by intelligence, produces knowledge. " To know " (*oida, eidenai*) is a word built into the fabric of Oedipus' name and ironically emphasized in line after line of the play. He speaks not only of his knowledge [74] but also, with fierce and conscious irony, of his ignorance. " I stopped her," he says of the Sphinx, " I, know-nothing Oedipus " (*ho mèden eidôs Oidipous*, 397).[75] This sarcastic phrase is an expression of contempt for the useless knowledge possessed by Tiresias, and the taunt is returned to him with interest. " Do you know [*oisth'*, 415] who your parents are? " Oedipus is ignorant of the one thing most men know, their parentage. It is not long before Oedipus begins to fear that his ironic boast of ignorance may have been a literal statement of the truth. " It seems," he tells Jocasta, " that it was myself I was subjecting to dreadful curses just now—without knowing it " (*ouk eidenai*, 745). With the arrival of the Corinthian messenger the ignorance of Oedipus is emphatically and repeatedly stressed: " You don't know what you are doing " (1008). " Don't you know that you have no just ground for fear? " (1014). " Know that he took you as a gift from my hand " (1022). And it is with this last word " know " (*isthi*, 1181) that the shepherd announces the monstrous truth: " if you are the man he says you are, know that you were born ill-fated." [76] Towards the end of the play Oedipus sums up the knowledge that remains with him. "This much at least I know" (*tosouton g' oida*, 1455), says the blind, ruined man; "no disease nor anything else could wreck me. For I would never have been saved from death, unless for some dreadful evil." It seems little enough but, unlike the knowledge he laid claim to before the catastrophe, it is real knowledge.

The knowledge attained by intelligent investigation fitted the exponents of the new scientific outlook to perform great services for their fellow men. They were equipped to find, to discover (the Greek word corresponding to these two means also "to invent"), to reveal, to make clear, to demonstrate, to teach. Their self-appointed task was to bring light where there was darkness, certainty where there was doubt, to replace confusion with clarity, and to train others in their methods and views. These are the attitudes and activities of an intellectual revolution, an age of enlightenment, and the words which describe them bulk large in the vocabulary of the *Oedipus Tyrannus*.

Heurein, "to find," is familiar even to the Greekless reader as a word associated with scientific discovery because of the story of Archimedes in the bath and his cry of (*h*)*eurêka*, "I have found it." But long before Archimedes ran naked through the streets of Syracuse in the third century B. C.,[77] this word was in common use to describe scientific discovery and invention. The Greek penchant for attributing every discovery or invention to a specific (and usually legendary) inventor (*heuretês*) is well known; *prôtos hêure*, "he was the first to discover" (or "invent"), is a formula which recurs incessantly in Greek histories of philosophy, mathematics, and science.[78]

It is a word used by Thucydides to describe the result of his historical method—the discovery of the past. The reader, he says, speaking of his own attempt to reconstruct ancient history, should "consider that the facts have been discovered

[*heurêsthai*] on the basis of the clearest evidence, as satis-
factorily as they could, considering that they happened long
ago." [79] In this sense it is a word exactly appropriate to the
search conducted by Oedipus; he too is a historian, trying to
discover the facts about the past on the basis of the clearest
evidence available. But the word is also applicable to discovery
in astronomy, technique, mathematics, in fact to the whole
range of discoveries and inventions which have made possible
human civilization. It is the verb which recurs most frequently
in Prometheus' account of his civilizing gifts to man; he uses
it of his discovery of number and writing (460), ships (468),
and metals (503).[80] The word occurs frequently also in the
myth of human progress told by Protagoras in the Platonic
dialogue: " man . . . invented [*hêureto*, 322a] houses, clothes,
shoes, blankets, and crops." So Palamedes, in the oration of
Gorgias, claims to have invented (*heurôn*, 30) " warlike forma-
tions . . . written laws . . . letters . . . weights and measures
. . . number . . . signal fires . . . and the game of checkers."
And the same word recurs in the fragments of the two
Sophoclean plays which dealt with Palamedes, the *Palamedes*
and the *Nauplius*.[81] It is used also in a magnificent passage
in one of the Hippocratic treatises, a passage which epitomizes
the confident, rational spirit of the new age. " Medicine,"
says the writer of the work entitled *On Ancient Medicine*,
" is not like some branches of enquiry [he has instanced
enquiries into things above and things below the earth] in
which everything rests on an unprovable hypothesis. Medicine
has discovered a principle and a method, through which many
great discoveries have been made over a long period, and what
remains will be discovered too, if the enquirer is competent,
knows what discoveries have been made, and takes them as the
starting point for his enquiry." [82]

In the opening scene of the play Oedipus, speaking to the

priest, calls his action in sending Creon to Delphi "the only healing treatment which after careful examination I was able to discover" (*hêuriskon*, 68). The result of that action is a call for further discovery, the investigation of the murder of Laius, an attempt to discover the past. Oedipus is at first appalled at the difficulty of the task—"Where shall the track be discovered?" (*heurêthêsetai*, 108)—but soon, as his questioning of Creon begins to elicit facts, he regains confidence. The witness who was present at Laius' death knew only one thing, says Creon deprecatingly, but Oedipus insists on knowing it. "For one thing might discover [the way] to learn many" (*exeuroi*, 120).

Oedipus begins as the discoverer, but as the investigation gets under way the confidence with which he uses the word evaporates. "Are these inventions [*tàxeurêmata*, 378] yours or Creon's?" he asks Tiresias (378) when the prophet accuses him; the word is profoundly ironic, for the accusation is not an invention but a discovery of truth. Tiresias in reply taunts him with his reputation as a discoverer. "You speak in riddles," Oedipus tells the prophet, and the answer is: "Are you not the best man alive at finding the answers to them?" (*heuriskein*, 440).

Oedipus accepts this taunt proudly. "Go on, reproach me, but it is in this, you will discover, that my greatness lies" (*heurêseis*, 441). And he applies himself energetically to the attempt first to discover the secret of Laius' murder, and later to solve the secret of his own birth, the riddle read him by Tiresias. When the Corinthian messenger makes clear that the shepherd who accompanied Laius is the key to the riddle of Oedipus' identity, Oedipus asks where the shepherd is to be found. "Inform me, this is the vital moment for these things to be discovered" (*heurêsthai*, 1050).[83]

But meanwhile a change has taken place in the relationship

between Oedipus and the process of discovery. "I found you," the Corinthian messenger says to him, "in the wooded glens of Cithaeron" (*heurôn*, 1026). This is a lie, and he later retracts it, but it raises for the first time the prospect of Oedipus not as discoverer but as discovered. And the chorus, in its optimistic speculations on the possibility that Oedipus is of divine birth, repeats the idea. "Did the Bacchic god who dwells on the mountains receive you as a lucky find from one of the nymphs of Helicon, with whom he often sports?" (*heurêma*, 1106).[85]

When the great discovery is finally made, the suggestion inherent in this change of relationship becomes clear statement. "All-seeing time has discovered you, against your will" (*ephêure*, 1213), sings the chorus, and Oedipus himself expresses the complete transition from active to passive, the *peripeteia* of the word. "Now I am discovered as base and of base birth" (*heuriskomai*, 1397); "I am discovered as base in every respect" (*ephêurêmai*, 1421). The finder has turned into the thing found, the discoverer into the thing discovered.

Phainein, "to bring to light, to make visible," is another of the words which are typical formulas of the scientific spirit of the age. It is of course a term associated with the legal process (to bring a criminal, or a crime, to light by informing the authorities), and this meaning is fully operative in the play, but so also are its wider scientific connotations, which are well exemplified by the passage in which Gorgias, in his defense of Helen, pays tribute to the power of words and mentions as an example of it "the words of the astronomers which have made things incredible and obscure visible [*phainesthai*] to the eyes of opinion."[86]

The truth about the murder of Laius belongs to the realm of things invisible, not revealed. "The Sphinx," says Creon, speaking of the murder of Laius, "forced us to dismiss what

was obscure, invisible " (tàphanê, 131). But Oedipus announces that he will " make a fresh start, and bring it to light "
(egô phanô, 132). The initial revelations, however, come from
others. Tiresias refuses to " reveal my sorrows, not to mention
yours " (ekphênô, 329), but he is goaded to speech by Oedipus
himself and ends their interview with a prophecy of revelations to come. " The man you seek is here . . . he shall be
revealed as a Theban born [phanêsetai, 453] . . . he shall
be revealed as father and brother of his own children "
(phanêsetai, 457). The next revelation comes from Jocasta,
and it is made in terms which forcefully suggest not only the
form but also the content of the new scientific doctrines:
" Listen to me and learn that no human creature has the
capacity to prophecy. I will reveal [phanô, 710] evidence to
prove it, and it will not take long." The evidence she brings
forward is an ambiguous proof at best, for it seems to prove that
though Apollo was wrong, Tiresias may have been right.
" Alas, it is clear as crystal now," says Oedipus when he hears
the details of the death of Laius; the word he uses, diaphanê
(754), comes from the scientific vocabulary.[87]

With the news from Corinth Oedipus recovers some of his
confidence, and once more assumes the title and performs the
function of the revealer. " It is impossible," he tells the dis-
traught Jocasta, " that with such evidence before me, I should
not reveal my origin " (phanô, 1059). But the revelation of his
origin is also the revelation of his pollution, and in his final
statements his use of this word is no longer active but passive.
" I am revealed," he cries, " unnaturally born and married, an
unnatural murderer " (pephasmai, 1184). " Revealed as unholy
by the gods " (phanent', 1383), he calls himself later, and in
one of his most terrible phrases he says that he has been
" revealed as a father who ploughed where he himself was

sown" (*ephanthên*, 1485). He is not only the revealer but also the thing revealed.

To "make visible" the obscure is to make it "clear," and it is characteristic of all ages of enlightenment that they are inclined to equate clarity with truth. The Greek word *saphês*, which in its earliest form in Homer, means "clear," [88] came to be used in the fifth century with something very like the meaning "true." Thucydides, for example, uses this word to recommend his austere history to those "who will want to examine the truth about [*to saphes*, "a clear picture of"] past events." [89] This insistence on clarity is typical of the temper of the new age: the *mythos* might be indirect, obscure, ambiguous, but the *logos* must be direct, clear, precise.[90] It is in these terms that Aristophanes makes his burlesque Euripides attack the dramatic writing of Aeschylus. "Not one thing he said was clear" (*saphes*, 927), says Euripides in the *Frogs*, and he attacks the Aeschylean prologue on the same basis: "He was obscure [*asaphês*, 1122] in his exposition of the facts."

The scientific spirit, which strives to make the invisible visible (*phainesthai ta aphanê*), attempts also to make the unclear clear. Oedipus, searching for clarity in the obscure affair of the death of Laius, is told by the chorus that from Tiresias he will learn the truth "most clearly" (*saphestata*, 286). Tiresias is a prophet, and the word *saphês* applied to prophets has a special force, for they were well known to deal in obscurity and ambiguity. A "clear" prophet can at least be judged by results; if his statement about the future can be clearly understood, it is at least possible to know, some day, whether it was also "true." [91] But what Tiresias says is something Oedipus cannot accept, and he retaliates by attacking the prophet's "clarity." "Tell me, how can you be called a clear [true] prophet?" (*mantis . . . saphês*, 390). This taunt is a reference to Tiresias' silence when the Sphinx ravaged

Thebes; Tiresias was no clear prophet at that time of danger—
he said nothing at all. And though he proceeds to prophecy
now, it is " riddling and unclear " (*ainikta kàsaphê*, 439). This
denunciation of Tiresias' obscurity (falsehood) is carried to
further lengths in Jocasta's claim that there is no foreknowledge
in all the universe: " there is no clear [true] foreknowledge
of anything " (*saphês*, 978).

There may be no foreknowledge, but Oedipus insists on
clarity, the clarity created by the human intelligence, which
in his person is now striving to discover not the future but the
past. " I will not be persuaded," he tells Jocasta, " not to learn
this [i. e. his origin] fully and clearly " (*saphôs*, 1065). But
the final clarity which he establishes proves the divine prediction both clear and true. " Alas," he cries, " then it would all
come out clear " (*saphê*, 1182). But these words also mean:
" Then the oracles must have turned out true." [92] Now he
sees clear for the first time in the play, but his eyes cannot
bear the clarity his intelligence has created and he rushes off
to put them out.

The man who has discovered, revealed, and made clear
becomes a demonstrator, a teacher. He makes evident (*dêloô*)
and points out (*deiknymi*). Both words mean also " to prove,"
and they are characteristic formulas of the great teachers of the
fifth century, the sophists.[93] They appear also in the *Oedipus
Tyrannus* and move in the pattern exemplified by the other
operative words of the Oedipean vocabulary, the pattern of
reversal from active to passive.

Oedipus undertakes to " make evident " an " unseen " murderer (*adêlon*, 475), to solve the mystery of an " unclear "
death (*adêlôn*, 497), but he is soon condemning Creon on " an
opinion which lacks evidence " (*adêlôi*, 608) and plunged into
darkness on the vital question of his own identity. The Corinthian messenger starts him off again on the search for clarity

by his mention of the all-important witness, the shepherd. "Who is that?" asks Oedipus. "Can you make him evident?" (*dêlôsai*, 1041). His identity is only too evident to Jocasta, but Oedipus has still some time to run before he shouts, to quote the messenger's words, for "someone to make evident to all Thebes the father-killer" (*dêloun*, 1287). The prophecy is fulfilled, that he would "make evident a progeny that man could not bear to see" (*dêlôsoim'*, 792).

His intention was to "point out" (*deiknymi*) the murderer. "I have no means of pointing out the killer" (*deiksai*, 278), says the chorus in answer to his proclamation. "You will point out [more clearly] if you will say one thing more" (*deikseis*, 748), says Oedipus to Jocasta, as he poses the final question which completes the revelation of the circumstances of the murder of Laius. And the word recurs in the terrible moment when the doors of the palace open, just before the blind and bloodstained Oedipus is revealed to the audience. "He will show you" (*deiksei*, 1294), says the messenger.[94] "The locks of these gates are opening. You will see a spectacle before long such that even one who hated him would pity."

The Greek words for "learn" and "teach" (*manthanein* and *didaskein*) occur frequently in the text of the play. It is true that they occur with great frequency in the text of almost any Greek play, for the word *manthanein* was commonly used in the general sense of "to find out" and *didaskein* with the simple meaning of "tell, inform." But in the *Oedipus Tyrannus* these words seem to be used in contexts and with a force which direct attention to their literal meaning.

They are of course words which in their literal sense re-create the atmosphere of the intellectual ferment of fifth-century Athens. The sophists who were subjecting every aspect of the traditional Athenian outlook to corrosive criticism were all of them professional teachers who for high fees trained listeners from all walks of life in the critical methods and the revolutionary doctrines of the new schools. This new education, an education for adults, was the burning question of the day, and even those who most severely criticized its products and results were molded by its disciplines and used its characteristic methods and formulas.

Oedipus is like the great teachers of the fifth century in one respect: he has no master from whom he learned, he is self-taught. "You had not been taught" (*ekdidachtheis*, 38), says the priest, expressing his admiration for Oedipus' solution of the riddle of the Sphinx, and Oedipus repeats the phrase in his proud claim that the solution of the riddle was a triumph of untrained intelligence. "I did not learn it from birds" (*mathôn*, 398). But though untaught himself, he assumes that others have had a teacher. "Who taught you that?" (*didachtheis*, 357) he asks Tiresias when he finds himself accused. "You did not learn it from your prophetic art." It is to Oedipus that others come for instruction. "Instruct me" (*didaske*, 554), says Creon, "what you claim to have suffered at my hands." "You are a skillful speaker," says Oedipus to Creon, "but I am a bad learner, from you" (*manthanein*, 545). "I have the right to learn from you" (*mathein*, 575), says Creon, and Oedipus answers: "Learn then, in full" (*ekmanthan'*, 576). "Instruct me" (*didakson*, 698), says Jocasta, asking Oedipus for an explanation of the quarrel with Creon, and Oedipus prefaces his account of his life before he came to Thebes with the words "I will instruct you" (*didaksô*, 839).

But as the action develops, the roles are reversed. Oedipus has a lesson read to him by Jocasta. "Listen to me," she tells him, in words that conjure up not only the atmosphere but also the doctrine of the sophistic schools; "Listen, and learn

136

that nothing human has the gift of prophecy" (*math'*, 708). And later Oedipus, now in truth the ignorant Oedipus of his own proud and sarcastic phrase, begs the Corinthian messenger for instruction. "My mother, or my father? Instruct me, in the gods' name" (*didaske*, 1009). The teacher becomes the learner, but he becomes something more. He turns into the "thing pointed out" (*paradeigma*, 1193), the paradigm, the example, the object lesson. "I have your destiny as an example," sings the chorus, "and call no man happy" (1193-5).

This same reversal is to be seen in the development of two other words which are typical titles of the champions of enlightenment in all ages, and which were in the Greek experience particularly associated with Athens in its role as the center of the political and intellectual revolution of the fifth century. Oedipus, like Athens,[95] and like the scientists and philosophers of the age,[96] is offered and accepts the titles "liberator" and "savior."

Prometheus, the mythical prototype of the scientist and sophist, proclaims himself, in Aeschylus' play, the liberator of mankind. "I liberated mortals," he says, "from going shattered to death" (*ekselysamên*, P. V. 235); the means of liberation, he tells us later, was the gift of fire, from which mankind learned the techniques of civilization. Many years later, when the liberating role of the new teachings was regarded with a less favorable and optimistic eye, Aristophanes in *The Clouds* made Strepsiades describe his son, a recent graduate *cum laude* of the sophistic school, as "a savior for my house . . . and a liberator from pain" (*sôtêr domois . . . kai lysanias*, 1161-2).

Oedipus is addressed by both titles in the opening speech of the priest. "You liberated the city of Cadmus [*ekselysas*, 35] . . . this land calls you savior . . ." (*sôtêra*, 48). And later, in the course of the quarrel with Tiresias, he adopts both of these titles himself. "How was it," he asks Tiresias, speaking of the time when Thebes was under attack by the Sphinx, "that you uttered no liberating word [*eklytêrion*, 392] for these fellow citizens of yours? No, *I* came . . ." And later, hard pressed by Tiresias, he retorts: "But if I saved this city, I don't care [what happens to me]" (*polin . . . eksesôs'*, 443).

But in the present crisis he finds himself unable either to liberate or to save. And soon the familiar rhythm of reversal becomes apparent in the language. "Why don't I liberate you from this fear?" (*ekselysamên*, 1003), the Corinthian messenger asks Oedipus, and the same officious informant a few lines later assumes the other title too. "I was your savior at that moment, my child" (*sôtêr*, 1030). "I liberated you from the fetters that pierced your feet" (*lyô*, 1034), he says later, and the shepherd adds the complementary verb—"he saved you . . . for disaster" (*esôsen*, 1180). Oedipus in his agony recognizes the Corinthian's claim. "Curse him," he cries, "curse the man who liberated me from my bonds [*elyse*, 1350] . . . and saved me . . ." (*kanesôsen*, 1351).[97] And later he repeats the shepherd's phrase. "I was saved [*esôthên*, 1457] . . . for some dreadful evil." The liberator turns out to be the liberated, the savior the saved.

In the reversal which is the pattern of development of these words in the play, the suffering of the tragic hero is projected on to a larger stage. The reversal of Oedipus becomes a demonstration (*paradeigma*) of the paradoxical nature of man's greatest achievements: his magnificent energy accomplishes his own ruin; his probing intelligence, pushing on to final solutions, brings him in the end face to face with a reality he cannot contemplate. His action defeats itself, or rather loses the name of action at all, for he is both actor and patient, the seeker and the thing sought, the finder and the thing found, the revealer and the thing revealed.

III

This same terrifying pattern is developed in detail in two more verbal complexes which suggest fresh images of the action and attitude of Oedipus. They are appropriate and significant images for the revolutionary nature of man's attempt to assert his mastery over nature by means of his intelligence, especially so for the fifth century, for it is from two of the greatest intellectual achievements of that century that they are drawn. Oedipus is presented in the figure of physician and mathematician.

The culminating achievement of man, in the history of human progress sketched in the choral ode of the *Antigone*, is the discovery of the art of medicine—" and from desperate diseases he has contrived means of escape." Medicine ranks high in the list of the inventions of Prometheus, the mythical founder of human civilization.[98] And it was, in fact, one of the great scientific achievements of fifth-century Greece. It is in the writings of the Hippocratic school that the most striking statements of the new scientific outlook are to be found. They exhibit an empirical spirit and an optimistic confidence which are not to be seen again in Western Europe until the nineteenth century after Christ. "Many discoveries have been made, and everything else will be discovered," is the sublimely confident statement of the author of the treatise *On Ancient Medicine*,[99] an argument in favor of the empirical method aimed against the importation into the art of medicine of philosophical hypotheses. "This disease," says the author of the treatise *On the Sacred Disease*, (5), "is in my opinion no more sacred than the rest of them. It has the same nature as other diseases, and, like them, a cause. It is also curable." The disease he is so confident can be cured is epilepsy. And the author of *On Ancient Medicine* propounds a medical adaptation of the Protagorean humanist thesis: "One must aim at some measure. But no measure, number or weight can you find, by reference to which you can attain exact knowledge, except the sensations of the body." [100] It is in the fifth-century medical writings that the spirit of the enlightenment is seen in its clearest colors and at its best. And one of the most fully developed images of the play presents Oedipus in these terms, as a physician.

As before, the metaphor has a solid basis in the dramatic situation. Oedipus is called upon to find the cause of the plague which afflicts the city, and to devise a remedy. The situation prepares the ground for the image, which is made precise and alive by the frequent appearance of words and usages which are drawn from and suggest the scientific vocabulary and style of the new medical science.

In the priest's speech at the beginning of the play there are a number of expressions which suggest that he is appealing to a physician on behalf of a sick patient. "The city," he tells Oedipus," . . . is storm-tossed, and cannot raise up [*anakouphisai*, 23] its head out of the depths of the bloody swell." This is figurative language which suggests a swimmer in a heavy sea, or a ship,[101] but it also weaves into the complex pattern the image of a patient fighting a disease, and this suggestion is strengthened by the word "bloody" (*phoiniou*, 24), which does not seem appropriate for either swimmer or ship. And the priest's word *anakouphisai*, "raise up," is echoed in a later speech of Oedipus, in a context which does not suggest ships or swimmers. "You might receive help and relief [*anakouphisin*, 218] from your troubles," he says to the chorus. The translation "relief" emphasizes what is in fact a common meaning of the word: *kouphizein*, "to lighten," is used almost as a technical term in medical language to describe "improvement" on the part of the patient, especially relief from fever. "Copious sweats," reads a Hippocratic description of the symptoms of a fever on the island of Thasos, "bringing no relief" (*kouphizontes ouden*).[102] In the *Philoctetes* Sophocles uses this word in the strictly medical sense: "I seem to be relieved" (*kouphizein dokô*, 735), says Philoctetes when Neoptolemus anxiously enquires about the condition of his disease.

In his description of the plague in Thebes the priest uses a word for "sterile" (*agonois*, 27) which occurs nowhere else in Sophocles and is a standard term of the Hippocratic writers and also of the later Greek medical literature.[103] And he appeals to Oedipus as "experienced" (*empeiroisi*, 44), using a word which is the highest term of praise the Hippocratic writers can bestow on a physician.[104]

Oedipus in reply uses similar language. "This one method of cure [*iasin*, 68] [105] which I found on examination [*skopôn*] I have already put into practice." Creon's arrival brings what corresponds to the diagnosis of the disease, for he brings an explanation of the cause of the plague, the murder of Laius, and also suggests a cure, the punishment of the murderer. His speech is scattered with words which come from the same source and suggest the same atmosphere. The news is "hard to bear," (*dysphor'*, 87); [106] he quotes Apollo as saying that the blood of Laius "brings a storm on the city" (*cheimazon polin*, 101), using a word which in medical literature describes the suffering of the patient at the height of the disease. "They feel pain on the third day, and are at their worst [*cheimazontai malista*—literally "are most storm-tossed"] on the fifth," says the author of the treatise *On Prognosis*.[107]

The chorus, in the opening stasimon, describes the plague from which Thebes is suffering. Here again, ornate and lyrical as their language is, and though the song they are singing is a prayer to the gods, many of the words they use are drawn from the vocabulary of the new scientific medicine. "The flame of pain" [*phloga pêmatos*, 166] is their phrase for the plague, and they describe its action as "burning" (*phlegei*, 192). The use of these and cognate words to describe fever and inflammation is characteristic of the Hippocratic writers and appears also in Thucydides' account of the Athenian plague.[108] "Children lie death-bringing on the ground" (*thanataphora*, 181), sings the chorus, and this adjective is common in medical texts.[109]

Oedipus now appears and promises them relief (*anakouphisin*, 218). He goes on to reproach them for the advanced stage the disease has attained, for according to him they could have prevented it by pressing the enquiry into the murder of Laius. "It was not right," he tells them, "for you to leave that affair unpurified, uncleansed" (*akatharton*, 256). This word occurs nowhere else in Sophocles but is a common term in the medical writers: they use it, for example, of an ulcer which has been neglected, or of a patient who has not been purged.[110]

All through the violent scenes of altercation, first with Tiresias and then with Creon, the metaphor is maintained,[111] but by the end of the scene with Creon a change has taken place in its application. "Such natures," says Creon, meaning Oedipus, "are, justly, most painful for themselves to bear" (*hai de toiautai physeis*, 674). This judgment on Oedipus is expressed in what are unmistakable medical terms. The use of the word "nature" (*physis*) in the plural is unexampled elsewhere in Sophocles and does not occur in Aeschylus either, but the whole phrase is a commonplace of the Hippocratic writings, where it is usually used to denote physical types. "Such natures" (*tas de toiautas physias*), says the author of *Ancient Medicine*, (12) "are weaker . . ." "Such natures" (*tas de toiautas physias*), says the writer of *Airs, Waters, Places* (4), "are necessarily given to eating much and drinking little." [112] The words of Creon are a diagnosis and Oedipus is the patient. Four lines later the chorus asks Jocasta: "Why do you delay to take this man into the house?" (*komizein*, 678). [113] They do not address Oedipus but appeal over his head to Jocasta; the solicitous tone of the request suggests that they think of Oedipus as a sick man. And it is in these terms that Jocasta speaks of him later, when Oedipus knows the circumstances of Laius' death. "He raises his passion too high with pains of all kinds" (*lypaisi*, 915). He is like a "stricken" pilot (*empeplêgmenon*, 922).

From this agony of spirit the great news brought by the Corinthian messenger gives him a temporary relief. Oedipus begins to probe and question once again. He asks how Polybus died. "By treachery, or by the visitation of disease?" (*nosou synallagêi*, 960). [114] The Corinthian messenger answers like a Hippocratic physician: "A small impulse brings aged bodies to their rest." [115]

This news brings Oedipus some comfort, and Jocasta claims the credit for the result. "Did I not foretell this long ago?" (*proulegon*, 973). The word she uses (and this is its only occurrence in Sophocles) is one of the key words in the Hippocratic discussions of the function of the doctor. "To declare the past, diagnose the present, foretell the future [*prolegein*], this should be your practice," says the author of the first book of *Visits*. [116] But it is typical of the irony of this play that Jocasta should use the word at this moment, for she now launches on a denial of the possibility of foretelling anything. Oedipus should not fear the prophecy of Apollo. "What should man fear, whose life is governed by the operations of chance, and for whom there is no clear [true] foreknowledge [*pronoia*, 978] of anything?" This is more than an attack on oracular prophecy, it is a nihilistic statement which rejects not only the religious viewpoint but the scientific one as well. *Pronoia*, "foreknowledge, foresight," is not only the basis of divine prophecy; it is also the ability which the physician, in the Hippocratic writings, is urged to cultivate above all others. "Practise foresight" (*pronoian*) begins the treatise *On Prognosis*; [117] this work is a full discussion of the art of making accurate forecasts as a necessary preliminary to treatment and as a means of inspiring confidence in the patient.

Jocasta rejects foresight and proclaims the rule of chance; the doctors, who teach both the possibility and the necessity of foresight, emphatically reject the concept of chance, both in the doctor's operations and in the functioning of the human body. "We ought not," says the writer of *On Ancient Medicine*, "to jettison the ancient art of medicine as nonexistent or bad research just because it does not have complete accuracy, but much rather, because of its capacity to advance by reasoning from deep ignorance to a point very near real accuracy, we should admire its discoveries as the product of good and correct research, and not of chance" (*V. M.* 12). The author of the treatise *On Places in Man* is even more explicit and indignant in his rejection of chance. "The whole of medicine has a sound basis," he says, "and the superb intellectual achievements which constitute it do not seem to have any need of chance. Chance is self-controlling, not subject to control, not even by prayer can you make fortune come; science is subject to control and has a fortunate result when the one who wishes to use it is an expert. What need has medicine of fortune [chance]? If there are clear [*saphê*, "true"] remedies for diseases, these remedies, it seems to me, do not wait for fortune to turn disease into health . . ." [118] The same point of view is developed in the treatise *On the Art*. Replying to those critics who malign the art of medicine because it does not heal all cases of sickness and who claim that even those patients who are healed by it owe more to chance than the medical art, the author states, in conciliatory form, a very unconciliatory opinion: "I do not myself deprive chance of any of its achievements, but I think that when diseases are badly treated the result is generally misfortune, and when they are well treated, good fortune." [119] The patients themselves, he goes on to point out, do not really believe that their cure was due to chance, since they submitted to medical treatment; "they were unwilling to look at the naked face of chance—they handed themselves over to the medical art." [120]

Jocasta's denial of foresight and exaltation of chance is a rejection of the possibility of that very forecasting in which she at first claimed to have been successful (*proulegon*, 973). And she proceeds to state the consequences which follow from the recognition of the dominion of chance in terms which, ironically, are the terms of medical science. They are terms which in themselves constitute a diagnosis of and a judgment on the course of conduct which she advocates. If chance governs all things, then "it is best to live recklessly [*eikê*, "haphazardly, without system," 979], as best one can." [121] This word *eikê* is used by Aeschylus' Prometheus to describe the chaotic nature of human life before civilization—"they confused everything at random" [*eikê*, *P. V.* 450]—and it is used in the doctors to describe the way of life which is unregimented, undisciplined, loose, one which gives no thought to the consequences. "Of those who were sick," says the writer of the first book of *Visits*, describing an epidemic on the island of Thasos," these mostly died: boys, young people, men in their prime . . . those who had lived recklessly [*eikê*] and at their ease [*epi to rathymon*]." [122] The second of these two phrases appears in Jocasta's next statement: "He who pays no attention to such things [as dreams] bears the burden of life most at his ease " (*rasta ton bion pherei*, 983).

But Oedipus has never lived "recklessly" or "at his ease," and when the messenger opens up a fresh avenue of investigation Oedipus continues to pursue the truth, to reach finally a point at which Jocasta, her eyes open at last, rushes into the palace to hang herself, after a last futile attempt to stop Oedipus' dogged probing. In the prolonged silence which follows this unexpected reaction [123] the chorus expresses its foreboding. "I fear that from this silence will break out evil" (*anarrêksei*, 1075). "Burst forth what will" (*rêgnytô*, 1076), Oedipus replies. This is generally taken to be a metaphor drawn from the "bursting out" of a storm: "the image," says Jebb, "is that of a storm bursting forth from a great stillness." It is noticeable, however, that the two parallels which Jebb quotes are both examples of e<u>k</u>rêgnysthai not a<u>narr</u>êgnysthai, and the effect of *ana* ("up") is to suggest rather an image of a volcanic eruption, or waters "bursting up" after an earthquake.[124] It suggests also an image from medical terminology, in which this word occurs frequently. The doctors use it of infections "chronic, troublesome, and often breaking out again" (*anarrêgnymena*), of air "breaking up the bubbles in which it is enclosed" (*anarrêksêi*)—a medical description of belching—of phlegm "bursting open the veins" (*anarrêgnyei*), of a flux "bursting upward" (*anarrêgnytai*), of blood "bursting open the passages" (*anarrêgnyei*).[125]

Evil "bursts up" as the chorus feared it would, and the messenger, after his clinical description of Oedipus' ghastly operation on his own eyes,[126] repeats the phrase: "This has broken out from two not one, evil mixed for husband and wife."[127] The messenger announces that Oedipus is about to come out of the palace. "But he needs strength, and someone to lead him on. For the disease is more than he can bear."[128]

Oedipus is a sick man, but he is also, in a terrible sense, the doctor, the surgeon who has just performed an operation on his own eyes. He justifies this action, and adds that if he had known how, he would have destroyed his hearing as well as his sight. This statement is made in words which suggest the medical vocabulary. "If there had been some way to obstruct [*phragmos*, 1387] the stream of hearing in the ears, I would not have refrained from shutting off [*apokleisai*, 1388] my wretched body entirely." Both these words are found only here in Sophocles, and both are common in the doctors.[129]

Oedipus goes on to recall the stages of his life, addressing himself to places and persons who have harbored and nurtured him, to Cithaeron, Polybus, Corinth. "You brought me up, a thing of beauty, but how festering with evil underneath the surface" (*kallos kakôn hypoulon*, 1396).[130] The festering sore of his hidden past has finally burst up, and Oedipus stands revealed not as the physician but as the sick man—in fact as the disease, for his presence in Thebes is the cause of the plague.[131]

IV

What is in some ways the most elaborately formulated and deeply suggestive image in the play is introduced by a bold phrase in the first speech of the priest in the prologue. "I do not regard you," he says to Oedipus, "as one equated to the gods [*theoisi . . . isoumenon*, 31] but as first of men." *Isoumenon*, "equated," is a mathematical term, and it is only one of a whole complex of such terms which is inextricably woven into the texture of the play's taut and suggestive language. To all the other achievements of mankind which are symbolized in the figure of Oedipus *tyrannos* is added what the Greeks regarded as a man's greatest, because most purely intellectual, discovery, mathematics.

In the Greek anthropological tradition, the discovery of number ranks very high among the steps towards man's understanding and hope of eventual control of his environment. It is claimed by Aeschylus' Promotheus: "and number too I discovered, outstanding among intellectual achievements" (*arithmon, P. V.* 459).[132] Palamedes, too, is credited with the discovery. "He discovered," says one of the characters in the lost *Nauplius* of Sophocles, "the inventions of weights, numbers, and measures . . . and first contrived ten out of one, and out of ten again units of fifty, and then thousands . . ."[133] The philosophic and scientific enquirers saw number as the basis of scientific cognition. "Everything that can be known has number," said Philolaos, "for it is impossible to grasp anything with the mind or recognize it without this."[134] And Aristotle mentions a proposed definition of man as "the creature which knows how to count."[135]

The word which the priest uses, *isoumenon*, "equated," refers to what the Greeks seem to have regarded as the central mathematical concept on which all the others depend, the idea of equality. "Geometrical equality," says Plato, "has great power among both gods and men."[136] And Jocasta, in the *Phoenissae* of Euripides, urging her son Eteocles to share power equally with his brother, describes equality as the directing creative force behind all mathematical relationships. "It was Equality which ordered measures for man, and divisions of weights, and defined number" (*isotês . . . kárithmon diôrisen, Ph.* 542).[137] When Euclid came to systematize the work of centuries of mathematical activity, he prefaced his book with the essential definitions, postulates, and axioms, the first four of which are concerned with equality. And when Diophantus, many centuries later, wrote his book on what we now know as algebra, he used this word which appears in the priest's speech to describe his fundamental operation, "to equate."[138]

Oedipus is not judged—not at any rate by the priest—as "equated to the gods," but this phrase is the prelude to the priest's demand that Oedipus find some way to equate himself to what he was once, when he answered the riddle of the Sphinx—the savior and liberator of Thebes. "With fair omens you brought us good fortune then, and now be equal to the man you were" (*tanyn isos genou*, 53). For the rejected equation of Oedipus to the gods the priest suggests a more appropriate one: he is asked to be equal to himself, to his own great reputation as the successful savior of Thebes.

But these two equations are only the beginning of a series. The play is full of equations, some incomplete, some false; the final equation shows man equated not to the gods but to himself, as Oedipus is finally equated to himself. For there are in this play not one Oedipus but two. One is the magnificent figure of the opening scenes, *tyrannos*, the man of wealth, power, and knowledge, "first of men," the intellect and the energy which drives on the search for the murderer of Laius. The other is the object of the search (*to zêtoumenon*), an obscure figure (*ton adêlon andra*) who has violated the most powerful human taboos, an incestuous parricide, "most accursed of men" (1345). In the end the one Oedipus finds the other, but even before he does so the two of them are already symbolically equated in the hero's name Oedipus, which connects the knowledge (*oida*) of the confident *tyrannos* with the swollen foot (*pous*) of Laius' outcast son. In the name they both bear is locked the secret of their identity, their equation, but Oedipus does not yet know the meaning of his name; that is what he is to find out. "Be now the equal of the man you were." The priest is right. Oedipus once answered a riddle and now he must answer another; but the answer to the riddle, once found, will equate him not to the foreigner who saved Thebes from the Sphinx but to the native-born king, the son of Laius and Jocasta.

Oedipus in his reply to the priest repeats the significant word: "Sick as you are, not one of you has sickness equal to mine" (*eks isou nosei*, 61). And he adds a word of his own, a characteristic metaphor—he is impatient at Creon's continued absence: "Measuring the day against the time [*ksymmetroumenon chronôi*, 73], I am anxious." And then, as Creon approaches, "He is now commensurate with the range of our voices" (*ksymmetros gar hôs klyein*, 84).[139]

Measure, like number, is one of the great instruments of human progress; weights and measures are among the discoveries of Palamedes, and figure in the list of ideas made possible by the conception of equality in the speech of Euripides' Jocasta. In the river valleys of the East centuries of mensuration and calculation had brought man to an understanding of the movements of the stars and of time; in the *Histories* of his friend Herodotus Sophocles had read of the calculation and mensuration which had gone into the building of the Egyptian pyramids. "Measure"—it is Protagoras' word: "Man is the measure of all things."

With these phrases of Oedipus the metaphor is set in train. Oedipus is the equator and measurer, and these are the methods by which he will reach the truth; calculation of time, measurement of age and number, comparison of place and description —these are the techniques which will solve the equation, establish the identity of the murderer of Laius. The tightly organized and relentless process by which Oedipus finds his way to the truth is presented by the language of the play as an equivalent of the activity of man's mind in almost all its aspects; it is the investigation by the officer of the law who identifies a criminal, the series of diagnoses by the physician who identifies the disease,[140] and it is also the working out of a mathematical problem which ends with the establishment of a true equation.

With Creon's entry the numerical aspect of the problem is emphasized at once. "One man of Laius' party escaped," he says, "and he had only one thing to say" (118-19). "What was it?" asks Oedipus. "One thing might find out a way to learn many" (120). The one thing the one man said was that Laius was killed not by one man but by many. This begins to sound like a problem in arithmetic,[141] and Oedipus undertakes to solve it. But the chorus, which enters at this point, has no such confidence; its note is one of despair. It makes its despondent statement about the plague in these same terms; it has its characteristic word, which like the priest and like Oedipus it pronounces twice. The chorus' word is *anarithmos*, "numberless, uncountable": "My sorrows are numberless" (*anarithma . . . pêmata*, 168), they sing, and later, "uncountable the deaths of which the city is dying" (*anarithmos ollutai*, 179). For the chorus the plague is something beyond the power of "number, outstanding among intellectual achievements."[142]

The prologue and the first stasimon, besides presenting the necessary exposition of the situation, present also the exposition of the metaphor. And with the entry of Tiresias, the development of the metaphor begins; its terrible potentialities are revealed. "Even though you are *tyrannos*," says the prophet at the height of his anger," we must be equated in the equality of the speeches we make against each other" (*eksisôsteon to goun is' antileksai*, 408-9). But he pushes the word to further lengths: "There is a mass of evils of which you are unconscious, which shall equate you to yourself and your children" (*ha s' eksisôsei soi te kai tois sois teknois*, 425).[143] This is not the equation the priest desired to see, Oedipus present equated to Oedipus past, the deliverer from the Sphinx, but a more frightening equation reaching further back into the past, Oedipus son of Polybus and Merope equated to Oedipus son of Laius and Jocasta, and equated to his own children, for he is the brother of his own sons and daughters. In his closing lines Tiresias explains this mysterious statement, and connects it with the as yet unrevealed murderer of Laius. " He will be revealed, a native Theban, one who in his relationship with his own children is both brother and father, with his mother both son and husband, with his father both marriage partner and murderer. Go inside the palace and reckon this up [*logizou*, 461] and if you find me mistaken [*epseusmenon*, 461] then say I have no head for prophecy." [144] Tiresias adopts the terms of Oedipus' own science and throws them in his face. But these new equations are beyond Oedipus' understanding; he dismisses them as the ravings of an unsuccessful conspirator with his back to the wall. Even the chorus, though clearly disturbed, rejects the prophet's words and stands by Oedipus.

After Tiresias, Creon; after the prophet, the politician. In Tiresias Oedipus faced a blind man who saw with unearthly sight, but Creon's vision, like that of Oedipus, is of this world. They are two of a kind, and Creon talks Oedipus' language; it is a quarrel between two calculators. " Hear an equal reply " (*is' antakouson*, 544), says Creon, and " long time might be measured since Laius' murder " (*metrêtheien chronoi*, 561). Tiresias was " equally honored then as now " (*eks isou*, 563). " You and Jocasta rule this land in equality of power " (*gês ison nemôn*, 579). And finally, " Am I not a third party equated to you two? " (*isoumai*, 581). Creon and Oedipus are not equated now, for Creon is at the mercy of the *tyrannos*, begging for a hearing; but before the play is over Oedipus will be at the mercy of Creon, begging kindness for his daughters, and he then uses the same word: "Do not equate them with my misfortunes" (*mêd' eksisôsêis*, 1507).

With Jocasta's intervention the enquiry changes direction. In her attempt to comfort Oedipus, whose only accuser is a prophet, she indicts prophecy in general, using as her example the unfulfilled prophecy about her own child, who was supposed to kill his father Laius. The child was abandoned on the mountainside, and Laius was killed by brigands at a place where three roads meet. "Such were the definitions [*diôrisan*, 723] made by prophetic voices," [145] and they were incorrect. But Oedipus is not for the moment interested in prophetic voices. "Where three roads meet." He once killed a man at such a place, and now, in a series of swift questions, he determines the relation between these two events. The place, the time, the description of the victim, the number in his party (five) all correspond exactly. His account of the circumstances of his own encounter at the crossroads includes a mention of Apollo's prophecy that he would kill his father and be his mother's mate. But this does not disturb him now. That prophecy has not been fulfilled, for his father and mother are alive in Corinth, where he will never go. "I measure the distance to the Corinthian land by the stars" (*astrois . . . ekmetroumenos*, 795).[146] What does disturb him is the possibility that he may be the murderer of Laius, the cause of the plague, the object of his own solemn excommunication. But he has some slight ground for hope. There is a discrepancy in the two corresponding sets of circumstances. It is the same numerical distinction which was discussed before, whether Laius was killed by one man or by many.[147] Jocasta said "brigands" and Oedipus was alone. This distinction is now all-important, the key to the solution of the equation. Oedipus gives orders to summon the survivor who can confirm or deny this saving detail. "If he says the same number as you, then

I am not the murderer. For one cannot be equal to many"
(*tois pollois isos*, 845). The Greek words which express this
closing thought suggest a general statement, and may fairly
be rendered: "In no circumstances can one be equal to more
than one." Oedipus' guilt or innocence rests now on a mathematical axiom.[148]

But a more fundamental equation has been brought into
question, the relation of the oracles to reality. Here are two
oracular "definitions," both the same, both apparently incorrect: the same terrible destiny was predicted for Jocasta's
son, who perished on the mountainside before he could fulfil
it, and for Oedipus, who has so far successfully avoided it.
One thing is clear to Jocasta. No matter who turns out to be
the murderer of Laius, the oracles were doubly wrong. "From
this day forward," she says, "I would not, on account of
prophecy, turn my head this way or that" (857-8). But this
is a far-reaching statement. If the equation of oracular
prophecy to reality is a false equation, then religion as a whole
is meaningless. Neither Jocasta nor Oedipus can allow the
possibility that the oracles may be right, and they accept the
consequences of this stand, as their subsequent statements make
clear. But they have gone too far for the chorus, which now
abandons Oedipus and turns instead to those "high-footed
laws [*hypsipodes*, 866] which are the children of Olympus
and not a creation of mortal man." The chorus calls on Zeus
to fulfil the oracles: "If these things do not coincide [*harmosei*,
902]"—if the oracles are not equated to reality—then "the
divine order is overthrown" (*errei ta theia*, 910).[149]

The oracles are now the central issue; the murder of Laius
is for the moment forgotten. A messenger from Corinth brings
news, news which will be greeted, he announces, "with an
equal amount of sorrow and joy" (*isôs*, 937).[150] "What is it,"
asks Jocasta, "which has such double power?" Polybus is

dead.[151] The sorrow equal to the joy will come later; for the moment there is only joy. The oracles are proved wrong again; Oedipus' father is dead, and not by the hand of Oedipus. Oedipus can no more kill his father than the son of Laius killed his. " Oracles of the gods, where are you now? " Oedipus is caught up in Jocasta's exaltation, but for him it does not last. Only half his burden is lifted from him. His mother still lives. He must still measure the distance to Corinthian soil by the stars.

Jocasta and the Corinthian messenger now try, in turn, to relieve him of this last remaining fear. Jocasta makes her famous declaration which rejects fear, providence—divine and human alike—and any idea of universal order. Her declaration amounts almost to a rejection of the law of cause and effect, and it certainly undermines the basis of human calculation. " Why should man fear? His life is governed by the operations of chance. Nothing can be accurately foreseen. The best rule is to live at random, as best one can." [152] It is a statement which recognizes and accepts an incalculable and meaningless universe. Oedipus would accept it too, but for one thing. His mother still lives. Try as he may to disregard the future, he still feels fear.

Where Jocasta failed, the Corinthian messenger succeeds. He does it by proving false the equation on which Oedipus' life is based. And he uses familiar terms: " Polybus is no more your father than I am, but equally so " (*ison*, 1018). Oedipus' reply is indignant: " How can my father be equal to a nobody, to zero? " (*eks isou tôi mêdeni*, 1019).[153] The answer to his question is: " Polybus is not your father, neither am I."

But that is as far as the Corinthian's knowledge goes; he was given the child Oedipus by another, a shepherd, one of Laius' men. And now the two separate equations begin to merge. " I think," says the chorus, " that this shepherd is the same man you have already sent for." The eyewitness to the death of Laius. He was sent for to say whether Laius was killed by one or many, but now he will bring more important news. He will finally lift from Oedipus' shoulders the burden of fear he has carried ever since he left Delphi. Oedipus brushes aside Jocasta's attempt to stop him and orders the shepherd to be brought in. Jocasta was right before. Why should he fear?

But Jocasta has already realized the truth. Not chance, but the fulfilment of the oracle; the prophecy and the facts coincide, as the chorus prayed they would. Her farewell to Oedipus expresses her knowledge and her agony by its omissions; she recognizes but cannot bring herself to pronounce the dreadful equations formulated by Tiresias. "Unfortunate." (*dustêne*). "This is the only name I can call you" (1071-72). She cannot call him husband. The three-day-old child she sent out to die on Cithaeron has been restored to her, and she cannot call him son.[154]

Oedipus hardly listens to her. He in his turn has scaled the same heights of desperate confidence from which she has toppled, and he goes higher still. Chance governs the universe, and Oedipus is her son. Not the son of Polybus, nor of any mortal man, but the son of fortunate chance. In his exaltation he rises in imagination above human stature: "The months, my brothers, have defined [*diôrisan*, 1083] me great and small." [155] He has waxed and waned like the moon, he is one of the forces of the universe, his family is time and space. It is a religious, a mystical conception; here is Oedipus' real religion: he is equal to the gods, the son of Chance, the only real goddess. Why should he not establish his identity?

The solution is only a few steps ahead. The shepherd of Laius is brought on. "If I, who never met the man, may make an estimate [*stathmasthai*, 1111],[156] I think this is the shepherd who has been for some time the object of our search [*zêtoumen*, 1112]. In age he is commensurate [*symmetros*, 1113] with this Corinthian here." With this significant prologue he plunges into the final calculation.

The movement of the next sixty lines is the swift ease of the last stages of the mathematical proof; the end is half foreseen, the process an almost automatic movement from one step to the next until Oedipus *tyrannos* and Oedipus the accursed, the knowledge and the swollen foot, are equated. "It all comes out clear," he cries at the end. The prophecy has been fulfilled. Oedipus knows himself for what he is. He is not the measurer but the thing measured, not the equator but the thing equated. He is the answer to the problem he tried to solve. The chorus sees in Oedipus a *paradeigma*, an example to mankind. In this self-recognition of Oedipus, man recognizes himself. Man measures himself, and the result is not that man is the measure of all things. The chorus which at the beginning of the play had no faith in number has now learned to count, and states what it understands to be the result of the great calculation: "Generations of mankind that must die, I add up the total of your life and find it equal to zero" (*isa kai to mêden . . . enarithmô*, 1187).

This despairing equation, though it is a natural reaction to the shock of the discovery, is not the play's last word. Man is not equated to zero, as the last section of the play makes clear, for Oedipus rises again from the ruin which inspired this starkly negative summation. But the culmination of the mathematical images in this phrase suggests something else. It proposes a formula for the solution of the problem discussed in the opening chapter, the relation between Oedipus' actions and the prophecy of Apollo. Oedipus' will was free, his actions his own, but the pattern of his action and suffering is the same as that of the Delphic prophecy. The relation between the prophecy and the hero's action is not that of cause and effect. It is the relation between two independent entities which are equated.

CHAPTER FOUR: GOD

When the priest, in the opening scene, tells Oedipus that he regards him not as " equated to the gods " but as " first of men," he is attempting, by means of this careful distinction, to clarify and correct an ambiguity inherent in his own speech and action. The beginning of the play suggests in both verbal and visual terms that Oedipus is in fact regarded as " equated to the gods." The priest of Zeus and selected young priests have come as suppliants to the palace of Oedipus; their action is parallel to that of other groups who, the priest tells us (19), have gone in supplication to the twin temples of Athena and the fire oracle of the Theban hero Ismenus. " You see us here," the priest says to Oedipus, " sitting in supplication at your altars " (*bômoisi tois sois*, 16). This is an extraordinary phrase for a priest to address to a *tyrannos*, and it did not escape the eye of the ancient commentators; " They come to the altars built in front of the palace as to the altars of a god," says the scholiast.[1] It is not until many hundred lines later (and after many events and revelations) that we find out from Jocasta that " your altars " are the altars dedicated to Lycean Apollo (919).

The equation is one that Oedipus does not reject. His first question to the suppliants contains an ambiguous pronoun (*moi*, 2) which suggests two different meanings for the sentence as a whole: " Tell me, what is the meaning of this supplicatory attitude? " or " What is the meaning of this attitude in which you supplicate me? "[2] And at the end of the chorus' appeal to the gods, an ode which is liturgical in form,[3] Oedipus addresses the chorus in words which, like his opening sentence, betray acceptance of the attitude towards him implicit in the tableau and speeches of the opening scene. " You are praying. And what you are praying for, if you are willing to hear and accept what I am about to say . . . you will receive . . ." [4] The words Oedipus chooses are symptomatic of a god-like attitude. They accept and promise fulfilment of the choral prayer (which was addressed to Athena, Artemis, Apollo, Zeus, and Dionysus) and are phrased in what is a typical formula of the Delphic oracle. "You are praying to me for Arcadia," the Pythian priestess answered the Spartans, according to Herodotus; "What you are praying for is a big thing. I shall not give it to you." "You come praying for good government," she said to Lycurgus; "I shall give it to you." [5]

These pointers would not have gone unrecognized in fifth-century Athens, for Oedipus is a *tyrannos* and the comparison of *tyrannis* to divine power is a commonplace of Greek literature. "He praises *tyrannis*," says Adeimantus in Plato's *Republic*, "as equal to godhead." The possessor of the ring of Gyges, in Glaucus' fable in the same work, is described as possessed of power to carry out any imaginable (and unlawful) act, and the catalogue of his powers concludes with the words, ". . . and act in other respects like one equal to the gods among men." [6]

The individual *tyrannos* is equal to the gods in his power, his prosperity, and his success. The *polis tyrannos*, Athens, assumes this same quasi-divinity; in the Periclean speeches in Thucydides the city replaces the gods as the object of man's veneration and devotion. In the three magnificent and lengthy speeches attributed to Pericles in the first two books of the *History*, the word *theos*, "god," does not occur even once. [7] The nearest thing to religious feeling which is to be found in them occurs in that section of the Funeral Speech where Pericles calls on the Athenians to "contemplate daily the power of the city and become lovers of Athens." "Athens," he says, in words more appropriate for a god than a state, "Athens alone comes to the test superior to report, Athens alone affords the attacking enemy no cause for annoyance at the character of the enemy by whom he is beaten and to the subject no cause for blaming his master as unworthy to rule." [8]

The city which thus in fifth-century Athens becomes the object of man's veneration is in the first place the creation of man, of his "attitudes which enable him to live in communities" (*astynomous orgas*), as Sophocles puts it in the chorus of the *Antigone*. If Athens can be spoken of in worshiping tones, what of man, who created the city? [9] The development of the new humanist view tended inevitably towards the substitution of man for god as the true center of the universe, the true measure of reality; this is what Protagoras meant by his famous phrase, "Man is the measure of all things." The rationalistic scientific mind, seeking an explanation of reality in human terms and assuming that such an explanation is possible and attainable, rejects the concept of God as irrelevant. If reality is fully explicable in human terms, the gods will automatically be disposed of when the complete explanation is worked out; meanwhile the important thing is the search for the explanation. The question of the existence or nonexistence of the gods is secondary and must be postponed; it is also a blind alley, for the answer to the question depends on the answer to another question, which the human intelligence *has* some hope of answering. "About the gods," so ran the opening sentence (all that we have left) of Protagoras' famous book *On the Gods*, "I have no means of knowing whether they exist or do not exist or what their form may be. Many things prevent [the attainment] of this knowledge, the obscurity [of the subject] and the fact that man's life is short." The word translated "obscurity" (*adêlotês*) disposes of the subject of the gods as one which does not allow of scientific method: nothing can be "made clear," "proved" (*dêlon, dêloun*). Everything connected with the gods is *adêlon*; they are, by their nature and by definition, beyond the reach of scientific understanding and discussion. And the concluding phrase—"the shortness of human life"—is not, as at first appears, a cynical quip at the impenetrability of the subject and the consequent futility of discussion about it; it is the serious statement of a man who sees other things to be understood which *can* be understood by the efforts of the human intelligence, though one man's life may not be long enough to reach the goal. "Life is short," runs the first Hippocratic aphorism, "the art long"; [10] here is the same feeling of pressure —there is so much to be learned, so little time to learn it. For such an attitude the existence or nonexistence of the gods is not the most urgent question; it is in fact a question to be excluded. And this is precisely what Plato makes Protagoras say in the *Theaetetus*, where Socrates imagines the great sophist reproving him and his fellow debaters for the irrelevancy of their discussions. "There you sit in a bunch making speeches, and bringing into the discussion the gods, while I exclude [*eksairô*] from both spoken and written discussion the whole question of their existence or nonexistence." [11]

With the gods excluded from discussion, and man the measure of all things, man's attempt to understand his environment and nature, if successful, will make him "equated to the gods." "The doctor who is also a philosopher," says the Hippocratic treatise *On Decorum*, "is the equal of the gods." [12] "Many are the wonderful and terrible things," sang the chorus of the *Antigone*, "and nothing more wonderful and terrible than man." But man with the attainment of complete understanding would be more than the equal of the gods, for if the scientific explanation of the universe made the concept of divine power unnecessary or demonstrably false, man would be revealed as the creator of the gods. This final stage is represented by a famous dramatic fragment of Critias, the leading spirit of the Thirty Tyrants; it describes the invention of the gods by a man of wisdom and intelligence whose object was to stabilize society by imposing on erring human beings an inescapable superior and a fear of superhuman vision and retribution.

> There was a time when the life of man was undisciplined, beastlike, and subject to superior strength, when there was no reward for the good and no punishment for the wicked. Then it was, in my opinion, that men made laws as correctors, so that Justice would be *tyrannos* . . . and have violence as its slave. A punishment was administered to anyone who acted wrongly. Then, when the laws prevented them from open acts of violence, they did them secretly. At that point, it seems to me, some man of deep wisdom and intelligence [*sophos gnomên*] invented [*ekseurein*] for mankind the fear of the gods . . . this was his reason for introducing divinity.

But long before Critias wrote these words which carry the doctrines of the enlightenment to a cynical extreme, the hopeful mood of its early stages—the vision of man in a universe he could fully understand and perhaps eventually control—had vanished. The Athenian confidence in their city's unconquerable destiny and fifth-century man's dream of a world understood and controlled by human intelligence—both alike collapsed in the horrors of the unexpected and inexplicable plague, in the growing misery and anarchy caused by the relentless and senseless war. The Protagorean "liberal" program of educating man to political justice was revealed as an idealistic illusion by the *Walpurgisnacht* of butchery and cynicism which Thucydides clinically analyzes in his accounts of the political massacres on Corcyra and the Athenian "negotiations" with Melos. The universe seemed to have been revealed not as a cosmos, an order, governed either by gods or by discoverable natural laws, but as a desperate chaos, governed by blind chance. "Whatever turns out contrary to calculation," said Pericles in the speech made just before the outbreak of the war, "we are accustomed to attribute to chance." [13] He is reminding the Athenians that in spite of their financial and technical superiority to the enemy they may suffer setbacks. But his remarks were grimly prophetic. Too many things "turned out contrary to calculation"; the plague, which Pericles describes as "sudden, unexpected, and happening contrary to all calculation," [14] was only the forerunner of a series of events which seemed to mock human calculation or foresight of any kind.[15]

The plays of Euripides reflect the growth in Athens of an increasingly reckless feeling that, as Jocasta puts it, "the operation of chance governs all things." Even in the prewar *Alcestis* (438 B.C.) Euripides prophetically expounds the desperate mood of the war years in the philosophizing of the drunken Heracles. "The course of chance—no one can see where it will go—this is not a thing which can be taught, or captured by technique . . . Enjoy yourself, drink, calculate that this day's life is yours—the rest belongs to chance." [16] In the later plays the mood is grimmer. This same Heracles, in a different Euripidean play, is struck by a series of calamities which defy human expectation and rational explanation; he rejects the solution which this terrible situation seems to call for, suicide, and determines to go on living, but in a world which he redefines as one subject to inexplicable chance. "Now, it seems, I must act as a slave to chance." [17] Menelaus, in the Euripidean *Orestes*, describes his situation in the same terms: "Now it is necessity that the wise should be slaves to chance." [18] The most uncompromising expression of this terrible doctrine is put into the mouth of Hecuba in the *Troades*, as she mourns over the mangled body of the child Astyanax. "Any mortal man that, seeming to prosper, rejoices as if his prosperity were solidly based, is a fool. For the turns of chance are like those of a crazed man, leaping now this way, now that . . ." [19]

This chance, which the Euripidean characters identify as the governing force of the universe, is clearly the philosophical "chance" of Thucydides, an abstraction of the absence of any causality comprehensible in human terms. But it was only to be expected, in fifth-century Greece, that this abstraction which now seemed to many the dominant factor in human life should be personified, should become in fact a god, or rather (since the word *tychê*, "chance," is feminine in Greek) a goddess. So Oedipus calls himself "the son of chance" (*paida tês tychês*), and Ion, in Euripides, addresses Chance as a divine being. "O you who have changed the fortunes of tens of thousands of mortals before now, making them unfortunate and then prosperous, Chance . . ." [20]

This personification was not unprecedented; in fact the unprecedented thing was the philosophical abstraction. Chance, in the older Greek poets, [21] and even in Herodotus, is often personified, and usually, far from indicating an absence of causality and order, it is associated with divine dispensation. In Herodotus' account of the founding of the Scythian royal line (a story told him by Greek colonists in Pontus), Heracles, driving the cattle of Geryon, comes to Scythia, and while he is asleep his cattle vanish "by divine chance" (*theiai tychêi*, iv. 8). It is, in other words, no chance at all, and the result of the disappearance of the cattle, the birth of Scythes, son of Heracles and the first Scythian king, was as the phrase indicates the divine purpose behind the apparently fortuitous disappearance of the cattle. So also in the Herodotean account of the founding of the Cypselid tyranny at Corinth (v. 92), the child Cypselus, later to be *tyrannos* of Corinth, is spared by his ten appointed executioners because when the first man of the ten took hold of the child, " by divine chance " it smiled, and the man had not the heart to kill it, nor had the others. The child " chanced " to smile, but this was not blind chance, for if the child had been killed the oracles predicting its eventual seizure of power in Corinth could not have been fulfilled.[22] This Chance, the instrument of the divine will, is addressed by Pindar as the " daughter of Zeus the liberator, saving chance," [23] and the poet Alcman called her, in an astonishing phrase, " sister of good government and Persuasion, daughter of Foreknowledge." [24]

That Chance, Tyche, should be personified and deified in Oedipus' confident outburst and other tragic passages is nothing new; what is new is the nature of the Chance which now assumes divinity. It is no longer the old instrument of the divine purpose, " daughter of Foreknowledge," but an autonomous goddess who personifies the absence of causal order in the universe. She is the principle of chaos. She presides not, as the older gods did, over an ordered universe but over a disorder in which " there is no clear foresight of anything." And this goddess cannot merely coexist with the other gods. She must be either, as the daughter of Forethought, divine Chance, their servant, or, as the absence of causality, blind Chance, their mistress. The very existence of this new goddess Chance makes the existence of the old gods meaningless. That the logic of this was apparent in the fifth century is demonstrated by a passage in Euripides' satyr-play *The Cyclops*. Odysseus, preparing to put out Polyphemus' eye, appeals to Hephaestus and Sleep to help him. " Do not," he says, " destroy Odysseus and his crew, after their glorious labors at Troy, at the hands of a man who cares nothing for gods or mortals. Otherwise we must think that Chance is a divinity, and "—here follows the logical conclusion—" that the power of the other divinities is inferior to that of Chance." [25]

This is of course exactly what was to happen in the long run; the other divinities receded before the figure of the new goddess Tyche. The pessimistic mood of the end of the fifth century deepened in the fourth as Greece, torn apart by incessant warfare, succumbed ignobly to the perseverance, intrigue, and raw aggressiveness of a half-savage Macedonian king. In this atmosphere of impotence and defeat the goddess Chance seemed to reign supreme. In spite of the efforts of the philosophers to reduce chance to a subordinate position (Plato, for example, counters the idea that "practically all human affairs are matters of chance" with a new version of the archaic relationship of "divine chance" to divine will—"All things are god, and with god chance and occasion "),[26] the goddess Chance, who symbolized the century's "sense of drift," [27] continued to be the obsessive refrain of the prayers and speculations of the ordinary man.[28] In the last years of the fourth century Demetrius of Phalerum wrote a book on Chance, and the historian Polybius approvingly quotes from it a passage which identifies Chance as the governing force in human history: "Chance, which makes no contracts with this life of ours, makes everything new contrary to our calulation and displays her power in the unexpected." [29] Though she had fewer temples,[30] the goddess Tyche superseded the Olympians in the mind of the common man; she was the only appropriate icon of a world which persistently mocked all human calculation and the logic on which it is based.

Such was the paradoxical ending of a search for truth which began by criticizing and then proceeded to abandon the Olympian deities as inadequate representatives of a cosmic order. The quest for rational principle and appropriate religious

personifications of a rational universe ended in the deification
of anarchy. The movement of more than a century of brilliant
and searching thought is movement not forward but back
to the starting point, from gods to goddess, from the Homeric
Olympians to the goddess Chance. But this circular progress
is not on one plane; the point of return is on a lower level.
The movement is a descending spiral.[31]

This self-defeating advance of the search for an intelligible
order in the universe is paralleled in Sophocles' tragedy by
the intellectual progress of Oedipus and Jocasta. Their successive changes of attitude towards the gods and the oracles which
represent the divine prescience in the play, brilliantly moti-
vated by the initial situation and the turns of the plot and
fully appropriate to the respective dramatic characters, are
yet symbolic of the mental agonies of a generation which abandoned a traditional order of belief with a hopeful vision of an
intelligible universe, only to find itself at last facing an incom-
prehensible future with a desperation thinly disguised as
recklessness.

The Oedipus of the opening scenes, formally pious in action
and speech but betraying in one phrase after another a confidence in man's worth as equal to that of the gods, is symbolic
of the mood of imperial Athens and bears a clear resemblance
to the representative figure who set the tone of the era and
gave it his name, Pericles. As an official of the Athenian state
Pericles performed religious acts (among which was presumably
the consultation of the Delphic oracle),[32] but if the oracle's
firmly expressed support of the Spartan cause against Athens
in 431 B. C. caused him any qualms, they find no reflection
in the confident speeches attributed to him by Thucydides in
the opening books of his *History*. In his funeral oration over
those who fell in the Samian War, Pericles compared the
Athenian dead to the gods, and the language he used is

typical of the rationalist spirit of the age. The Athenian dead are immortal, like the gods—so the historian Stesimbrotus reports his argument—"for we do not see the gods, but infer [*tekmairometha*] their immortality from the honors which they receive and the benefits which they confer upon us."[33] This is a statement which illustrates clearly the application of the Protagorean dictum, "Man is the measure of all things." The immortality of the gods is deduced from the fact that man honors them (in spite of their invisibility) and the fact that they confer benefits on man. And by the same tokens Pericles proves the immortality of the Athenian dead who gave their lives for the city.

The mood of the Athenian leadership at the beginning of the war was one of outer conformance and inner skepticism. The skepticism would come out into the open only if circumstances forced it; but the calamitous surprises of the war quickly achieved precisely that effect. In the inferno produced by the plague, which made no discrimination between the just and the unjust, the conviction grew that "it made no difference whether one worshiped the gods or not"; and in the frequent Euripidean attacks on the Delphic oracle (in plays produced at a religious festival in the city's name) we have some measure of the strong Athenian reaction against Delphi's enthusiastic encouragement of the Spartans at the beginning of the war.

So with Oedipus. His true feelings do not find open expression until the prophet of Apollo accuses him of the murder of Laius. Immediately the respectful, almost adulatory tone of Oedipus' first address to Tiresias (300-15) is replaced by incredulous and contemptuous fury. All the opprobrious epithets which fifth-century Athens could invent for cynical peddlers of superstition are hurled at the blind prophet's head: "intriguing quack," Oedipus calls the representative of Apollo, "deceitful huckster, with an eye for profit, and for nothing else."[34]

That a king should attack a prophet is nothing new in Greek literature. In the first book of the *Iliad* Agamemnon threatens Chryses, the priest of Apollo, with physical violence (i. 26-8) and angrily reviles the prophet Calchas for taking the priest's part (i. 105 ff.). But Oedipus' attack on the prophet is not like Agamemnon's. Agamemnon reviles Calchas as a "prophet of evil," but he does not question the truth of the prophet's statement (though it accuses him of wrongdoing), and he proceeds to follow the prophet's advice. Oedipus not only rejects the prophet's statement but also goes on to attack the claims of prophecy itself. He contrasts the failure of Tiresias to solve the riddle of the Sphinx with his own success; his words imply a contemptuous comparison between the sources of information open to the prophet (the birds, 395, and the god, 396), and his own intelligence, which without any source of information stopped the Sphinx. Oedipus has rejected the statement of a prophet "in whom alone," according to the chorus, "truth is inborn" (299), who "sees the same things as Lord Apollo" (284-5), and in Oedipus' proud words can be seen the outline of the next step in his progress, the rejection of all prophecy, including the prophecy of a god.

But for the chorus the first step is disturbing enough. At first they "neither accept nor reject" (485-6) the prophet's words; they "can find nothing to say." But in the end they reach a formula which seems appropriate: Tiresias is after all a man, and therefore fallible—to reject his words does not necessarily mean that one rejects Apollo. "Zeus and Apollo have understanding and know the deeds of mortals. But when it comes to men—that a prophet is more right than I am, there is no true judgment of this" (498-501). So the complicated rhythm of the development is established: as Oedipus' words reveal that he is ready to take the next step towards total rejection of prophecy, the chorus draws the line where it formulations [*diôrisan*, 723] of prophetic voices. Do not concern yourself with prophecies. For whatever the god seeks and needs he will easily make clear himself " (720-5).

This is an extraordinary statement. The false oracle came not from Apollo but from his " ministers." Who were they? Not, this time, Tiresias, for if so Jocasta would have named him—the case against the prophet's fallibility would be clear and sufficient. She must be referring to Apollo's " ministers " at Delphi, the priests or the priestess responsible for the delivery of the prophecy. The ministers gave voice to the prophecy,[36] but Apollo did not bring it to fulfilment; it was not his prophecy. If he needs to say anything he will reveal it in person, not through " ministers." Here is subtle doctrine. It avoids indicting Apollo, but delivers a death blow to Apolline prophecy, which had from time immemorial been delivered through his ministers at Delphi. How is Apollo to prophesy, if not through human beings who serve him? " There is no human creature," Jocasta said, " which possesses the art of prophecy "; as she explains that statement it becomes clear that she might just as well have added " and no god either."

Before the scene is over this is precisely what she does say, fully and clearly. As was to be expected of the superlative plotting of this play, she does so in reaction to a fresh revelation. Her first attack on prophecy, which was intended to comfort Oedipus, has had the paradoxical effect of plunging him into fear that Tiresias may be right. He is unimpressed by her general argument; he can see nothing but the incidental detail: the fact that Laius was killed at the junction of three roads. To explain his fears to Jocasta he gives her an account of his life previous to his arrival at Thebes, and this account includes the prophecy given to him by Apollo at Delphi: that he would kill his father and beget children by his mother. Oedipus does not try to belittle this prophecy as the work of

Apollo's " ministers." " Phoebus," he says unequivocally, " spoke and foreshadowed dreadful disasters " (788-90).

Jocasta has dismissed the prophet Tiresias and exposed the falsity of the prophecy made by the " ministers " of Apollo; if she is to be of any comfort to Oedipus now she must extend her indictment to include what Oedipus himself calls the word of Phoebus. She does not hesitate: she now makes a significant correction of her first hesitant formulation and states openly what she previously implied. The eyewitness of Laius' death, she says, may possibly go back on what he said, but he cannot demonstrate that the death of Laius was consistent with the prophecy. " Loxias plainly said that he was to die at the hands of my son." [37] The oracle to Laius, she now says, came not from " ministers " but from the god himself. To counter the words of Tiresias all she needed was a false oracle from Apollo's human ministers; to counter the oracle given to Oedipus by Apollo she needs a false oracle delivered by Apollo himself; and by this bold correction she makes the same oracle serve both arguments. The oracle, man-given or god-given, is false and will be forever false, for the son who was to kill his father died first. When she sums up her argument with her famous defiance of prophecy— " From now on I would not, for the sake of a prophecy, look this way, or that " (857-8)—she is dismissing all the prophecies so far revealed: the accusations of Tiresias, the oracle given by Apollo's ministers, or rather by Apollo, to Laius, and the oracle given by Apollo to Oedipus. The logic of the changing situation drives her to the position that was in any case implicit in her first statement, the rejection of all prophecy, human and divine alike.[38]

The chorus could doubt Tiresias but not Apollo. It reacts violently against Jocasta's defiance of prophecy, and its attitude is colored by other aspects of the scene it has just witnessed.

Since it last expressed its unimpaired loyalty to Oedipus (691 ff.) it has learned much. It has heard that Jocasta's child by Laius was exposed on the mountainside in a particularly barbarous fashion, and that this was done to prevent the fulfilment of a Delphic oracle; that Oedipus, the savior of Thebes, came to the city stained with blood, possibly the blood of Laius; that Oedipus is a fugitive from a Delphic oracle which predicts for him the same unhallowed destiny as that foretold for Laius' son. All these dreadful revelations of pollution, actual and threatened, combined with Jocasta's proud rejection of prophecy and Oedipus' firmly expressed approval of her statement,[39] impel the chorus to disassociate itself from the rulers of Thebes. It appeals to higher authorities and laws in terms which reject implicitly and explicitly the whole philosophical outlook on which Oedipus and Jocasta now base their hope and action.

"May destiny [*moira*, 863] be with me," the chorus sings. The word is carefully chosen; it is the word Jocasta used when she described the prophecy given to Laius, "that destiny [*moira*, 713] would come to him, to die at the hands of his son." Prophecy and destiny are linked; Jocasta explicitly rejects the first, and implicitly the second; the chorus, which will end by vindicating prophecy, begins by accepting destiny. It prays for "reverent purity of word and deed" (*hagneian*, 864). Both Oedipus and Jocasta, the one as the main actor and the other as the accomplice in the taking of human life, are "impure" and both are irreverent in word. Their deeds no one in Thebes dare question, but the chorus appeals to the "high-footed laws proclaimed, brought to birth [*teknôthentes*, 867] in the clear air of heaven, whose father is Olympus alone—no mortal nature of human kind begot [*etikten*, 870] them." The images here reflect the chorus' horror at the tainted births foretold in the oracles delivered to Oedipus; the appeal to the higher laws emphasizes the inadequacy of man-made law—the law in Thebes is Oedipus, he is *tyrannos*.

The chorus realizes that it is facing a harder choice than before; once it had to choose between Oedipus and Tiresias, now between Oedipus and Apollo. It does not hesitate: "I shall not cease to hold the god as my champion" (*prostatên*, 882). The word they use is the Athenian political term used to describe the position of the dominating personality in Athenian affairs, and its appearance here stresses the fact that this statement is a transfer of allegiance. But if Apollo is to be their champion, he must vindicate himself; the oracles must be fulfilled (902-3). The old oracles given to Laius (which Jocasta has apparently proved can never be fulfilled in any circumstances) are "dying"; Oedipus and Jocasta are "excluding" (*eksairousin*, 907) the oracles, as Protagoras did the gods. Apollo is no longer "made manifest by the honors paid him." [40] The power of the gods is overthrown.

But the chorus is overestimating the confidence of its rulers. In spite of Jocasta's comforting demonstrations of the falsity of prophecy, Oedipus is a prey to agony and fear, and, with the pilot stricken, Jocasta herself is afraid. She appears with garlands and incense, announcing her intention to visit "the temples of the gods" (911). But every word she says shows that this is not in any sense a recantation. She has not changed her opinion of oracles, old or new (915-16); it is an erratic move, the unreasoning expression of fear. [41] "The idea occurred to me [*doksa moi parestathê*, 911]," she says, "to come as a suppliant to the temples of the gods." The reason (*gar*, 914) is the agitation of Oedipus, which she regards as a sign that he has lost control of himself (915-16), and which she tried to overcome by advice (918). Only when her attempt to stiffen Oedipus' resolution failed did she come as a suppliant to the gods. She now addresses herself to the altar at which the priest sat in supplication at the opening of the play. "I have come in supplication, with these symbols of prayer, to you, Lycean Apollo, for you are the nearest." [42] This is surely an unusual formula of prayer. True enough, Apollo's altar is the nearest, and it is only natural that her visit to the "temples of the gods" should begin with it, but to tell him so in the invocation of the prayer argues at least a religious insensibility.

With the electrifying news brought by the Corinthian messenger Jocasta's confidence surges back, for here is further proof of what she tried to demonstrate to Oedipus by inference: the "new" oracles given to him at Delphi are proved as false as the "old" oracles given to Laius at Thebes. [43] "Prophecies of the gods," she cries, "where are you?" And more precisely still: "See what the awful oracles of the gods have come to" (952-3). [44]

The proofs now seem overwhelming, and Oedipus matches Jocasta's confident scorn. "Why should one carefully observe the hearth of the Pythian prophet or the birds that scream over our heads . . . ?" He dismisses the prophetic art of Tiresias and of Apollo in the same breath: "Polybus has taken the present prophecies with him to Hades where he lies hidden—they are worthless" (971-2). [45]

This is not quite true, as he at once realizes. Polybus has taken only half the prophecies with him; there remains still the fear of the marriage with his mother. And here, as before, Jocatas is one step ahead of Oedipus, and now presents him with a philosophical basis for release from this and every other fear. "What has man to fear, whose life is governed by the operation of chance?" [46]

This word *tychê*, "chance," has been used often before in the course of the play; its explosive epiphany in these lines has been well prepared. In the earlier scenes it is used in the old sense: fortune, good or bad, viewed as the expression, not the negation, of divine order. "You brought us fortune then, with auspicious bird omens" (*tychên*, 52), says the priest to Oedipus, associating the liberation of Thebes from the Sphinx with Tiresias' art of divination from birds, and thus placing Oedipus' great achievement in a context of meaningful relationship between god-given signs and human intelligence and action.[47] This context Oedipus will soon deny (398), but for the moment he himself prays, when Creon returns from Delphi with the oracular response: "O Lord Apollo, may he walk in the brightness of some saving fortune" (*tychêi . . . sôtêri*, 80-1), thus associating *tyche* directly with the god and the oracle which he impatiently awaits.[48] He later twice uses this word of the misfortunes of Laius (102, 263), the second time in a striking personification: "now Tyche has jumped on his head," a metaphor drawn from the *pancration*, the merciless "all-in" fighting event of the Greek athletic games.[49] The word is used here in a different sense, for the death of Laius is not, so far as Oedipus can see, an event associated with divine plan or order: it is something terrible which simply "happened" (*etychen*). As the action unfolds further, this word is made to express the feeling of both Oedipus and Jocasta about events which they cannot comprehend; it begins to assume the meaning assigned to it by Pericles—"to chance we ascribe whatever turns out contrary to calculation." So Jocasta, when asked by the chorus to take Oedipus into the palace, replies: "Yes, I will, when I know the nature of what has chanced" (*tychê*, 680). She is referring to the apparently irrational quarrel between Oedipus and Creon. "To whom else should I confide," says Oedipus later, just before he tells his story to Jocasta, "passing through such chance as this?" (*tychês*, 773). He is referring to the chance discovery [50] that the place where Laius was killed was the same as the scene as his mother lives he cannot banish fear. Strong as the evidence is, he cannot yet accept the universe of chance.

It is the Corinthian messenger who now delivers the convincing argument. Oedipus is not the son of Polybus and Merope. His whole life history is a striking example of the operation of chance. Found on the hillside by one shepherd (or so the Corinthian messenger believes), passed on to another, given to the childless king Polybus, brought up as the heir to a kingdom, Oedipus went to Delphi as a result of a chance remark made by a drunkard, to hear a dreadful prophecy which made him a self-banished exile from Corinth forever. He came to Thebes a homeless wanderer, answered the riddle of the Sphinx, and won the *tyrannis* of the city and the hand of a queen. Even his name he owes to chance. "You were named the man you are from this chance" (*ek tychés tautés*, 1036), the messenger reminds him. The whole story, the beginning of which is only now being brought to light, seems like a powerful demonstration that Jocasta was right. Such a fantastic series of coincidences seems expressly designed to mock the idea that human destiny is predictable; it is a paradigm of the inconsequent anarchy of the universe.

Jocasta was right, but for Oedipus in his present mood she seems to have stopped short of the full truth. He accepts the rule of chance, but it is not, for him, a blind chance which nullifies human action and condemns man to live at random. Chance is a goddess, and Oedipus is her son.[55] She is "the good giver,"[56] and he will not be dishonored when his real identity is at last established. It is typical of Oedipus that he accepts a doctrine which is offered to him as a warrant for "living at random" and transforms it into a basis for controlled action; as the son of Tyche he will press on the search to the end—his parentage is a guarantee of success. He makes out of Jocasta's nihilizing chance a goddess who controls the universe and has selected him as her chosen vessel: he is kin to the moons that mark the months for all men and for Oedipus the ebb and rise of his own great destiny.[57]

The implication of this magnificent speech of Oedipus is clearly that he is equated to the gods. The chorus, breathtaken at the sudden and (apparently) auspicious revelations, inspired by Oedipus' courage and infected by his enthusiasm for the unimaginable vistas that now open up before him, proceeds to make the idea explicit.[58] Oedipus, they sing, will prove to be not a foreigner but, to their great joy, a Theban; his nurse and mother is revealed as the Theban mountain Cithaeron (1089 ff.). But his real parentage must be greater yet. Which of the mountain nymphs bore him to Pan? To Apollo? Or was his father Hermes? Or the Theban divinity Dionysus? [59]

These exultant speculations, put forward as prophetic (*mantis*, 1086) and addressed to Apollo for his approval (1096-97), are the penultimate step in the long search for the origins of Oedipus. "My father," Oedipus told Jocasta, "was Polybus of Corinth, my mother Merope, a Dorian." But that was before the Corinthian messenger released Oedipus from fear. Since then his mother, in his mind and in that of the chorus, has appeared to the imagination in a variety of identities, which run the gamut from small to great : a third-generation slave (1063), the goddess Tyche, the mountain Cithaeron, a long-lived nymph, a nymph of Helicon. And the image of his father, once stable in the figure of Polybus of Corinth, has been tentatively identified with the Corinthian messenger,[60] Apollo, Pan, Hermes, and Dionysus. As the last notes of the chorus' joyful song die away, Oedipus begins the final enquiry which will bring the search for the truth to an end; he will soon know his parents as Jocasta, who has already gone off into the palace to hang herself, and Laius, whom he killed at the crossroads so many years ago.[61] He is the son not of Chance but of mischance, as the herdsman tells him (1181);[62] the revelation of his parentage, far from raising him to the level of the gods, reduces him below the level of all normal humanity. And the vicissitudes of his astonishing career are revealed as the working not of Jocasta's blind chance nor the anarchic goddess Chance but of the old "divine chance," *theia tychê*, the expression in action of divine foreknowledge, the mode of fulfilment of Apollo's oracle.

This intellectual progress of Oedipus and Jocasta, which parallels the intellectual progress of the age of enlightenment, has been carefully set in an ironic dramatic framework where it is exposed as wrong from the start. At one point after another the words which characterize the power, decision, and action of Oedipus find a significant echo in contexts which emphatically oppose to his human greatness the power, decision, and action of the gods. The assumption of divine stature implicit in Oedipus' attitude is thus made explicit and at the same time exposed as false. The priest, for example, addresses Oedipus as " the one in power " (*all' ô kratynôn*, 14), and the chorus, much later, at the point where it transfers its allegiance from the *tyrannos* to the god, uses exactly the same words to address Zeus (*all' ô kratynôn*, 904). The priest hails Oedipus as " savior " (*sôtêra*, 48), a title which Oedipus accepts (*eksesôs'*, 443);[63] the priest meanwhile has prayed that " Apollo will come as savior" (*sôtêr*, 150). Oedipus claims that he has " stopped " the Sphinx (*epausa*, 397), but it is on Apollo that the priest calls to " stop " the plague (*paustêrios*, 150). Oedipus claims to " wield the power " in Thebes (*kratê . . . nemô*, 237), but Zeus, the chorus sings, " wields the power of the lightning" (*astrapan kratê nemôn*, 201). Oedipus calls himself "great" (*megan*, 441; cf. 776), but the god, says the chorus, is "great" in his laws (*megas theos*, 872).[64] Oedipus has "empire" (*archê*, 259, 383), but the "empire" of Zeus is immortal (*athanaton archan*, 905). Oedipus promises "strength" (*alkên*, 218; cf. 42) but it is to Athena that the chorus prays for "strength" (*alkan*, 189). Oedipus talks to the Thebans like a father to his children (*tekna*, 1; cf. 6),[65] but the chorus finally appeals to "father Zeus" (*Zeu pater*, 202). Oedipus "destroyed" the Sphinx (*phthisas*, 1198), but it is to Zeus that the chorus appeals to "destroy" the plague (*phthison*, 202).[66] All these echoes are like a mockery of Oedipus' pretensions,[67] and in addition the language of the play rings with sardonic puns on his name which seem to find their way into the speech of the characters like echoes of some far-off grim laughter. *Oidipous*—"Swollen-foot"—the name emphasizes the physical blemish which scars the body of the splendid *tyrannos*, a defect he would like to forget [68] but which reminds us of the cast-out child he once was and forshadows the outcast man he is soon to be. The second half of his name, *pous*, "foot," recurs constantly in passages which, though the speaker is usually not conscious of the force of his speech, refer to Oedipus' real identity as the murderer of Laius. "The Sphinx," says Creon, replying to Oedipus' veiled reproach that he had not exerted himself enough in the original search for the murderer of Laius, "the Sphinx forced us to look at what was at our feet" (*to pros posi skopein*, 130). Tiresias invokes the "dread-footed curse of your mother and father" (*deinopous ara*, 418). And two of the choral odes heavily emphasize this word by repeating it in strophe and antistrophe. "It is time [for the unknown murderer] to set his foot in motion in flight" (*phygai poda nôman*, 468), they sing, and in the corresponding antistrophe they describe the murderer as " a wild beast, alone, cut off," *meleos meleôi podi chêreuôn* (479)—a phrase which can be taken metaphorically, as Jebb does (" forlorn on his joyless path "), but which means literally " forlorn and miserable with miserable foot." In the next choral ode, the one in which they abandon Oedipus and pray for the fulfilment of the oracles, the chorus' words repeat the same pattern: " The laws of Zeus are high-footed " (*hypsipodes*, 866) is answered in the antistrophe by " pride . . . plunges into sheer necessity wherein no service of the foot can serve " (Jebb's translation of *ou podi chrêsimôi chrêtai*, 877). These words literally mean " where it uses a useless foot "; they repeat in a negative form the " miserable foot " (*meleôi podi*) of the previous ode. These phrases all point with terrible irony to the maimed foot of Oedipus which is the basis of his name and the key to his identity; two of them, *hypsipodes* and *deinopous*, are like punning forms of the name itself.

These mocking repetitions of the second half of the hero's name evoke the Oedipus who will be revealed, the hunted murderer. The equally emphatic repetitions of the first component of his name stress a dominant characteristic of the imposing *tyrannos*. *Oidi-* means " swell," but it is very close to *oida*, " I know," [69] and this is a word that is never far from Oedipus' lips; his knowledge is what makes him the decisive and confident *tyrannos*. *Oida* recurs throughout the text of the play with the same grim persistence as *pous*,[70] and the suggestion inherent in the name of the *tyrannos* is ironically pointed up in a group of three assonantal line-endings which in their savage punning emphasis are surely unparalleled in Greek tragedy. When the messenger from Corinth comes to tell Oedipus that his father Polybus is dead, he enquires for Oedipus, who is inside the palace, in the following terms (924-6):

Strangers, from you might I *learn where*
is the palace of the *tyrannos Oidipous,*
best of all, where he himself is, if you *know where.*

Here it is in the original:

Ar' an par' hymôn ô ksenoi mathoim' hopou
ta tou tyrannou dômat' estin Oidipou
malista d' auton eipat' ei katoisth' hopou.[71]

These violent puns,[72] suggesting a fantastic conjugation of a verb " to know where " formed from the name of the hero who, as Tiresias told him, does not know where he is—this is the ironic laughter of the gods whom Oedipus " excludes " in his search for the truth. They watch the critical intelligence work its way laboriously and courageously through to the absolutely clear vision which, once found, it cannot bear to face. Their presence is manifested in this intrusive ironic pattern in the language of the characters, which is a riddling reminder that there is a standard beyond man by which Oedipus is measured. As Oedipus finds out in the end, man is not the measure of all things; rather, as Plato was to say much later, " the measure of all things is—the god." [73]

CHAPTER FIVE: HERO

But the play does not end with the proof of divine omniscience and human ignorance. It ends, as it begins, with Oedipus. "Equal to zero"—the chorus' estimate, proposed at the moment when Oedipus learns who he is, seems right and indeed inevitable. But it is hard to accept. It means that the heroic action of Oedipus, with all that his action is made to represent, is a hollow mockery, a snare and a delusion. It suggests that man should not seek, for fear of what he will find. It renounces the qualities and actions which distinguish man from the beasts, and accepts a state of blind, mute acquiescence no less repugnant to the human spirit than the recklessness demanded by Jocasta's universe of chance. And yet at that moment it seems the only possible conclusion. With Oedipus as their paradigm, it is difficult to see what other estimate the chorus can make.

A different estimate is proposed, not in words but in dramatic action, by the final scene of the play. For Oedipus, the paradigm, on whom the chorus' despairing estimate is based, surmounts the catastrophe and reasserts himself. He is so far from being equal to zero that in the last lines of the play ¹ Creon has to tell him not to try to "rule in everything" (1522). This last scene of the play, so often criticized as anticlimactic or unbearable, is on the contrary vital for the play, and a development which makes its acceptance possible. It shows us the recovery of Oedipus, the reintegration of the hero, the reconstitution of the imperious, dynamic, intelligent figure of the opening scenes.

This is an astonishing development, for Oedipus, when he comes out of the palace, is so terrible a sight that the chorus cannot bear to look at him (1303), and his situation is such

that the chorus expresses a wish that it had never known him
(1348). It approves his wish that he could have died on the
mountainside before he reached manhood (1356), and tells
him that he would be better dead now than alive and blind
(1368). This despair is reflected in the words of Oedipus
himself: they are the words of a broken man.

The first lines present us with an Oedipus who speaks
in terms we can hardly recognize: he speaks of his movements, voice, and destiny as things alien to him, utterly
beyond his control. "Where am I being carried? How does
my voice fly about, carried aloft? O my destiny, to what
point have you leaped out?" (1309-11).[2] These are the words
of a blinded man awakening to the realization of his terrible
impotence, but they express also a feeling that Oedipus is no
longer an active force but purely passive. This impression
is enforced by his next words, an address to the darkness in
which he will now forever move, and a reference to the pain
which pierces his eyes and mind alike (1313-18). The climax
of this unnatural passivity is reached when Oedipus first
becomes aware of the presence of the chorus (1321). His
realization takes the form of a grateful recognition of their
steadfastness in "looking after the blind man" (1323). This
is an expression of his utter dependency on others; he is so
far from action now that he needs help even to exist. He seems
indeed a zero, equal to nothing.

It is precisely at this point that the chorus reminds us, and
him, that part at any rate of his present calamitous state, his
blindness, is his own choice, the result of his own independent
action after the recognition of the truth. This was not called
for by the prophecy of Apollo, nor was it demanded in the
oracle's instructions about the murderer's punishment or the
curse on him pronounced by Oedipus. It was Oedipus' autonomous action, and the chorus now asks him why he did it:

" You have done dreadful things " (*deina drasas*, 1327). They use the word for action which was peculiarly his when he was *tyrannos*, and the question they ask him suggests an explanation. "Which of the divinities spurred you on?" Oedipus' reply defends his action and rejects the chorus' formula, which would shift the responsibility for the blinding off his shoulders. Apollo, he says, brought my sufferings to fulfilment, but " as for the hand that struck my eyes, it was mine and no one else's " (1330-1). He confirms what the messenger has already told us; the action was " self-chosen " (*authairetoi*, 1231), and a few lines later the chorus reproves him for it. It was in fact an action typical of Oedipus *tyrannos*, one which anticipated the reaction, advice, and objection of others, a *fait accompli*, a swift decisive act for which he assumes full responsibility and which he proceeds to defend. And now, as if the chorus' reminder of his own action had arrested the disintegration of his personality which was so terribly clear in the first speech after his entrance, the old Oedipus reappears. As he rejects the chorus' suggestion that the responsibility was not his, grounds his action logically, and (as his lines make the transition from the lyric of lamentation to the iambic of rational speech), rejects their reproaches, all the traits of his magnificent character reappear. It is not long before he is recognizably the same man as before.

He is still the man of decisive action, and still displays the courage which had always inspired that action. His attitude to the new and terrible situation in which he now finds himself is full of the same courage which he displayed before: he accepts the full consequences of the curse he imposed on himself, and insists stubbornly, in the face of Creon's opposition, that he be put to death or exiled from Thebes. He brushes aside the compromise offered by Creon with the same courage that dismissed the attempts of Tiresias, Jocasta, and

the herdsman to stop the investigation. The speed and impatience of his will is if anything increased; *tachys*, "swift,"
is still his word. "Take me away from this place as quickly
as possible" (*hoti tachista*, 1340). "Hide me away as quickly
as possible" (*hopôs tachista*, 1410). "Throw me out of this
land as quickly as may be" (*hoson tachisth'*, 1436).

As before, he has no patience with half-measures or delay;
the oracle and his own curse call for his exile or death, and
he sees nothing to be gained by prolonging the inaction. The
same analytical intelligence is at work; he is right, and, as we
know, Creon finally does late what Oedipus wanted done
early—he exiles Oedipus from Thebes. The same hard intelligence which insisted on full clarity and all the facts is
displayed in his remorseless exploration and formulation of the
frightful situation in which he finds himself. He spares himself
no detail of the consequences of his pollution for himself and
for his daughters. It is typical that while Creon's reaction is
to cover and conceal (1426 ff.), Oedipus brings everything out
into the open, analyzing in painful detail his own situation
and that of his children. The intelligence of Oedipus is at
work even at the high pitch of semihysterical grief;[3] even
in his outburst of lamentation he distinguishes between what
he regards as the gods' responsibility and his own. And an
extraordinary thing emerges as Oedipus abandons the wild
lament of his first reaction for the reasoned speech of the
last part of the play: it becomes apparent that even the self-
blinding was based on the deliberation and reflection which
in Oedipus *tyrannos* always preceded action.[4] To the chorus'
reproach that he had "made a bad decision" (1367) in
blinding himself he replies with the old impatience and a touch
of the old anger. "Do not read me a lesson or give me any
advice, to the effect that I have not done the best thing" (1369-
70). And he goes on to describe in detail the reasoning by

which he arrived at the decision to put out his eyes (1370-83). Sophocles makes it clear that this is an account of past reflection preceding the action (and not a present rationalization of it) by his use of the past tense throughout the speech.[5] Oedipus is fully confident of the rightness of the action and the thought which preceded and produced it. And all through this scene he maps out the future for himself and his family, giving Creon instructions for the burial of Jocasta, his own expulsion from Thebes, and the upbringing of his sons and daughters.

The old confidence in his own intelligence and action is still there, but the exaggerated and vaulting hopefulness is gone. And yet there is still a kind of hope; he becomes certain, after his initial wish for death, that he is destined to live, that he is in some sense indestructible. "This much I know [*oida*]: that not disease, nor anything else can destroy me. For I would never have been saved from death in the first place [i. e. as a child on the mountainside] except for some strange and fearful evil" (*deinôi kakôi*, 1457). He feels himself as eminent in disaster as he once was in prosperity— "my sufferings are such as no one could bear but me" (1414-15); whatever his end will be, it will be out of the ordinary, like everything else about him. "But let my destiny go, wherever it is going" (1458).

The devotion to the interests of the city which was so marked a feature of the attitude of the *tyrannos* might be expected to become dormant in the man who is now a polluted outcast from society, but on the contrary it is still active in Oedipus. His anxiety to have the terms of his own curse and the command of the oracle exactly and immediately fulfilled springs partly from his sense of the city's need of release from the plague, which can come only through the punishment of the murderer of Laius. It is in terms of the interest of the city that he states his desire for exile, speaking this time not as *tyrannos* but with a consciousness of his newly revealed position as the hereditary monarch: " Let not the city of my fathers be condemned to have me as a living inhabitant " (1449-50).

And Oedipus is still adaptable, quick to align himself with changed circumstances. The process of his swift adjustment to his blindness is carefully delineated. After the helpless desperation of the opening lines, in which he is oblivious of any reality outside himself, he comes to realize that he has still some power of perception and recognition—he can hear. " You are not unperceived," he tells the chorus; " I distinguish clearly [*gignôskô saphôs*, 1325] your voice at any rate, plunged in darkness though I am." And from the point at which he recognizes the possibilities as well as the limitations of his new state, he never turns back. He begins to adapt himself to the larger aspects of the situation, and makes the transition from passive back to active.

The adaptability of Oedipus surmounts the most terrible reversal of relationships imaginable. Oedipus is now an outcast, and, as Tiresias told him he would be, a beggar. The wealthy *tyrannos* expressed his wish as an order, but the beggar lives by insistent appeals, by emphatic and often importunate pleading. When Creon appears, Oedipus shows himself to be as insistent a beggar as ever lived; the formulas of supplication come as easily from his lips as the imperative words, and they are charged with the same fierce energy. Once Oedipus is told that Creon has not come to mock him, he shows himself an adept in his new role; appeal and entreaty follow each other swiftly—Creon is given no breathing space. " By the gods ... do what I ask," he says (1432); begging to be expelled from the city, and Creon recognizes the tone of his speech, for he replies " You importune me " (*lipareis*, 1435), the appropriate word for the action of the beggar. In the subsequent appeal to be allowed the privilege of saying farewell to his children, Oedipus achieves a wheedling importunacy which is formally emphasized by the breaks in the regularity of the verses: 1468, 1471, and 1475 are cut off short before the end of the first measure. "Let me touch them, and weep for their sorrows. Grant it, my lord. Grant it, you who are noble in birth." This last phrase is a reference to his own polluted fatherhood; it is the beggar's characteristic contrast between the nobility of his patron's birth and the humble nature of his own circumstances. Oedipus greets the granting of his request with the beggar's typical blessing of his bene-factor—"May you be fortunate . . ." (1478)—and the same flattering contrast of circumstances—"May a divinity prove a better guardian to you than it did to me" (1479). Later he makes another appeal to Creon's pity, this time on behalf of his daughters: "Do not let them wander husbandless as beggars, do not make their fortune the equivalent of mine" (1505-7)—a phrase which indicates his conception of his own status as a beggar. "Pity them," he continues (1508); "Nod your head in sign of acceptance, noble man, touch them with your hand" (1510). Oedipus has made a swift and strikingly successful adjustment to his new role. As a beggar he is irresistible.[6]

For this abject and insistent supplication is full of an imperiousness that recalls the *tyrannos*. When he first hears the voice of Creon, whom he had wrongly condemned to death, he is abashed and at a loss for words (1419), yet in a few moments he is arguing stubbornly with him, and finally gives him his instructions in a magnificent phrase which combines the attitude of the *tyrannos* and the beggar: "I make you responsible and I beg you . . ." (*episkêptô te kai prostrepsomai*, 1446). The first word is the same one which he used before, when as *tyrannos* he ordered the people of

Thebes to cooperate with him in his search for the murderer of Laius.

It is a surprising word, and even more surprising is the fact that Creon does not protest. The last scene of the play presents us with an unpredictable situation: in spite of his tremendous reversal, Oedipus is still the active force which binds men and circumstances to its will. His reflection and intelligence assure him that he must go immediately into exile, and to this point of view he clings stubbornly, urging it persistently and imperiously on Creon until the man who now has the power to "decide and act" (1417) yields to the will of the blind beggar. At the last moment, when Creon orders him into the house, Oedipus imposes conditions (1517); the conditions are the same demand he has so stubbornly repeated throughout the scene—that Creon immediately exile him from Thebes (1518). Creon's attempt to shift the responsibility by consulting Delphi is rejected by Oedipus, and he is right; according to the original oracular advice, and also the curse pronounced by Oedipus, the murderer of Laius must be exiled. "I come as one most hateful to the gods," says Oedipus (1519). Creon yields to his demands, but in an ambiguous phrase: "For that reason you will swiftly get what you want" (1519)—which might mean either "I will exile you" or "the gods, since they hate you, will, through the agency of the oracle, command your banishment." Oedipus demands a clear promise: "You consent, then?" (1520). And Creon finally does consent, and though the terms of his consent are still ambiguous they commit him much more strongly than his previous statement. "It is not my custom to say idly what I do not think" (1520).[7] It is a phrase worthy of Creon the politician, but Oedipus accepts it as a definite promise, and allows himself to be led into the palace. Before he does, he makes an attempt to take the children with him, but at this point Creon finally asserts himself and separates the children from their father. He takes the occasion to reprove Oedipus for his imperious tone. "Do not wish to exercise power [*kratein*, 1522] in everything. For the power which you won [*hakratêsas*, 1522] has not accompanied you to the end of your life." He does not get his way in everything, but in most he has, including the most important issue of all, his expulsion; in this the blind beggar has imposed his will on the king.

The final phrase of Creon—"Do not wish to exercise power in everything"—brings us full circle; it is an echo of the first words addressed to Oedipus in the play; "Oedipus, you who exercise power in my country," the priest said to him at the beginning (*kratynôn*, 14). Creon actually has to remind the blinded polluted man that he is no longer *tyrannos*; the will of Oedipus is reasserting itself, and Creon suddenly sees that "action and deliberation," the functions which he assumed when Oedipus was revealed as the son of Laius, are slipping from him. The swiftness and force of Oedipus' recovery from the shock of self-recognition can be gauged from the fact that in the very last line of the play Oedipus has to be reminded of his reversal.

This recovery is all the more astonishing because there is no reference in Sophocles' lines to the justification of Oedipus and his elevation to the status of divine hero which is the subject of the later play *Oedipus at Colonus*.[8] There is, at most, a sense that Oedipus has a special destiny, an invulnerability to ordinary calamities, but this special destiny Oedipus can only refer to as a "dreadful evil" (*deinôi kakôi*, 1457). The reassertion of Oedipus' forceful personality rests on no change in his situation, no promise or assurance, human or divine; it is, like every one of his actions and attitudes, autonomous, the expression of a great personality which defies human expectation as it once defied divine prophecy.

The closing note of the tragedy is a renewed insistence on the heroic nature of Oedipus; the play ends as it began, with the greatness of the hero. But it is a different kind of greatness. It is now based on knowledge, not, as before, on ignorance,[9] and this new knowledge is, like that of Socrates, a recognition of man's ignorance. " Apollo and Zeus," the chorus sang, " have understanding and knowledge of things human " (497-9); and Oedipus now directs the full force of his intelligence and action to the fulfilment of the oracular command that the murderer of Laius be killed or exiled. Creon, who resists the appeals of Oedipus, can taunt him with his former lack of belief—" You would have faith in the god now " (1445) —but Oedipus does not deign to answer this sarcastic rebuke. He hammers away insistently at his demand that the command of the oracle be literally and immediately fulfilled. The heroic qualities of the *tyrannos*, once exercised against prophecy and the destiny of which it is the expression, are now ranged on its side. And Creon's refusal to fulfil the oracle's command presents us with a situation in which Oedipus' acceptance of what he once rejected demands and produces not passivity but action, not acquiescence but struggle. The heroic qualities of Oedipus are still to be given full play, but now with, not against, the powers that shape destiny and govern the world. " May Destiny be with me . . ." the chorus sang when it abandoned Oedipus (863); that prayer is fulfilled for the hero. Destiny is with him; the confidence which was once based solely on himself is now more firmly based; it proceeds now from a knowledge of the nature of reality and the forces which govern it, and his identification with their will. In the last scene he champions the command of the oracle against the will of Creon, the new ruler of Thebes; it is Creon now who displays a politic attitude towards the Delphic oracle, and Oedipus who insists on its literal fulfilment. He is now blind like Tiresias, and like Tiresias has a more penetrating vision than the ruler he opposes; in this scene he has in fact become the spokesman of Apollo, " seeing," as the chorus said of Tiresias, " the same things as the lord Apollo." Now that his will is identified with *moira*, " destiny," his action ceases to be self-defeating, for it is based on true knowledge. The greatness of Oedipus in his ruin is no less, and in some senses more, than the greatness of the *tyrannos*.

Oedipus is a paradigm of all mankind, and of the city which is man's greatest creation. His resurgence in the last scene of the play is a prophetic vision of a defeated Athens which will rise to a greatness beyond anything she had attained in victory, a vision of man, superior to the tragic reversal of his action and the terrible success of his search for truth, reasserting his greatness, not this time in defiance of the powers which shape human life but in harmony with those powers. "All things are born to be diminished," Pericles reminded the Athenians; the tragic vision of Sophocles accepts this melancholy recognition and transcends it, to see beyond the defeat of man's ambition the true greatness of which only the defeated are capable.

The *Oedipus Tyrannus* of Sophocles combines two apparently irreconcilable themes, the greatness of the gods and the greatness of man, and the combination of these themes is inevitably tragic, for the greatness of the gods is most clearly and powerfully demonstrated by man's defeat. " The god is great in his laws and he does not grow old." But man does, and not only does he grow old, he also dies. Unlike the gods, he exists in time. The beauty and power of his physical frame is subject to sickness, death, and corruption; the beauty and power of his intellectual, artistic, and social achievement to decline, overthrow, and oblivion. His greatness and beauty arouse in us a pride in their magnificence which is inseparable from and increased by our sorrow over their immanent and imminent death. Oedipus is symbolic of all human achievement: his hard-won magnificience, unlike the everlasting magnificence of the divine, cannot last, and while it lives, shines all the more brilliant against the somber background of its impermanency. Sophocles' tragedy presents us with a terrible affirmation of man's subordinate position in the universe, and at the same time with a heroic vision of man's victory in defeat. Man is not equated to the gods, but man at his greatest, as in Oedipus, is capable of something which the gods, by definition, cannot experience; the proud tragic view of Sophocles sees in the fragility and inevitable defeat of human greatness the possibility of a purely human heroism to which the gods can never attain, for the condition of their existence is everlasting victory.

The abbreviations for authors and works are those used in the ninth edition of Liddell and Scott's *Lexicon*; and their methods of reference are used except in the case of Plutarch's *Moralia*, where I give the title of the essay as well as the Wyttenbach page number. The abbreviations for periodicals are those used in *L'année philologique*.

1. Other centuries claim him too. Sir Richard Jebb in *Sophocles. Oedipus Tyrannus* (Cambridge, Univ. Press, 1887), Intro., p. xxvii, remarks: " As regards Oedipus, it might be said that, in this particular aspect [i. e. the sense in which he is conceived to be placed at issue with religion] he is a modern character, and more especially, perhaps, a character of the nineteenth century."

2. I quote Freud's remarks merely as a fine illustration of the view under discussion, not as a target for another classical volley against Freud. As will be clear, I have considerable respect for his views. His discussion of the *Oedipus* does not deserve the strictures which many classical scholars have wasted on it, since he is concerned not so much with Sophocles' play as with the basic mythic material. He states this clearly himself: " The form which it [the Oedipus fable] subsequently assumed [i. e. the *Oedipus Tyrannus*] was the result of an uncomprehending secondary elaboration of the material, which sought to make it serve a theological intention "(*The Interpretation of Dreams*, N. Y., Modern Library, 1938, p. 309). Freud himself obviously never entertained the notion of a Freudian interpretation of the Sophoclean play: that unenviable task was assumed by his disciples. A recent product of the school is worth quoting briefly as an example of what happens when the *epigonos* rushes in where his predecessor feared to tread: *The Muse at Length*, by Arthur Wormhoudt, Ph. D., Boston, The Christopher Publishing House, 1953.

From this work (pp. 118-23) it appears that Jocasta "instead of stiffening Oedipus' courage as we should expect in the positive Oedipus complex . . . makes him back down in accord with her role as finger symbol in the breast complex or feminine identity and ring symbol in the negative Oedipus complex." "Laius' . . . double-pronged goad represents the two breasts transferred from the pre-oedipal to the oedipal level." "Mount Cithaeron . . . Parnassus . . . and Helicon . . . are breast symbols which represent the poet's ability to substitute words or symbols for the milk of which he wants to be masochistically deprived." Mr. Wormhoudt neatly resolves the much discussed problem of the exodus of the *Oedipus Tyrannus*: "what Oedipus accomplishes in the last scene of the play . . . is the substitution of exhibitionism for voyeurism."

As for the *Oedipus at Colonus*: "Polynices describes the filthy garments in which Oedipus is dressed, and accepts the anal guilt which these imply himself. The reason then for Oedipus' violent rejection of him is that in this way he executes the punishment of castration upon himself."

The author, to give him his due, does not expect such radical reinterpretations to be accepted overnight: "the resistance to the scientific study of literature is much greater than to astronomy, chemistry or biology (great as that was), because it touches matters closer to home" (pp. 9-10).

3. Ibid., pp. 108-9.

4. These last two actions are described by the messenger as ἐκόντα κοὐκ ἄκοντα: "willed, not against the will" (1230); and αὐθαίρετοι: "self-chosen" (1231). For the first of these two phrases cf. Macaria's description of her act of self-sacrifice in E. *Heracl.* 531: ἑκοῦσα κοὐκ ἄκουσα.

5. οὐ γάρ σε μοῖρα πρός γ' ἐμοῦ πεσεῖν, ἐπεὶ ἱκανὸς Ἀπόλλων, ᾧ τάδ' ἐκπρᾶξαι μέλει. So all the modern editors and translators.

6. "Nempe Tiresias plane contrarium dicit illius quod dicere debuit . . . Facile, imperitis describentibus librariis, pronomina commutari potuerunt."

7. This papyrus (POxy. 22) dates from the fifth century A.D. and is thus our earliest manuscript of the passage. It reads [   ] ΜΕ ΜΟΙΡΑ ΠΡΟΣ ΓΕ ΣΟΥ ΠΕΣΕΙΝ ΕΠΕΙ. One recent MS (cod. Abbat. 41, 14th century, Jebb's Δ) reads σε, but no MS reads γ' ἐμοῦ.

8. οὐ γάρ με μοῖρα πρός γε σοῦ . . . See Pearson's apparatus.

9. It was first challenged by Gilbert Murray in his book *The Rise of the Greek Epic* (3d ed. Oxford, Clarendon Press, 1924), p. 87, n. 1. The gist of the note is: "Oed. 'Thou art a child of unbroken night, so that neither I nor any other who sees the light would (ἂν) ever harm thee.' Tir. 'It is not my doom to fall by thy hand' &c. So Mss. and cf. 448 below where Tiresias repeats the same statement." To this there is little to add: for the omission of the object ("you") in the MS version cf. 1045 below, ὥστ' ἰδεῖν ἐμέ, which must mean "so that I may see [him]." Murray attributes Oedipus' announcement that he would not harm Tiresias to αἰδώς (and is on this ground rightly challenged by A. C. Pearson, "Sophoclea II," 374-5, in *CQ* 23 [1929], 94); Oedipus' motive in sparing Tiresias is not respect but contempt (cf. the scathing contempt of 348-9); Tiresias is beneath his notice. Pearson's other objection, that "the ruin of Oedipus, not of Tiresias, is the main question raised by 372 sq." does not take account of the threats to punish Tiresias which Oedipus repeatedly makes (cf. 355, 363, 368). Sir John Sheppard's objection (p. 125) does not allow for the possibility that τάδ' may refer to Tiresias' hypothetical fall instead of "this present business."

10. With Brunk's emendation this question seems to be a complete change of direction; not impossible, of course, but the logical advance indicated by the MS reading is much more like Oedipus.

11. So, apparently, W. C. Greene, *Moira* (Cambridge, Mass., Harvard Univ. Press, 1948), p. 155: "Granted, however, that Oedipus is already guilty of parricide and incest, there will

be no tragedy if these facts do not transpire. But in that case, too, the old oracles and their god, Apollo, will be in disrepute, as the chorus will protest. Consistency demands therefore that the agencies of fate discover the facts which fate has already caused; the plague which is afflicting Thebes is the force which initiates the events leading to the discovery."

12. *Il.* i. 52: πυραὶ νεκύων καίοντο θαμειαί.

13. For the connection of the plague and the oracle in the minds of the Athenians see Th. ii. 54.

14. For Apollo as plague averter in historical times cf. Paus. x. 11. 5 (Cleonae, ca. 429 B.C.); I. 3. 4 (Athens): τὴν λοιμώδη σφίσι νόσον ὁμοῦ τῷ Πελοποννησίων πολέμῳ πιέζουσαν κατὰ μάντευμα ἔπαυσε⟨ν ἐκ⟩ Δελφῶν.

15. The Homeric hymn to Ares, which lists 16 epithets of the god in the first five lines, has nothing which even vaguely hints at plague. The closest approximation to this striking identification in the Sophoclean passage is to be found in the *Suppliants* of Aeschylus. In two passages (659-66 and 678-85) the chorus couples plague and Ares: λοιμός . . . Ἄρης in the first case, and Ἄρη . . . νούσων in the second. But, though associated, they are not identified, as they are in the Sophoclean lines. For the bearing of this identification on the problem of the date of the play see Knox, "The Date of the *Oedipus Tyrannus*," *AJP*, 78 (1956), 133 ff.

16. It is interesting to compare this initial imperative, which a religious mind may attribute to the gods but which is none the less a fact of common human experience, disease, with the initial imperative in *Hamlet*, which is a demand for vengeance expressed by a father's ghost.

17. Cf. David Grene, *Three Greek Tragedies in Translation* (Chicago, 1942), p. 79.

18. ἐξαγγέλλεται. For this sense of the word cf. E. *Heracl.* 531,

where Macaria volunteers to die for her brothers: κἀξαγγέλ-
λομαι θνῄσκειν. . . .

19. Cf. C. Robert *Oidipus* (Berlin, 1915), p. 291: "Der aber,
der den schweigenden Zeugen die Zunge löst, der das längst
Vergangene wieder aufleben lässt, der fast einzig und allein die
Entdeckung herbeiführt, das ist . . . Oidipus selbst."

20. Cf. the scholiast's comment on 1062: οἴεται [sc. Οἰδίπους]
τὴν Ἰοκάστην . . . κωλύειν τὴν ζήτησιν.

21. On this see the stimulating article of R. A. Pack, "Fate,
Chance, and Tragic Error," *AJP*, 60 (1939), 350 ff.

22. It is difficult to follow the reasoning behind A. J. A. Waldock's statement (*Sophocles the Dramatist*, Cambridge University Press, 1951, p. 144) that the character of Oedipus is
"not very clearly defined," and the further statement that he
"does not possess . . . an intelligence of piercing quickness
or very remarkable reach" though he "has at least an average
mind." Elsewhere he states (p. 168): "There is no meaning
in the *Oedipus Tyrannus*," and exposes attempts to "smuggle
significance" into the work (p. 159).

23. Cf. W. Nestlé, "Hippocratica," *Hermes*, 73 (1938), 13:
"das natürliche Genie des *self-made man* . . ." (on Thucydides'
portrait of Themistocles).

24. For δρᾶν cf. 72, 77, 145, 235, 640, 1327, and 1402. For
πράσσειν cf. 69, 287, and 1403.

25. ὅ τι δρῶν ἢ τί φωνῶν. . . . For this formula cf. D. xliii, 66
(text of an Athenian consultation of the Delphic Oracle):
ἐπερωτᾷ ὁ δῆμος ὁ Ἀθηναίων περὶ τοῦ σημείου τοῦ ἐν τῷ οὐρανῷ
γενομένου ὅ τι ἂν δρῶσιν Ἀθήναιοις ἢ ὅτῳ θεῷ θύουσιν ἢ εὐχομένοις
εἴη ἐπὶ τὸ ἄμεινον ἀπὸ τοῦ σημείου.

26. This is implied in 73-5.

27. Indicated in Oedipus' correction of Creon's "brigands"
(λῃστὰς 122) to "the brigand (ὁ λῃστής, 124). The point of

the correction is that if the murderer of Laius was alone he must have been the agent of a powerful conspiracy, and the man who would benefit from the death of Laius was Creon, the next in line for the throne. Oedipus' next question (128-9) is a veiled accusation that Creon did not want a real investigation of the death of Laius.

28. Cf. ξένος, 219, 220; ὕστερος γὰρ ἀστὸς εἰς ἀστοὺς τελῶ, 222; τοὐπιόντος . . . ἀνδρός, 393; ἐγὼ μολών, 396.

29. Line endings: ἄγνωτά μοι, 58; ὡς ἐγώ, 60; ἡ δ' ἐμή, 63; μ' ἐξεγείρετε, 65; ἐγὼ κακός, 76; ἐγὼ φανῶ, 132; κἀμὲ σύμμαχον, 135; ἐμαυτὸν ὠφελῶ, 141; σημαίνειν ἐμοί, 226; κλύειν ἐμοῦ, 235; ἀρτίως ἐμοί, 243; ἐμοῦ συνειδότος, 250; κυρῶ τ' ἐγώ, 258; τοὐμοῦ πατρός, 264. Line beginnings: ἀγώ, 6; ἐμοῦ, 12; καί μ', 73; ἄναξ ἐμόν, 85; ἀλλ' αὐτός, 138; κἄμ' ἄν, 140; ὡς πᾶν ἐμοῦ, 145; ἀγώ, 219; ἴχνευον αὐτός, 221; τῆσδ' ἧς ἐγώ, 237; ἐγώ, 244; ἐν τοῖς ἐμοῖς, 250; ὑπέρ τ' ἐμαυτοῦ, 253; ἀνθ' ὧν ἐγώ, 264; ἤκουσα κἀγώ, 293.

30. Cf. the chorus' phrase: ἐπὶ τὰν ἐπίδαμον φάτιν . . . Οἰδιπόδα (495-6).

31. His attitude bears a remarkable resemblance to that of Pericles in the last speech reported by Thucydides, after the plague (ii. 61 especially). Pericles terms the plague " sudden, unexpected, and completely beyond calculation " (αἰφνίδιον καὶ ἀπροσδόκητον καὶ . . . πλείστῳ παραλόγῳ ξυμβαῖνον) and bids the Athenians " withstand their misfortunes " (ξυμφοραῖς . . . ὑφίστασθαι). His description of the Athenian reaction to the plague—" pain possesses the feelings of each one of you " (τὸ μὲν λυποῦν ἔχει . . . τὴν αἴσθησιν ἑκάστῳ)—resembles O. T. 62 ff.

32. Hdt. i. 99: μήτε ἐσιέναι παρὰ βασιλέα μηδένα, δι' ἀγγέλων δὲ πάντα χρᾶσθαι, ὁρᾶσθαί τε βασιλέα ὑπὸ μηδενός.

33. It is a carefully couched diplomatic formula which reveals nothing except to those who can relate it to the facts. It begins with ἐσθλήν· (" Good news! ") and proceeds to δύσφορ' (" it may not sound so good ") and ends with εὐτυχεῖν (" everything is going to be all right ").

34. For this exact shade of ἔπος cf. Th. ii. 54. 2.

35. The closing word ἔσω may have been accompanied by a gesture towards the door of the palace, or even a movement towards it.

36. Σ on 1: φιλόδημον καὶ προνοητικὸν τοῦ κοινῇ συμφέροντος τὸ τοῦ Οἰδίποδος ἦθος.

37. Cf. Σ on 124: τείνει δὲ τοῦτο εἰς Κρέοντα ὡς αὐτοῦ συνθεμένου τῷ τοῦ Λαΐου φονεῖ διὰ τὴν βασιλείαν.

38. Cf. Chap. 2, pp. 74-5 and C. H. Whitman, *Sophocles* (Cambridge, Mass., Harvard Univ. Press, 1951), p. 268, n. 31: "I think the lively Athenians would . . . approve of his shrewdness in smelling a plot."

39. Cf. 380-3.

40. Elsewhere in Sophocles this word is used to describe veneration of a god (or a place), never of a man. Cf. O. C. 1654, *Ph.* 657: προσκύσαι θ᾽ ὥσπερ θεόν (the bow of Heracles); *El.* 1374: ἕδη θεῶν, *Ph.* 533, 776, 1408.

41. The dynamics of the altercation between Oedipus and Tiresias make a curious pattern. Tiresias challenges Oedipus to do the worst his anger can suggest to him, and is surprised by the result (343-56). But then the roles are reversed. "Shall I say something else, to make you more angry?" asks Tiresias (364), and Oedipus tells him to say whatever he likes—it will have no result (μάτην εἰρήσεται, 365). He in his turn is surprised. Tiresias surpasses his expectations—it is tit for tat.

42. This τῶνδε is the expression Creon used for the suppliants, and which Oedipus mildly reproved.

43. See Whitman, pp. 33 ff. and references there.

44. *Poetics* 1452ᵇ. 13. Cf. the enlightening discussion in Greene (1), pp. 92-3, especially n. 16.

45. Ibid. 1452ᵃ. 11.

46. The process is emphasized by the reversals of relationship implied in a number of words which contrast the *tyrannos* and the fallen man. He " feels pity " (κατοικτίρων, 13), and in the end is himself a sight such as " even one who hates him would pity " (καὶ στυγοῦντ' ἐποικτίσαι, 1296). He does not ask for anything (οὐκ αἰτητόν, 384), others ask him (αἰτεῖς, 216), but in the end he asks for a sword to kill himself (ἐξαιτῶν, 1255) and for banishment (αἰτεῖς, 1518). He orders Tiresias to be taken away (κομιζέτω, 445); in the end Creon orders him too to be taken away (ἐσκομίζετε, 1429). He orders the shepherd to be led on (ἄξει τις, 1069) and in the end begs to be led off (ἀπάγετ', 1340, 1341, cf. 1521). These last two examples stem of course from his violent transformation from seeing to blind: on which see W. C. Helmbold, " The Paradox of the *Oedipus*," *AJP*, 72 (1951), 293 ff.

47. This oracular prediction was apparently (in Sophocles' version at any rate) unsolicited. The phrase used by Jocasta (χρησμὸς γὰρ ἦλθε Λαΐῳ ποτ', 711) recalls unsolicited oracles in Herodotus (e. g. Hdt. ii. 133: ἐλθεῖν οἱ μαντήιον ἐκ Βουτοῦς πόλιος [Mycerinus].

48. " Fate " serves as a stock translation equivalent for, among others, the following Greek words: μοῖρα, μόρος, μόρσιμον, εἱμαρμένη, πεπρωμένον, αἶσα, πότμος, ἀνάγκη, χρεών, δαίμων—all of which have different connotations.

49. Cf. Greene (1), chap. 8, and his article " Fate, Good, and Evil in Pre-Socratic Philosophy," *HSPh*, 47 (1936), 85-129.

50. Cf. Knox, " The Hippolytus of Euripides," *YClS*, *13* (1952), 1-31.

51. Hdt. vii. 12 ff.

52. Cf. also Pylades' famous three lines in the *Choephoroe* which spur on the halting Orestes, and the epiphany of Heracles in the *Philoctetes*.

53. Hdt. i. 53-4.

54. Ibid. i. 91.

55. Ibid. vii. 37.

56. Ibid. i. 209-10.

57. Ibid. vii. 142.

58. Ibid. vii. 57: ἐν οὐδενὶ λόγῳ ἐποιήσατο καίπερ εὐσύμβλητον ἐόν.

59. Ibid. i. 59: οὐκ ὢν ταῦτα παραινέσαντος Χίλωνος πείθεσθαι θέλειν τὸν Ἱπποκράτεα.

60. Ibid. viii. 77: ἐναργέως λέγοντας. . . .

61. Servius on *Aen.* iv. 696 distinguishes between *fata denuntiativa* and *fatum condicionale.* As an example of the former he gives: "'Pompeius ter triumphaturus est' (fata decernunt ut ubicumque terrarum fuerit, ter triumphet, nec potest aliter evenire)." His example of the second type is: "Pompeius si post Pharsalicum bellum Aegypti litus attigerit, ferro peribit." He also adduces the speech of Achilles (*Il.* xviii. 88 ff.) in which the hero describes the alternatives prophesied for him by Thetis. On these two examples Servius comments: "vides igitur condicionem fati sub duplici eventus expectatione pendere. . . ." and later uses the clever formula "gemina fati auctoritate." The application of these categories to the oracle in the *O. T.* is discussed by Pack.

62. Hdt. vii. 220. The text of the oracle is given there.

63. Ibid.: ταῦτά τε δὴ ἐπιλεγόμενον Λεωνίδην. . .

64. Ibid. i. 13.

65. Ibid. viii. 19.

66. Ibid. viii. 96: τὸ ἐλελήθεε πάντας τοὺς Ἕλληνας. . . .

67. Ibid. i. 120.

68. Jebb on OT 971.

69. Hdt. vi. 107.

70. Ibid. vi. 80.

71. Ibid. ii. 133: θέλων τὸ μαντήιον ψευδόμενον ἀπόδεξαι. . . .

72. Ibid. i. 91.

73. His angry and contemptuous rejection of the Erinyes, to take only one example, is clearly not the attitude of Zeus.

74. For a full examination of the subject see Greene (1), especially app. 6.

75. Augustinus, De libero arbitrio iii. 2: "Maximam partem hominum ista quaestione torqueri quomodo non sint contraria et repugnantia ut et Deus praesciens omnium futurorum sit et nos non necessitate sed voluntate peccemus." Cf. also the brilliant discussion of the whole problem in De civ. dei v. 8-10.

76. Ev. Matt. 26: 34-5, 69-75. Ev. Marc. 14: 29-31, 66-72. Ev. Luc. 22: 34, 54-62. Ev. Jo. 13: 36-8, 18: 25-7.

77. In Sophocles' version an unqualified, unconditional prophecy, not, as in Aeschylus and Euripides, a command which he might have obeyed but did not.

78. This is a deliberate omission, for in both Aeschylus (Th. 742 ff.) and Euripides (Ph. 13 ff.) Laius disobeys Apollo's command (thrice repeated in Aeschylus' account) not to have children. In this version of the legend Oedipus is paying for the sin of Laius. Sophocles allows no such easy way out. Cf. Helmbold, p. 294, n.3: "There is a complete suppression of the reason why Laius, and consequently his son, was doomed."

79. Cf. D. Chr. x. 29 (a comic denigration of the Oedipus story): [Οἰδίπους] . . . ἠγανάκτει καὶ ἐβόα μέγαλα, ὅτι τῶν αὐτῶν πατήρ ἐστι καὶ ἀδελφὸς καὶ τῆς αὐτῆς γυναικὸς ἀνὴρ καὶ υἱός· οἱ δὲ ἀλεκτρυόνες οὐκ ἀγανακτοῦσιν ἐπὶ τούτοις οὐδὲ οἱ κύνες οὐδὲ τῶν ὄνων οὐδείς. . . .

80. Hdt. viii. 77: Χρησμοῖσι δὲ οὐκ ἔχω ἀντιλέγειν ὡς οὐκ εἰσὶ

ἀληθέες, οὐ βουλόμενος ἐναργέως λέγοντας πειρᾶσθαι καταβάλλειν, ἔς τοιάδε πρήγματα ἐσβλέψας . . . ἐς τοιαῦτα μὲν καὶ οὕτω ἐναργέως λέγοντι Βάκιδι ἀντιλογίας χρησμῶν πέρι οὔτε αὐτὸς λέγειν τολμέω οὔτε παρ' ἄλλων ἐνδέκομαι.

81. Th. ii. 54.

82. Ibid. vii. 50: θειασμῷ τε καὶ τῷ τοιούτῳ. . . .

83. Ibid. vi. 89: ὁμολογουμένης ἀνοίας. . . .

84. Ibid. ii. 8: πολλὰ μὲν λόγια ἐλέγετο, πολλὰ δὲ χρησμολόγοι ᾖδον.

85. Ibid. v. 26: τοῖς ἀπὸ χρησμῶν τι ἰσχυρισαμένοις μόνον δὴ τοῦτο ἐχυρῶς ξυμβάν. Ironically enough, even this prophecy is true only on the basis of Thucydides' computation of the duration of the war, which was not generally accepted.

86. The *locus classicus* is *Hel.* 744-57. Cf. also *I. A.* 956-8.

87. 954-9: Φοῖβον ἀνθρώποις μόνον χρῆν θεσπιῳδεῖν, ὃς δέδοικεν οὐδένα. Cf. idem, *El.* 399-400.

88. Apollo's plan (described in detail by Hermes, 67-73) is to tell Xuthus a lie (that Ion is the son of Xuthus) and so establish Ion in Athens. Xuthus will think Ion his son, Creusa will know that he is actually hers by Apollo (γνωσθῇ Κρεούσῃ, 72), and Apollo's rape of Creusa will remain a secret (γάμοι τε Λοξίου κρυπτοὶ γένωνται, 72-3). This design, based on a false oracular statement and contemplating the permanent deception of Xuthus, is a miserable failure, for Creusa publishes the whole story of her rape by Apollo, nearly kills Ion, and is in turn almost killed by him. Ion challenges the story that Apollo is his father, and is only prevented from asking the god at his oracle for an explanation by the arrival of Athena, who comes because Apollo did not think it right (οὐκ ἠξίου, 1557) to appear in person—he might be blamed for the preceding events (1558).

89. H. Diels and W. Kranz, *Die Fragmente der Vorsokratiker* (10th ed. Berlin, 1960), Protagoras B1. The usual interpretation of this famous statement is that of Plato (*Tht.* 152a, *Cra.* 385e, etc.): the individual man is his own measure of reality. But the statement can also be taken to mean that mankind as a whole is the criterion, as Plato in fact implies by his parody of the phrase (*Tht.* 161c: "Why didn't he say that a pig is the measure of all things?"). This interpretation is offered by Sextus Empiricus (Diels-Kranz, Protagoras A14) in his summary; in addition to the "relative" interpretation, he offers also the interpretation that "all things which appear to men exist, and the things which do not appear to any man do not exist." Cf. also Kurt von Fritz, ΝΟΥΣ, ΝΟΕΙΝ, and Their Derivatives," Pt. II, *CP*, 41 (1946), 22; and Kathleen Freeman, *The Pre-Socratic Philosophers* (Oxford, 1949), p. 349. A full discussion of the implications of Protagoras' statement for the *Oedipus* is to be found in chap. 4 of this book.

90. Diels-Kranz, Antipho. A9.

91. E. *Hel.* 757; cf. idem, Fr. 973 (Nauck²).

92. Cf. especially *Eq.*, passim, and the oracle-monger in *Aves.*

93. See Herodotus' account of the use made by the Pisistratidae of the oracle-monger Onomacritus to influence Mardonius (vii. 6). *The Knights* of Aristophanes makes much capital out of the use of oracles as political ammunition. They are presented as one of Cleon's most important techniques for controlling Demos (cf. 61), and Cleon finally loses his power by being beaten in a contest between the oracles of Bakis and those of Glanis. The subjects of the oracles of Bakis are: "Athens, Pylos, you, me, everything" (1005-6), and those of Glanis: "Athens, lentil soup, the Spartans; fresh mackerel, short-weight barley-sellers in the market place, you, and me and everything" (1007-10).

94. Th. viii. 1: ὠργίζοντο δὲ καὶ τοῖς χρησμολόγοις τε καὶ μάντεσι

καὶ ὁπόσοι τι τότε αὐτοὺς θειάσαντες ἐπήλπισαν ὡς λήψονται Σικελίαν.

95. Martin, P. Nilsson, *Greek Popular Religion* (N. Y., Columbia Univ. Press, 1940), p. 136. Cf. idem, *Geschichte der Griechischen Religion*, I (Munich, C. H. Beck, 1955), 768: "Es ist sehr wahrscheinlich dass in betreff der Entstehung der Religionsprozesse der springende Punkt in der Rivalität zwischen den Wahrsagen und der Naturphilosophie zu suchen ist."

96. Jebb's "Religion, both faith and observance" is not strong enough. True, this is the meaning of the parallel which he quotes from *O. C.* 1537, but in *Ph.* 452 (τὰ θεῖ᾽ ἐπαινῶν τοὺς θεοὺς εὕρω κακούς) it means something like "divine action, dispensation," and in Herodotus τὸ θεῖον generally stands for divinity itself (cf. i. 32, iii. 108). Θεῖος is to θεός as ἀνθρώπινος is to ἄνθρωπος, and ἕρρει τὰ ἀνθρώπινα would mean something like "man's power has vanished" or "humanity no longer exists." In any case this final phrase must be climactic. The statement progresses from the discounting of prophecy to the discounting of the particular god who made it (Apollo is no longer honored), and if the third statement be understood to mean "faith and observance of the gods is perishing" the whole structure collapses into anticlimax, for this merely repeats the second statement in a more general form. The real process is that which Jocasta and Oedipus actually go through: the discounting of prophecy makes necessary disregard for Apollo, and this leads to disregard for his father Zeus and all the gods and to rejection of divine order as a whole. Such a statement of disbelief in divine order is explicitly made by Jocasta in the next scene, and is implied in Oedipus' proclamation that he is "the son of Chance."

97. Cf. Phrynichus, Fr. 9 (Kock): ἀνὴρ χορεύει καὶ τὰ τοῦ θεοῦ καλά. This is discussed by Victor Ehrenberg in *The People of Aristophanes* (2d ed. Oxford, 1951), p. 23.

98. Whitman is right when he takes the ode to be "a prayer

for the fulfilment of the oracle given to Laius rather than for the mere discovery of the murderer" (p. 269, n. 42). The oracle given to Laius (or about Laius) is in fact mentioned specifically in the final statement of the ode (906). But Whitman's reading of the ode as a whole is an ingenious attempt to minimize its importance—as he must do, for this ode is a substantial thorn in the flesh of his basic thesis. The fact that the chorus previously refused to believe Tiresias (Whitman, p. 134) is no grounds for saying that their attitude in this ode has a "disquieting current of real unbelief"; as Whitman agrees, they are singing about a different subject, the oracle given to Laius, not the identity of his murderer, and they are dealing now with a prophecy made not by a man but by a god.

The admitted fifth-century prejudice against oracle-mongers (on which Whitman relies greatly) has nothing to do with this case, for although Jocasta, with her ὑπηρετῶν ἄπο (712), has tried to shift the question from the area of divine to that of human prophecy, nobody believes her, and she does not even believe it herself, for at the end of the scene (853) she attributes the prophecy squarely to Apollo. What is involved now is the categorical, unambiguous prophecy of a god, and whereas Tiresias' prophecies might be doubted without irreverence, Apollo's may not. "They threaten Zeus and Apollo with neglect and contempt unless the oracle does come true," says Whitman. Rather, they pray to Zeus to fulfil the oracle (as Whitman says himself in the note): that is, they pray for something which is, as far as they can see, impossible—that Laius' son, who is dead, should kill his father, who is also dead. If this is not "faith with fervor" what would be? It sounds like the faith which moves mountains. In the circumstances, the fact that the chorus takes the oracle with any seriousness at all is a signal proof of faith. And in any case, they do profess "faith with fervor" in the opening strophe where they sing of the sublimity of the divine laws, pure in conception, superhuman, unforgetting: "In these the god is great, and does not grow old." This is a faith that is directly menaced by the attack on prophecy, for prophecy is a pronouncement stemming from these laws, and if prophecy is false the laws and the order they create do not exist.

Whitman's rather satirical paraphrase of the ode (p. 134) misses its point: " I believe this prophecy is probably true, but if I see no evidence, so much for prophecies and the gods in general." A more accurate paraphrase would run: "The god is great in his everlasting laws which are beyond human understanding. Oedipus and Jocasta are defying those laws through their defiance of the prophecy which stems from them. They seem to be right—the prophecy has not been fulfilled and cannot be fulfilled. If they are right, worship of the gods will cease, the gods are dishonored, they disappear. The oracle *must* be fulfilled, in a spectacular way, so that all men will be impressed. Zeus, make it come true."

This is hardly "the somewhat confused morality of the bourgeoisie who can feel that the times want stabilizing" (Whitman, p. 135). The only character who is trying to "stabilize the times" in this play is Jocasta, who would be content to live with all the questions unanswered, and who can reject Apollo's prophecy and then pray to him for help.

All this is not to say, with Pohlenz, that the ode is "forcibly dragged in as a protest against *Freigeisterei*" (Whitman is, as often, devastatingly right in his dismissal of this thesis), nor that it is "a pronouncement *ex cathedra* from the poet himself" or a "credo from the poet" (Whitman, pp. 133, 135). Like everything else in the play the ode is magnificently functional: it puts the question raised by the situation (the validity of divine prophecy), in its larger framework, the validity of the traditional religious view as a whole.

99. See Chapter 4 for a full discussion. For some perceptive comments cf. Cleanth Brooks and R. B. Heilman, *Understanding Drama* (N. Y., 1948), pp. 574-7.

100. Creon later, without consulting the oracle, keeps Oedipus

in Thebes, in spite of his promise to exile him and in spite of the original oracular response and the curse.

101. The text of this passage is corrupt, but the Λοξίου of 1102 is sound, and the analogy of Πανὸς in 1100 leaves no doubt about the meaning.

NOTES FOR CHAPTER TWO: ATHENS

1. τύραννος and τυραννίς occur 14 times in the play: three times applied by Oedipus to his own position (380, 535, 541), five times used of him or his power by others with respect or at least no hint of criticism (Creon, 514, 588, 592, the Corinthian, 925, the chorus, 1095). In the *Antigone*, where Creon is surely a more "tyrannical" figure than Oedipus in this play, the words occur only four times: three times used of Creon by his critics (Antigone, 506, Ismene, 60, Tiresias, 1056), and once in a general passage on the instability of human fortune (1169). Creon never uses either word in connection with himself.

2. Aristotle calls it simply "The Oedipus"; cf. *Poetics* 1452[a]. 1454[b], etc.

3. Euripides goes so far as to make a chorus of Athenian citizens refer to Demophon, son of Theseus, an Attic king and a pattern of Athenian bravery and piety, as *tyrannos* (*Heracl.* 111). Cf. also idem, *El.* 877.

4. Cf. Pl. R. ii. 361b: διὰ παρασκευὴν φίλων καὶ οὐσίας. Hdt. i. 64: ἐρρίζωσε τὴν τυραννίδα ἐπικούροισί τε πολλοῖσι καὶ χρημάτων συνόδοισι.

5. Cf.219-20 and 222.

6. i. 13: τυραννίδες ἐν ταῖς πόλεσι καθίσταντο τῶν προσόδων

μειζόνων γιγνομένων (πρότερον δὲ ἦσαν ἐπὶ ῥητοῖς γέρασι πατρικαὶ βασιλεῖαι). For this same distinction cf. Arist. *Pol.* 1285ᵃ. 3.

7. Cf. Pl. *Alc.* i. 120a: ἡγεμὼν . . . τῆσδε τῆς πόλεως.

8. He had left Corinth to settle his doubts once for all by consulting the Delphic Oracle, but was sent away unanswered; ἄτιμον is his word (789), which in the context simply means "with my request unfulfilled" (cf. ἀτιμάζεις, 340, and Pl. *Euthphr.* 15d), but also implies "without honor," i. e. the doubt about his birth still unresolved.

9. Cf. the situation in the *Odyssey*, where the hand of Penelope is evidently regarded as a basis for the assumption of royal power.

10. ἐξ οὗ καὶ βασιλεὺς καλῇ ἐμὸς καὶ τὰ μέγιστ' ἐτιμάθης . . . καλῇ is ambiguous, for in such a construction it refers to both past and present (cf. W. W. Goodwin, *Syntax of the Moods and Tenses of the Greek Verb*, Boston, 1890, sec. 26), but the present reference is emphasized by the change in tense from this verb to the next (ἐτιμάθης) where there is no ambiguity at all (naturally, for this second statement can refer only to the past). Normal construction, however, would demand that this verb too be in the present tense. The effect is to stress the reference to the present in καλῇ, which might not have been emphatic without the change of tense from the first verb to the second.

11. Cf. 834.

12. Archilochus, Fr. 22 (Diehl), and cf. the second hypothesis of the O. T. The statement that the word *tyrannos* first occurs in Archilochus is there attributed to Hippias the sophist, who either did not know the Homeric hymn to Ares (cf. 5) or thought that it was composed after the time of Archilochus.

13. Ar. *Th.* 329: τελέως δ' ἐκκλησιάσαιμεν, Ἀθηναίων εὐγενεῖς γυναῖκες.

14. See Xenophon's account of the establishment of a *tyrannis* by Euphron at Sicyon: καὶ τῶν συναρχόντων δὲ τοὺς μὲν δόλῳ ἀπέκτεινεν, τοὺς δὲ ἐξέβαλεν . . . ὥστε πάντα ὑφ' ἑαυτῷ ἐποιήσατο καὶ σαφῶς τύραννος ἦν (*H. G.* vii. 1. 44-6). Cf. Hdt. v. 92ε; Arist. *Pol.* 1311ᵃ. 7; E. *Supp.* 444-55.

15. For these characteristic actions cf. Hdt. iii. 80 and E. *Supp.* 447-9.

16. Cf. Hdt. iii. 39 (Polycrates), v. 92ε (Cypselus); E. Fr. 605 (Nauck²).

17. Cf. Hdt. iii. 80; *Ion* 627-8.

18. Cf. E. *Ion* 621-8, X. *Hier.* ii. 8-10.

19. Cf. Th. i. 130; X. *Hier.* viii. 10; Pl. *R.* viii 567d; Arist. *Pol.* 1285ᵃ, 1311ᵃ.

20. In the *Agamemnon* of Aeschylus Aegisthus has a bodyguard of spearmen (λοχῖται, 1650) whom he calls in to overawe the chorus; his assumption of power is described as *tyrannis* in 1355, 1365, and 1633. In the *Choephoroe* he is tricked into coming to the palace without his bodyguard (λοχίταις, 768; δορυφόρους ὀπάονας, 769). In the Euripidean *Electra* Aegisthus has his guard with him when Orestes and Pylades kill him; they have to be won over by the murderers (λόγχας δὲ θέντες δεσπότου φρουρήματα / δμῶες, 798-9. They are numerous— πολλοί, 845.) In the Sophoclean *Electra* the bodyguard of Aegisthus is away with him in the country; Orestes is urged to kill Clytemnestra before Aegisthus and his guards return. (1370-71: σοφώτεροις ἄλλοισι τούτων πλείοσιν μαχούμενοι. "ἄλλοισι are the bodyguards," says Jebb, ad loc.) Aegisthus seems in fact to be the type of the tragic *tyrannos*, against whom killing was "no murder"; it is significant in this respect that Electra's speech to Chrysothemis, in which she urges the murder of Aegisthus (S. *El.* 975-85), recalls the formulas of the famous *scolion* in praise of Harmodius and Aristogeiton.

21. One of them is ordered to twist the shepherd's arms behind his back (1154).

22. Cf. 91-3.

23. Cf. 144: ἄλλος δὲ Κάδμου λαὸν ὧδ' ἀθροιζέτω, and see Earle's note (M. L. Earle, *The Oedipus Tyrannus*, N. Y., American Book Co., 1901).

24. Th. ii. 63. So striking a phrase would hardly have been attributed to Pericles unless he had actually said something of this kind.

25. Plu. Per. xii: καὶ δοκεῖ δεινὴν ὕβριν ἡ Ἑλλὰς ὑβρίζεσθαι καὶ τυραννεῖσθαι περιφανῶς. . . . In this passage Plutarch is summarizing the arguments of the fifth-century opposition to the Periclean policies. For the Athenian Demos as *tyrannos* cf. Ar. *Eq.* 1111 ff.: ὦ Δῆμε καλήν γ' ἔχεις / ἀρχήν, ὅτε πάντες ἄνθρωποι δεδίασί σ' ὥσπερ ἄνδρα τύραννον.

26. Th. vi. 85: ἀνδρὶ δὲ τυράννῳ ἢ πόλει ἀρχὴν ἐχούσῃ. . . .

27. Ibid. i. 122: τύραννον δὲ ἐῶμεν ἐγκαθεστάναι πόλιν, ibid. 124: τὴν καθεστηκυῖαν ἐν τῇ Ἑλλάδι πόλιν τύραννον. . . . Cf. ibid. iii. 10 (the Mitylenean envoys on Athenian policy): ἐπὶ καταδουλώσει τῶν Ἑλλήνων . . . τὴν δὲ τῶν ξυμμάχων δούλωσιν. . . .

28. For example, the sophistic tone of Creon's speech in his own defense; the contemporary reference of such terms as μέτοικος (452) (used by Tiresias, of all people) and προστάτης (411); the use of the word δασμός (36) to describe the "tribute" exacted by the Sphinx (on which cf. Earle, ad loc.); the plague, the topical references in the *parodos* (on which see Knox [1]). On the whole subject see now V. Ehrenberg, *Sophocles and Pericles* (Oxford, 1954), chap. 1, "Tragedy and History."

29. For a recent example cf. P. Masqueray's note (*Sophocle*, Paris, Budé, 1929) on 411. On "anachronism" cf. Ehrenberg (2), pp. 15-16.

30. For a brilliant analysis of the political framework of the play see George Thomson's *Aeschylus, Prometheus Bound,* Cambridge, 1932.

31. The fifth century is, after all, the period of the birth of historical writing and the historical consciousness.

32. Lycus, 157-64; Amphitryon, 188-203. For a most remarkable example of "anachronism" (one that if attributed to carelessness convicts the poet as a botcher and if to "absence of historical sense" as a moron) see E. *Supp.* 404-9. Theseus, king of Athens, informs a Theban herald that Athens is not ruled by one man but is a free city. "The people rules, by yearly succession of offices in turn. . . ." Theseus is presumably *archon basileus.*

33. *Julius Caesar* I. i; *Macbeth* II. iii.

34. *Amphitruo* 149, 164; *a portu*; 460: *ibo ad portum.*

35. It seems to have caused some misgiving in ancient times, for the scholium takes pains to explain that it does not mean what it says. The comment is obscure, but seems to suggest that ναῦς in this line is used metaphorically for "city." This is of course impossible, in view of the combination of ναῦς and τεῖχος.

36. The bases of the power of Athens after the Persian invasion were the fleet and the walls (both of them the creation of the policies of Themistocles; cf. Pl. *Grg.* 455e), and the conditions of the Athenian surrender in 404 B.C. were the destruction of the walls and the confiscation of the ships (And. iii. 11: τὰ τείχη καθαιρεῖν καὶ τὰς ναῦς παραδιδόναι. Cf. ibid. 37, 39). Cf. also Lys. xii. 68, xiii. 14, xxviii. 11; Ar. Fr. 220; Demetrius, Fr. 2 (Kock, 1, 796); Lycurg., *In Leocratem* 139. For Themistocles on walls and ships cf. Th. i. 93. Destruction of walls and surrender of ships were the regular conditions of capitulation for rebellious Athenian allies; cf. Th. i. 101 (Thasos), 117 (Samos), iii. 50 (Mitylene; cf. iii. 2 and 3).

For this same combination in Sophocles cf. *Antigone* 954: οὐ πύργος οὐχ ἁλίκτυποι κελαιναὶ νᾶες.

37. For a full discussion of this subject see Knox (1).

38. Cf. Hdt. v. 70.

39. Th. ii. 65: ὑπὸ τοῦ πρώτου ἀνδρὸς ἀρχή, i. 139: ἀνήρ . . . πρῶτος . . . (cf. *O. T.* 33: ἀνδρῶν δὲ πρῶτον). Add Plu. *Per.* 3: οἴκου δὲ καὶ γένους τοῦ πρώτου κατ' ἀμφοτέρους, 16: πρωτεύων. The title seems, however, not to have been confined to Pericles: cf. Cratinus, Fr. 1. 3-4: πάντ' ἀρίστῳ τῶν Πανελλήνων πρώτῳ Κίμωνι. . . .

40. Plu. *Per.* 3 (Kock, Fr. 240). With μέγιστον cf. *O. T.* 776.

41. Plu. *Per.* 39: ἐπίφθονος ἰσχύς . . . μοναρχία λεγομένη καὶ τυραννίς. Cf. *O. T.* 380 ff.: ὦ πλοῦτε καὶ τυραννί . . . ὅσος παρ' ὑμῖν ὁ φθόνος φυλάσσεται. . . .

42. Plu. *Per.* 16. His teacher Damon was ostracized as "friendly to tyranny," φιλοτύραννος (ibid. 4).

43. Earle (p. 53), sums up the case well: "Periclean traits do appear—one might almost say inevitably—in Sophocles' Oedipus."

44. Th. i. 80: πλούτῳ τε ἰδίῳ καὶ δημοσίῳ . . . (Archidamus); ii. 64: πόλιν τε τοῖς πᾶσιν εὐπορωτάτην . . . ᾠκήσαμεν (Pericles). For Athenian wealth cf. also Th. ii. 13 (Pericles' inventory of Athenian reserves) and vi. 31 (Thucydides' comment on the cost of the expedition to Sicily). Cf. also Eupolis, Fr. 307: πόλιν . . . ἀφθονεστάτην . . . χρήμασιν. . . .

45. Siegecraft. Th. i. 102, 142. For the Peloponnesians as "farmers" cf. Th. i. 141 (Pericles). For Athenian skill and inventiveness cf. Isoc. 4. 40 (a tribute to Athens' role as the inventor and transmitter of technical progress. : καὶ μὲν δὴ καὶ τῶν τεχνῶν τάς τε πρὸς τἀναγκαῖα τοῦ βίου χρησίμας καὶ τὰς πρὸς ἡδονὴν μεμηχανημένας, τὰς μὲν εὑροῦσα, τὰς δὲ δοκιμάσασα χρῆσθαι

τοῖς λοιποῖς παρέδωκεν, and Plu. *De glor. Ath.* 345F: μητὴρ καὶ τροφὸς . . . τεχνῶν. For Athenian "trades" in the fifth century cf. [X.] *Ath.* 12: δεῖται ἡ πόλις μετοίκων διά τε τὸ πλῆθος τῶν τεχνῶν. . . .

46. Th. i. 71: πολλῆς καὶ τῆς ἐπιτεχνήσεως δεῖ. . . .

47. Ibid. ii. 87: ἄνευ δὲ εὐψυχίας οὐδεμία τέχνη πρὸς τοὺς κινδύνους ἰσχύει . . . τέχνη δὲ ἄνευ ἀλκῆς οὐδὲν ὠφελεῖ.

48. Ibid., i. 121: ἐπιστήμη.

49. Ibid. i. 142: τὸ δὲ ναυτικὸν τέχνης ἐστίν, ὥσπερ καὶ ἄλλο τι . . . .

50. Ibid. i. 75: ἆρ᾽ ἀξιοί ἐσμεν . . . καὶ προθυμίας ἕνεκα τῆς τότε καὶ γνώμης ξυνέσεως ἀρχῆς γε ἧς ἔχομεν τοῖς Ἕλλησι μὴ οὕτως ἄγαν ἐπιφθόνως διακεῖσθαι; The parallels to the language of the Sophoclean play are striking: τῆς πάρος προθυμίας (48), γνώμῃ κυρήσας (398), τῆσδέ γ᾽ ἀρχῆς οὕνεχ᾽ (383), ὅσος . . . φθόνος (382). For the same sentiment cf. Lys. ii. 48.

51. Th. ii. 64: εἰ δέ τις μὴ κέκτηται, φθονήσει. . . .

52. Th. ii. 62: μετὰ πόνων καὶ οὐ παρ᾽ ἄλλων δεξάμενοι.

53. Ibid. i. 75: ἐλάβομεν οὐ βιασάμενοι . . . αὐτῶν δεηθέντων ἡγεμόνας καταστῆναι 76 ἀρχὴν διδομένην ἐδεξάμεθα. Cf. *O. T.* 383 ff.: ἀρχῆς . . . ἣν ἐμοὶ πόλις δωρητὸν οὐκ αἰτητὸν εἰσεχείρισεν. Cf. also Th. vi. 76 (Hermocrates on the Athenians): ἡγέμονες γὰρ γενόμενοι ἑκόντων τῶν τε Ἰώνων. Isoc. 4. 72: δόντων μὲν τῶν ἄλλων Ἑλλήνων. Din. i. 37.

Like Oedipus, Athens was πρῶτος (cf. *O. T.* 33 and Th. iv. 95: ἀξίως . . . τῆς τε πόλεως ἣν ἕκαστος πατρίδα ἔχων πρώτην ἐν τοῖς Ἕλλησιν ἀγάλλεται and Hdt. ix. 27) and μέγας (cf. Hdt. v. 66: Ἀθῆναι ἐοῦσαι καὶ πρὶν μεγάλαι . . . ἐγίνοντο μέζονες. . . . Th. ii. 61: πόλιν μεγάλην οἰκοῦντας. Ar. *Eq.* 178, 180, 838, *Av.* 37; and Th. i. 23 and ii. 64 where the word occurs over and over again like a refrain). Like Oedipus (8, 1207) Athens was κλειναί cf. S. *Aj.* 861, Fr. 323; Eub. 10 (Kock ii); Pind, Fr. 64 (Bowra); E. *Heracl.* 38).

54. Eulogistic portraits of the Athenian character are common too (Sophocles' Theseus in the *O. C.*, Euripides' Demophon and Theseus).

55. Th. ii. 64: ταῦτα ὁ μὲν ἀπράγμων μέμψαιτ' ἂν, ὁ δὲ δρᾶν τι καὶ αὐτὸς βουλόμενος ζηλώσει. For δρᾶν in the *O. T.* cf. Chap. 1, n. 24.

56. Th. ii. 64: οἵτινες πρὸς τὰς ξυμφορὰς γνώμῃ μὲν ἥκιστα λυποῦνται, ἔργῳ δὲ μάλιστα ἀντέχουσιν, οὗτοι καὶ πόλεων καὶ ἰδιωτῶν κράτιστοί εἰσιν. Cf. *O. T.* 618 ff. and also Th. vi. 87 (Athenian πολυπραγμοσύνη).

57. Th. i. 70: μήτε ἑορτὴν ἄλλο τι ἡγεῖσθαι ἢ τὸ τὰ δέοντα πρᾶξαι. This sounds like a malicious hit at the Spartan practice of avoiding critical action by celebrating a convenient festival (cf. Hdt. vi. 106, Marathon; vii. 206, Thermopylae; ix. 7, the second Persian attack on Athens).

58. Th. i. 70: πεφυκέναι ἐπὶ τῷ μήτε αὐτοὺς ἔχειν ἡσυχίαν μήτε τοὺς ἄλλους ἀνθρώπους ἐᾶν. For ἡσυχία cf. *O. T.* 620. For Athenian vigor in general see (in addition to Th. i. 70) Hdt. ix. 60 (Pausanias on the Athenians); Th. i. 74 (the Athenian envoys at Sparta), vi. 18 (Alcibiades' appeal to the tradition of Athenian activity).

59. Th. vii. 61: ὅσοι τε Ἀθηναίων πάρεστε, πολλῶν ἤδη πολέμων ἔμπειροι. . . .

60. Ibid. ii. 89.

61. Hdt. ix. 46: ὑμεῖς ἐπίστασθε . . . ἡμεῖς δὲ ἄπειροι.

62. Th. i. 71: τὰ τῶν Ἀθηναίων ἀπὸ τῆς πολυπειρίας ἐπὶ πλέον ὑμῶν κεκαίνωται. Cf. also Th. i. 142 (Pericles on Athenian experience on land and sea), i. 80: θαλάσσης ἐμπειρότατοι (Archidamus on the Athenians), vi. 36: δεινοὶ καὶ πολλῶν

ἔμπειροι (Athenagoras on the Athenians), iv. 10; Isoc. 4. 21:
ἐμπειροτάτους.

63. They support their claim by an appeal to ancient history
(the wars against Eurystheus, the Amazons, the Trojans)
and to the more recent victory at Marathon. Hdt. ix. 27:
ἡμῖν πατρώιόν ἐστι ἐοῦσι χρηστοῖσι ἀεὶ πρώτοισι εἶναι.

64. Th. i. 90; φοβουμένων . . . τὴν ἐς τὸν Μηδικὸν πόλεμον τόλ-
μαν. . . .

65. Th. i. 102: δείσαντες τῶν Ἀθηναίων τὸ τολμηρόν. . . .

66. Ibid. ii. 88.

67. Th. ii. 41: ἐσβατὸν τῇ ἡμετέρᾳ τόλμῃ (Pericles); vii. 28: τὸν
παράλογον . . . τῆς δυνάμεως καὶ τόλμης.

68. Ibid. i. 144: τόλμῃ μείζονι ἢ δυνάμει (Pericles); i. 70: παρὰ
δύναμιν τολμηταί . . . (Corinthians).

69. Ibid. i. 74: προθυμίαν δὲ καὶ πολὺ τολμηροτάτην . . . ἀπό τε
τῆς οὐκ οὔσης ἔτι ὁρμώμενοι καὶ ὑπὲρ τῆς ἐν βραχείᾳ ἐλπίδι οὔσης
κινδυνεύοντες. Cf. [Lys.] Epitaph. 58: ἐπέδειξαν δὲ καὶ ἐν ταῖς
δυστυχίαις τὴν ἑαυτῶν ἀρετήν. For other references to Athenian
courage see Th. i. 70: ἄοκνοι, ii. 39, 89, vi. 31, 33.

70. Th. i. 70: ἐπινοῆσαι ὀξεῖς καὶ ἐπιτελέσαι ἔργῳ ἃ ἂν γνῶσιν . . .
μόνοι γὰρ ἔχουσί τε ὁμοίως καὶ ἐλπίζουσιν ἃ ἂν ἐπινοήσωσι διὰ τὸ
ταχεῖαν τὴν ἐπιχείρησιν ποιεῖσθαι ὧν ἂν γνῶσιν.

71. Ibid. i. 57: προκαταλαμβάνειν, iii. 3. προκαταλαβεῖν. Cf. the
advice of the Corcyreans (Th. i. 33): ἡμέτερον δέ γ᾽ αὖ ἔργον
προτερῆσαι . . . καὶ προεπιβουλεύειν αὐτοῖς μᾶλλον ἢ ἀντεπιβου-
λεύειν with O. T. 618-21.

72. For the walls of Athens cf. Th. i. 93: ἐν ὀλίγῳ χρόνῳ, for
Syracuse vi. 98: ἔκπληξιν . . . παρέσχεν τῷ τάχει τῆς οἰκοδομίας.
Cf. also iv. 8 (the fortification of Pylos): οἰκοδόμημα διὰ ταχέων
εἰργασμένον, and vii. 42 (Demosthenes at Syracuse).

73. [Lys.] Epitaph. 26: οὕτω δὲ διὰ ταχέων. . . . For Athenian

speed cf. also Isoc. 4. 87; Plu. *Per.* xiii (the Periclean building program): μάλιστα θαυμάσιον ἦν τὸ τάχος.

74. Hdt. v. 89: οὐκ ἀνέσχοντο ἀκούσαντες ὅκως χρεὸν εἴη ἐπισχεῖν. . . . For the impatience of Oedipus cf. Chap. 1, p. 17. When Themistocles, in Thucydides' account of the building of the walls of Athens, excuses himself for not appearing before the Spartan assembly on the ground that his colleagues have not yet arrived, he uses a phrase reminiscent of the remark of Oedipus waiting for Tiresias: θαυμάζειν ὡς οὔπω πάρεισιν (Th. i. 90); cf. *O. T.* 289: πάλαι δὲ μὴ παρὼν θαυμάζεται.

75. Th. ii. 40: τολμᾶν τε οἱ αὐτοὶ μάλιστα καὶ περὶ ὧν ἐπιχειρήσομεν ἐκλογίζεσθαι.

76. Hdt. i. 60: τοῖσι πρώτοισι λεγομένοισι εἶναι Ἑλλήνων σοφίην.

77. Th. i. 75: προθυμίας ἕνεκα τῆς τότε καὶ γνώμης ξυνέσεως. . . .

78. Ibid. i. 144: γνώμῃ τε πλέονι ἢ τύχῃ. Cf. *O. T.* 398.

79. Ibid. ii. 40: φιλοσοφοῦμεν ἄνευ μαλακίας.

80. Ibid. ii. 62: καταφρόνησις δὲ ὃς ἂν καὶ γνώμῃ πιστεύῃ τῶν ἐναντίων προύχειν. . . .

81. Ibid. ii. 62: δύο μερῶν τῶν ἐς χρῆσιν φανερῶν. . . . For these two "elements" cf. S. *Ant.* 335-8.

82. Th. ii. 42: σφίσιν αὐτοῖς ἀξιοῦντες πεποιθέναι. Contrast what Thucydides says about the Mityleneans (iii. 5): οὔτε ἐπίστευσαν σφίσιν αὐτοῖς.

83. Ibid. i. 70 ὀλίγα πρὸς τὰ μέλλοντα τυχεῖν πράξαντες.

84. Ibid., iv. 10: ἀπερισκέπτως εὔελπις.

85. Ibid. vii. 77: ἐλπίδα χρὴ ἔχειν . . . ἐλπὶς . . . θρασεῖα. Cf. *O. T.* 835: Cho. . . . ἔχ' ἐλπίδα. Oed. καὶ μὴν τοσοῦτον γ' ἐστί μοι τῆς ἐλπίδος. . . .

86. Th. i. 70: ἐν τοῖς δεινοῖς εὐέλπιδες. Cf. Εὐελπίδης, the Athen-

ian in the *Birds* of Aristophanes. Ehrenberg (1), p. 57, n. 2, quotes this parallel from Croiset, and adds Th. vi. 24 (εὐέλπιδες ὄντες σωθήσεσθαι) and iv. 10.

87. Th. ii. 39: ῥαθυμίᾳ μᾶλλον ἢ πόνων μελέτῃ . . . τρόπων ἀνδρείας.

88. Ibid. i. 138: οἰκείᾳ γὰρ ξυνέσει καὶ οὔτε προμαθὼν ἐς αὐτὴν οὐδὲν οὔτ᾽ ἐπιμαθών . . . ὧν δ᾽ ἄπειρος εἴη, κρῖναι ἱκανῶς. Cf. O. T. 37-8: οὐδὲν ἐξειδὼς πλέον οὐδ᾽ ἐκδιδαχθείς, 398: γνώμῃ κυρήσας οὐδ᾽ ἀπ᾽ οἰωνῶν μαθών.

89. Th. ii. 41: τὸν αὐτὸν ἄνδρα παρ᾽ ἡμῶν ἐπὶ πλεῖστ᾽ ἂν εἴδη καὶ μετὰ χαρίτων μάλιστ᾽ ἂν εὐτραπέλως τὸ σῶμα αὔταρκες παρέχεσθαι. Cf. O. T. 11-12: ὡς θέλοντος ἂν ἐμοῦ προσαρκεῖν πᾶν, 145: ὡς πᾶν ἐμοῦ δράσοντος. . . .

90. Th. i. 138. For another example of Athenian adaptability see iv. 9.

91. Ibid. ii. 60: φιλόπολις. Cf. O. T. 510: ἁδύπολις.

92. Th. ii. 43: ἐραστὰς γιγνομένους αὐτῆς. Cf. O. T. 601: ἐραστὴς τῆσδε τῆς γνώμης (Creon). This is the only occurrence of the word in Sophocles.

93. Th. i. 70: τοῖς μὲν σώμασιν ἀλλοτριωτάτοις ὑπὲρ τῆς πόλεως. . . .

94. Cf. Whitman, p. 268, n. 31: "I think the lively Athenians would . . . approve of his shrewdness in smelling a plot."

95. Th. i. 107: δήμου καταλύσεως ὑποψίᾳ.

96. Ibid. vi. 53: πάντα ὑπόπτως ἀποδεχόμενοι . . . πάντα ὑπόπτως ἐλάμβανεν (sc. ὁ δῆμος); 60: ὁ δῆμος . . . χαλεπὸς ἦν τότε καὶ ὑπόπτης.

97. Ibid. ii. 13: μηδεμίαν οἱ ὑποψίαν κατὰ ταῦτα γίγνεσθαι. . . .

98. Ibid. iii. 43: ὑποπτεύηται κέρδους μὲν ἕνεκα τὰ βέλτιστα δὲ ὅμως λέγειν.

99. Hdt. v. 70: τούς ἐναγέας ἐπιλέγων. . . .

100. Ibid., v. 72: ἀπικόμενος δὲ ἀγηλατέει ἑπτακόσια ἐπίστια ᾿Αθηναίων. Cf. O. T. 402: ἀγηλατήσειν. This word occurs only here in Sophocles.

101. Th. i. 126: τὸ ἄγος ἐλαύνειν. Cf. 127.

102. Ar. V. 343-45: οὐ γὰρ ἄν ποθ᾽ οὗτος ἀνήρ τοῦτ᾽ ἐτόλμησεν λέγειν εἰ μὴ ξυνωμότης τις ἦν. Cf. O. T. 124-5: πῶς οὖν ὁ λῃστής, εἴ τι μὴ ξὺν ἀργύρῳ ἐπράσσετ᾽ ἐνθένδ᾽ ἐς τόδ᾽ ἄν τόλμης ἔβη;

103. This action is cited approvingly by Lycurg. *In Leocr.* 122.

104. Th. ii. 60: προσδεχομένῳ μοι τὰ τῆς ὀργῆς ὑμῶν, 59: ἐβούλετο . . . ἀπαγαγὼν τὸ ὀργιζόμενον τῆς γνώμης. . . .

105. Ar. *Pax.* 606-7: Περικλέης φοβηθεὶς . . . τὰς φύσεις ὑμῶν δεδοικὼς καὶ τὸν αὐτοδὰξ τρόπον.

106. Th. vi. 60: αὐτῶν . . . ὀργιζομένων, viii. 1: ὠργίζοντο δὲ καὶ τοῖς χρησμολόγοις.

107. Ar. *Eq.* 41-2: γερόντιον . . . ἄγροικος ὀργὴν . . . δύσκολον.

108. Ibid., 537: Κράτης ὀργὰς ὑμῶν ἠνέσχετο. . . .

109. Ar. V. 243: ἡμερῶν ὀργὴν τριῶν πονηράν. . . .

110. Antipho. 5. 71: μὴ μετ᾽ ὀργῆς καὶ διαβολῆς. . . .

111. Ibid. 69: ὀργῇ μᾶλλον ἢ γνώμῃ. Cf. O. T. 524: ὀργῇ βιασθὲν μᾶλλον ἢ γνώμῃ φρενῶν.

112. Cf. Th. iii. 36: μετάνοιά τις εὐθὺς ἦν αὐτοῖς . . . .

113. Cf. X. H. G. i. 7. 35: μετέμελε τοῖς ᾿Αθηναίοις. . . .

114. A. Eu. 682: πρώτας δίκας κρίνοντες. . . .

115. See D. L. v. 17 for Aristotle's remark: τοὺς ᾿Αθηναίους . . . εὑρηκέναι πυροὺς καὶ νόμους. Cf. Ael. V. H. iii. 38: δίκας τε δοῦναι καὶ λαβεῖν ηὗρον ᾿Αθηναῖοι πρῶτοι. Isoc. 4. 39 (quoted below,

n. 116); Cic. *Pro Flacco* 62: Athenienses . . . unde . . . iura, leges ortae; Lucr. vi. 3; Stat. *Theb.* xii. 501.

116. Cf. Isoc. 4. 39: αὐτὴν παράδειγμα ποιήσασα· πρώτη γὰρ καὶ νόμους ἔθετο.

117. Ar. *Nu.* 208: δικαστὰς οὐχ ὁρῶ καθημένους. Cf. idem, *Pax.* 505, *Av.* 40-41.

118. [X.] *Ath.* iii. 2: δίκας καὶ γραφὰς καὶ εὐθύνας ἐπιδικάζειν ὅσας οὐδ᾽ οἱ σύμπαντες ἄνθρωποι ἐπιδικάζουσι. Cf. X. *Mem.* iii. 5. 16: πλείστας δίκας ἀλλήλοις δικάζονται.

119. Th. i. 77: φιλοδικεῖν δοκοῦμεν. . . .

120. 110: ἐν τῆδ᾽ ἔφασκε γῆ. . . .

121. 102: ποίου γὰρ ἀνδρὸς τήνδε μηνύει τύχην;

122. And so could not bring an εἰσαγγελία. See Meier-Schömann-Lipsius, *Der Attische Process* (Berlin, 1883-87), pp. 330-2.

123. For the role of Apollo as μηνυτής cf. the story of Sophocles and Μηνυτὴς Ἡρακλῆς (*Vita* 12).

124. 110-11: ἐν τῆδ᾽ ἔφασκε γῆ· τὸ δὲ ζητούμενον
ἁλωτόν, ἐκφεύγει δὲ τἀμελούμενον.

125. Cf. D. xxiv. 11: ἐλέσθαι ζητητάς, εἰ δέ τις οἶδέ τιν᾽, . . . μηνύειν πρὸς τούτους. For the rewards (μήνυτρα) cf. Th. vi. 27, And. i. 27-8, and also *O.T.* 231-2: κέρδος . . . χάρις. For *O.T.* 228: αὐτὸς καθ᾽ αὑτοῦ see Th. vi. 60: ὁ μὲν [Andocides] αὐτός τε καθ᾽ ἑαυτοῦ καὶ κατ᾽ ἄλλων μηνύει.

126. Cf. the formal curse on Alcibiades pronounced by all the priests and priestesses in Plu. *Alc.* xxii.

127. Th. vi. 27: τοὺς δράσαντας ᾔδει οὐδεὶς (cf. *O.T.* 293: τὸν δὲ δρῶντ᾽ οὐδεὶς ὁρᾷ, 246: τὸν δεδρακότ᾽) ἀλλὰ μεγάλοις μηνύτροις δημοσίᾳ οὗτοί τε ἐζητοῦντο (cf. *O.T.* 232: κέρδος τελῶ 'γώ, 266: ζητῶν τὸν αὐτόχειρα) καὶ προσέτι ἐψηφίσαντο καὶ εἴ τις ἄλλο τι

οἶδεν ἀσέβημα γεγενημένον (cf. *O. T.* 230: εἰ δ' αὖ τις ἄλλον οἶδεν ἐξ ἄλλης χθονός) μηνύειν ἀδεῶς τὸν βουλόμενον (cf. *O. T.* 227-9) καὶ ἀστῶν καὶ ξένων καὶ δούλων.

128. Cf. And. i. 14: ἦσθα ζητητής, ὦ Διόγνητε, ὅτε . . . μηνύσαντα 'Ανδρόμαχον. . . .

129. There is a passage in Demosthenes (xlvii. 68-70) which describes the dilemma of a man who cannot prosecute those whom he considers responsible for the death of an old house-servant: he is not related to her and since she has no living relatives he cannot find anyone entitled to bring suit. He is advised by the *exegetae* that all he can do is to make a proclamation banishing them from civic and religious functions, but without naming them; he must refer to them only as "those who did the deed and killed": ὀνομαστὶ μὲν μηδενὶ προαγορεύειν, τοῖς δεδρακόσι δὲ καὶ κτείνασιν. For a detailed discussion of this passage see R. Bonner and G. Smith, *The Administration of Justice from Homer to Aristotle* (Chicago, 1938), 2, 217 ff.

130. The process may be inferred from Antipho. 2. γ. 2: τὸ κακούργημα ἂν ἐκηρύσσετο and ibid. 8.6: εἰ δὲ ἐκηρύσσοντο ἢ μὴ ἄλλοι τινὲς κακοῦργοι . . . ἀφανοῦς δὲ ὄντος τοῦ κηρύγματος. For κηρύσσειν in this sense cf. *O. T.* 737: ταῦτ' ἐκηρύχθη πόλει (i. e. the murder of Laius).

131. Pl. Lg. ix. 874a, b: ἐὰν δὲ τεθνεὼς μὲν αὖ τις φανῇ, ἄδηλος δὲ ὁ κτείνας ᾖ (cf. *O. T.* 475-6) καὶ μὴ ἀμελῶς ζητοῦσιν ἀνεύρετος γίγνηται (cf. *O. T.* 110-11) τὰς μὲν προρρήσεις τὰς αὐτὰς γίγνεσθαι καθάπερ τοῖς ἄλλοις, προαγορεύειν δὲ τὸν φόνον τῷ δράσαντι (cf. *O. T.* 293, 296) καὶ ἐπιδικασάμενον ἐν ἀγορᾷ κηρῦξαι (cf. *O. T.* 450) τῷ κτείναντι τὸν καὶ τὸν καὶ ὠφληκότι φόνου (cf. *O. T.* 511) μὴ ἐπιβαίνειν ἱερῶν μηδὲ ὅλης χώρας τῆς τοῦ παθόντος (cf. *O. T.* 236-40).

132. Cf. (for example) Antipho. 6. 35-6: προαγορεύειν . . . εἴργεσθαι τῶν νομίμων, and ibid. 45-6 for the activities proscribed by the ban.

133. 297: οὐξελέγξων.

134. Cf. (for example) D. lix. 1, xviii. 103, 278, xxi. 176, lvi. 4; Pl. *Ap.* 29c, *Grg.* 522b; D. xix. 2: πρὶν γὰρ εἰσελθεῖν εἰς ὑμᾶς καὶ λόγον δοῦναι. "εἰσάγω, εἰσέρχομαι, εἴσοδος are the proper terms in speaking of a court," says John Burnet (Plato, *Euthyphro, Apology, and Crito*, Oxford, Clarendon Press, 1924) on Pl. *Ap.* 17c5. εἰσέρχεσθαι in Sophocles means "to go into something" (e. g. a house, a tent) except in *El.* 685 and 700, where it means "enter the lists" for a race. In *O. C.* 907, οὗσπερ αὐτὸς τοὺς νόμους εἰσῆλθ' ἔχων, the meaning is surely, as in *O. T.* 319, legal; "he will be made to conform," says Theseus of Creon, "to those same laws with which he himself came into court." In the *O. T.* passage the literal meaning "come in" will not do: Tiresias has not "come in" to anything, for the interview takes place in the open air. This is not, however, an objection to taking the word in a legal sense, for murder trials in fifth-century Athens did take place in the open air.

135. Cf. (for example) D. xlii. 32, xxii. 4; Antipho, 2, *a*. 2; Ar. *V.* 922.

136. Cf. D. xxiii, 86: οὐ γὰρ δήπου . . . ταῦτ' ἐν ψηφίσματι γράψας τις ἔννομ' ἂν εἰρηκὼς εἴη, 95: ἔστι δ' οὐδὲν . . . τοῦτο σημεῖον τοῦ τοῦτον ἔννομ' εἰρηκέναι. Cf. also Aeschin. iii. 23, 48, 193, 230. This is the only occurrence of ἔννομος in Sophocles.

137. *O. T.* 330; ξυνειδὼς οὐ φράσεις; Cf. Pl. *Lg.* 742b: ὁ συνειδὼς καὶ μὴ φράζων. And. i. 41, 47.

138. Cf. Gorg. *Pal.* 27: ἀντικατηγορῆσαι. Antipho. 4 β 6; Lys. xxv. 30 ff. Cf. also Arist. *Rh. Al.* xxxvi. 1442b: τὰς πράξεις . . . εἰς τοὺς ἀντιδίκους ἀποτρέψεις . . . τὴν αἰτίαν εἰς τοὺς ἐναντίους τρέποντες.

139. Cf. for speaker's record of service Lys. vii. 30 ff. xviii. 7, xix. 29, 57, xxi 1 ff., xxv. 12; for contrast of records Antipho. 2 β 12; Lys. x. 27-9.

140. *O. T.* 408-9: ἐξισωστέον τὸ γοῦν ἴσ' ἀντιλέξαι. This right to reply at equal length (ἀντιλέγειν) was exactly regulated in the courtroom by the water-clock: prosecution and defense had exactly the same amount of time.

141. *O. T.* 409: τοῦδε γὰρ κἀγὼ κρατῶ. Cf. Antipho. 6. 18: αἰτιάσασθαι μὲν οὖν καὶ καταψεύσασθαι ἔξεστι τῷ βουλομένῳ. αὐτὸς γὰρ ἕκαστος τούτου κρατεῖ. Also Gorg. *Pal.* 2: τοῦ μὲν ὑμεῖς ὅλου κρατεῖτε, τοῦ δ' ἐγώ, τῆς μὲν δίκης ἐγώ, τῆς δὲ βίας ὑμεῖς . . . κρατεῖτε γὰρ καὶ τούτων, ὧν οὐδὲν ἐγώ τυγχάνω κρατῶν.

142. Cf. (for example) Lys. xiii. 18, 64, xxx. 1-2.

143. *O. T.* 420-1; ποῖος οὐκ ἔσται λιμήν / ποῖος Κιθαιρὼν οὐχὶ σύμφωνος τάχα;

144. Antipho. 6. 49: ποίαν δίκην οὐ δικάσαιντ' ἂν ἢ ποῖον δικαστήριον οὐκ ἐξαπατήσειαν; Cf. ibid. 51, Lys. xiii, 46: ποίαν τινα οἴεσθε γνώμην περὶ τούτου ἔχειν, ἢ ποίαν τινα ἂν ψῆφον θέσθαι . . . ; Idem, xxxi. 31: ποίων . . . ὅρκων φροντίσαι . . . ἢ ποῖα ἂν ἀπόρρητα τηρῆσαι; Idem, vi. 33.

145. Cf. D. xviii. 12, xxiii. 89; [And.] 4. 16, 21; etc.

146. *O. T.* 429: ἦ ταῦτα δῆτ' ἀνεκτὰ πρὸς τούτου κλύειν; Cf. Ar. *Ach.* 618: ὦ δημοκρατία, ταῦτα δῆτ' ἀνασχετά; D. xxv. 17; Aeschin. i. 34.

147. *O. T.* 432: εἰ σὺ μὴ 'κάλεις. Cf. (for example) Andoc. 1. 14: καί μοι κάλει Διόγνητον, ibid. 18, etc. Other reminiscences of the legal atmosphere in the Tiresias scene are as follows: *O. T.* 351, κηρύγματι . . . ἐμμένειν (cf. D. lvii. 12: τούτοις ἐμμένειν, idem, xli. 14, xxv. 17, xxvii. 1); *O. T.* 363: οὔ τι . . . χαίρων (cf. Andoc. 1. 101; δοκεῖς οὖν χαιρήσειν); *O. T.* 378: Κρέοντος ἢ σοῦ ταῦτα τἀξευρήματα (cf. Antipho. i. 15: αὐτῆς μὲν τοῦτο εὕρημα, ἐκείνης δὲ ὑπηρέτημα); *O. T.* 401; χὡ συνθεὶς τάδε (cf. Gorg. *Pal.* 3: συνέθηκε ταύτην τὴν αἰτίαν, Antipho. 5. 25: ἐξ ἐπιβουλῆς συνέθεσαν ταῦτα, Ar. *V.* 693: ξυνθέντε τὸ πρᾶγμα);

O. T. 441: τοιαῦτ' ὀνείδιζ' οἷς ἔμ' εὑρήσεις μέγαν (cf. D. xlv. 78: μὴ οὖν μοι ταῦτ' ὀνείδιζε, ἐφ' οἷς ἐπαίνου τύχοιμ' ἂν δικαίως); *O. T.* 445: παρὼν . . . ὀχλεῖς (cf. D. xliv. 45, xxi, 189, xviii. 4; Din. i. 2); *O. T.* 455: πτωχὸς ἀντὶ πλουσίου ξένην ἔπι (cf. Antipho. 2. β. 9: γέρων καὶ ἄπολις ὢν ἐπὶ ξενίας πτωχεύσω; Lys. xxxii. 17: ἀντὶ πλουσίων πτωχούς).

148. Their intervention in the quarrel itself (404-7) was judicial in tone, deprecating anger, and attempting to restore relevancy.

149. Antipho. 5. 57: οὐδὲ γὰρ ἔχθρα οὐδεμία ἦν ἐμοὶ κἀκείνῳ. Cf. idem, 2. *a.* 5: ἐκ παλαιοῦ γὰρ ἐχθρὸς ὢν αὐτοῦ (from the prosecutor's speech).

150. *O. T.* 501: κρίσις οὐκ ἔστιν ἀληθής. Cf. Antipho. 3. β. 2: δόξῃ καὶ μὴ ἀληθείᾳ τὴν κρίσιν ποιήσασθαι. . . . Gorg. *Pal.* 35: μετὰ . . . τῆς ἀληθείας τὴν κρίσιν ποιήσατε. Pl. *Lg.* ii. 663c: τὴν δ' ἀλήθειαν τῆς κρίσεως. . . .

151. For σοφὸς ὤφθη cf. Lys. xxvii. 3: ὤφθησαν ἀδικοῦντες, ibid. 6.

152. *O. T.* 513-14: δειν' ἔπη . . . κατηγορεῖν. Cf. Andoc. 1. 7: δεινὰ κατηγορήσαντες. D. xix. 9: πολλὰ δὲ καὶ δεινὰ κατηγορεῖν ἔχων.

153. *O. T.* 518: οὗτοι βίου μοι τοῦ μακραίωνος πόθος. Cf. Aeschin. ii. 5: ἀβίωτον εἶναί μοι τόν λοιπὸν βίον νομίζω. Gorg. *Pal.* 20: πῶς οὐκ ἂν ἀβίωτος ἦν ὁ βίος μοι πράξαντι ταῦτα;

154. *O. T.* 533: τόλμης πρόσωπον. Antipho. 1. 28: θαυμάζω δὲ ἔγωγε τῆς τόλμης τοῦ ἀδελφοῦ, idem, 3. γ. 1: τολμηρός, 2: τολμῶν, 5: ἐς τοῦτο . . . τόλμης ἥκει, idem, 4. γ. 4: ἐτόλμησε, 6: ἐς τοῦτο τόλμης, idem, 5. 15; And. 1. 100; Lys. xii. 22; Gorg. *Pal.* 24.

155. *O. T.* 534; φονεὺς ὢν τοῦδε τἀνδρὸς ἐμφανῶς. Cf. D. xxi. 106: αὐτὸν . . . νομίζω αὐτόχειρά μου γεγενῆσθαι. Antipho. 4. β. 7: φονῆς τέ μου γίγνονται, 4. γ. 1: ζῶν τε καὶ βλέπων φονέας αὐτοῦ φησιν εἶναι. Cf. also idem, 5. 59.

156. Cf. Antipho. 6. 34.

157. *O. T.* 576: οὐ γὰρ δὴ φονεὺς ἀλώσομαι. Cf. Antipho. 2. β. 2: αὐτὸς καταδοχθεὶς φονεὺς εἶναι ἀνοσίως ἁλώσομαι.

158. See Th. viii. 68 for Thucydides' high estimate of it.

159. Text in K. J. Maidment, *Minor Attic Orators* (London, 1941), *1*, 294, 296. For a similar argument cf. Hdt. v. 106.

160. For the responsibilities of an ambassador cf. D. xix. 4 (a politico-legal text which throws light on Oedipus' impeachment and Creon's defense): λογίσασθε τίνων προσήκει λόγον παρὰ πρεσβευτοῦ λαβεῖν· πρῶτον μὲν τοινυν ὧν ἐπήγγειλε, δεύτερον δὲ ὧν ἔπεισε.... Cf. *O. T.* 604: εἰ σαφῶς ἤγγειλά σοι..., 555: ἔπειθες ἢ οὐκ ἔπειθες... ;

161. 32: εἰ μὲν τι ἠσέβηκα ... ἀποκτείνατέ με. Cf. *O. T.* 605-6: ἐάν με ... λάβῃς ... μὴ μ᾽ ἁπλῇ κτάνῃς ψήφῳ, διπλῇ δὲ.... Cf. also D. xviii. 10: εἰ μὲν ἴστε με τοιοῦτον ὄντα οἷον οὗτος ᾐτιᾶτο ... ἀναστάντες καταψηφίσασθ᾽ ἤδη. Isoc. 15. 51; Lys. iii. 4.

162. *O. T.* 613-15: ἀλλ᾽ ἐν χρόνῳ γνώσῃ τάδ᾽ ἀσφαλῶς ἐπεὶ χρόνος δίκαιον ἄνδρα δείκνυσιν μόνος. Antipho. 5. 86: ἀλλὰ δότε τι καὶ τῷ χρόνῳ μεθ᾽ οὗ ὀρθότατα εὑρίσκουσιν οἱ τὴν ἀκρίβειαν ζητοῦντες τῶν πραγμάτων. Cf. ibid. 71. Cf. also Lys. xix. 61: πιστεῦσαι ... τῷ χρόνῳ. Gorg. *Pal.* 34.

163. It occurs in what seems to be this technical sense in Gorg. *Pal.* 3: εἰ δὲ φθόνῳ καὶ κακοτεχνίᾳ καὶ πανουργίᾳ συνέθηκε ταύτην τὴν αἰτίαν....

164. For κακοτεχνεῖν cf. D. xliii. 2, xlvi. 25, κακοτεχνία xlvii. 2, xlix. 56; Pl. *Lg.* xi. 936d.

165. *O. T.* 656-7: τὸν ἐναγῆ φίλον μήποτ᾽ ἐν αἰτίᾳ σὺν ἀφανεῖ λόγῳ σ᾽ ἄτιμον βαλεῖν. Antipho. 5. 59: ἐν ἀφανεῖ λόγῳ ζητεῖς ἀπολέσαι. For ἐναγής cf. Aeschin. iii. 110.

166. D. xlv. 88: τὸν πεπονθότ᾽ ἐλεινότερον τῶν δωσόντων δίκην

ἡγεῖσθε. Cf. Antipho. i. 25-7, Gorg. *Pal.* 33. D. xxv. 76 contains a prosecutor's analysis of and attack on the appeal to pity.

167. Antipho. 3. β. 2, 11. Cf. also idem, 2. β. 13, 3. a. 2, 5. 73; Lys. iv. 20; Andoc. 1. 67; D. xxi. 99; Aeschin. ii. 179. For Socrates' refusal to ask for pity cf. Pl. *Ap.* 34c.

168. *O. T.* 732: ποῦ 'σθ' ὁ χῶρος . . . ; 735: καὶ τίς χρόνος . . . ; 740: τὸν δὲ Λάιον φύσιν τίν' εἶρπε, φράζε, τίνα δ' ἀκμὴν ἥβης ἔχων; 750: πότερον ἐχώρει βαιός, ἢ πολλοὺς ἔχων . . . ; Cf. Gorg. *Pal.* 22; φράσον τούτοις ⟨τὸν τρόπον⟩ τὸν τόπον, τὸν χρόνον, πότε, ποῦ, πῶς . . . and for ⟨τρόπον⟩ cf. *O. T.* 99: τίς ὁ τρόπος τῆς ξυμφορᾶς;

169. 2. γ. 10: ἡμῖν μὲν προστρόπαιος ὁ ἀποθανὼν οὐκ ἔσται, ὑμῖν δὲ ἐνθύμιος γενήσεται. Idem, 3. δ. 9: τοῖς καταλαμβάνουσι μεῖζον τὸ ἐνθύμιον γενήσεται.

170. Lys. xii. 4: οὑμὸς πατὴρ Κέφαλος ἐπείσθη μὲν ὑπὸ Περικλέους εἰς ταύτην τὴν γῆν ἀφικέσθαι.

171. D. lvii. 37: Ἐμοὶ γὰρ ἦν πάππος, ὦ ἄνδρες Ἀθηναῖοι, τῆς μητρὸς πατήρ, Δαμόστρατος Μελιτεύς. Cf. also idem, xxvii. 4: Δημοσθένης γὰρ οὑμὸς πατήρ, xl. 6: ἡ γὰρ μήτηρ ἡ ἐμὴ. . . .

172. Cf. D. xliv. 16, 19. For a full discussion see W. Wyse's note on Is. iii. 62. 4 (*The Speeches of Isaeus*, Cambridge, 1904, p. 345). This technical sense is appropriate at E. *El.* 595 and 1251.

173. *O. T.* 828-9: ἆρ' οὐκ ἀπ' ὠμοῦ ταῦτα δαίμονος τις ἂν κρίνων . . . ; D. xxv. 83: ὠμῶς καὶ πικρῶς εἶχε. Ibid. 84: πικρία καὶ μιαιφονία καὶ ὠμότης. Cf. also idem, xxi. 97: τὸν οὕτως ὠμόν, ibid. 109.

174. *O. T.* 848-9: φανέν γε τοὔπος . . . κοὐκ ἔστιν αὐτῷ τοῦτό γ' ἐκβαλεῖν πάλιν. Cf. Pl. *Cri.* 46b: τοὺς δὴ λόγους οὓς ἐν τῷ ἔμπροσθεν ἔλεγον οὐ δύναμαι νῦν ἐκβαλεῖν. . . .

175. Antipho. 2. a. 10: ἄναγνον . . . ἀγνείαν, 2, β, 11.

176. D. xxiv. 191: μὴ λανθανέτω ψευδόμενος ὑμᾶς. Cf. idem, xix. 239, xlviii. 40, xxvii. 64, xxxiv. 31.

177. *O.T.* 902: χειρόδεικτα. Cf. D. xxv. 68: δακτυλοδεικτεῖτ' ἐπὶ τῷ πονηρότατον τῶν ὄντων ἁπάντων δεικνύναι.

178. Cf. the end of Demosthenes' first speech against Aristogeiton (xxv. 98 ff.) where the judges are asked how, if they bring in an acquittal, they can "go to the sanctuary of the mother-goddess . . . to consult the laws as if they were still valid" or "climb the Acropolis on the first day of the month and pray to the gods."

179. See the discussion of the passage in Chap. 1, p. 19.

180. *O.T.* 1121-2: οὗτος σὺ πρέσβυ δεῦρό μοι φώνει βλέπων ὅσ' ἂν σ' ἐρωτῶ. Pl. *Ap.* 24c: μοι δεῦρο ὦ Μέλητε εἰπέ. Cf. Andoc. I. 18: βλέπετε εἰς τούτους καὶ μαρτυρεῖτε. . . .

181. For ἐρωτᾶν cf. *O.T.* 740, 1119, 1122.

182. *O.T.* 1122-3: Λαΐου ποτ' ἦσθα σύ; ἦ. Andoc. I. 14: Ἦσθα ζητητής . . . ; ἦ. Lys. xii. 25: Ἦσθα δ' ἐν τῷ βουλευτηρίῳ . . . ; ἦ.

183. *O.T.* 1133: ἀναμνήσω νιν. For ἀναμιμνήσκω in the orators cf. D. xviii. 17, 60, idem, xxiv. 12. Similarly ὑπομνῆσαι in Gorg. *Pal.* 28, 31, 37. For "forgetful" witnesses cf. Lycurg. *In Leocr.* 20.

184. D. xxv. 77-8. For ὦ τᾶν used in the same way (in the mouth of an imaginary and swiftly confuted objector) cf. idem, i. 26, iii. 29, xviii. 312.

185. *O.T.* 1147; κόλαζε, 1148; κολαστοῦ. Cf. Andoc. 4. 4: κολάζειν ἐξὸν . . . , Pl. *Lg.* 863a. For κολάζειν cf. also Antipho. 4. a. 6 and 7, 3. δ. 8; Lys. xii. 36, Ar. *V.* 258, 406, 927, and for κολαστής Lys. xxvii. 3.

186. The technical word βάσανος is used metaphorically (*O.T.* 494 and 510) in the chorus' judicial summation.

187. Antipho. 5. 32, 50. For a general discussion of this aspect of evidence given under torture cf. Arist. *Rh.* i. 15. 26 (1376b-1377a). Cf. also idem, *Rh. Al.* xvi. 1432a; βάσανος δ' ἐστὶ μὲν ὁμολογία παρὰ συνειδότος ἄκοντος δέ.

188. *O. T.* 1214-15: δικάζει τὸν ἄγαμον γάμον. . . .

189. For the conviction of the defendant as a παράδειγμα cf. Lys. xiv. 12, 45, xvi. 14; D. xxi. 76, 97, 227; Lycurg. *In Leocr.* 27, 150.

Other passages which reinforce the legal emphasis of the language are: *O. T.* 136: γῇ τῇδε τιμωροῦντα τῷ θεῷ θ' ἅμα (cf. Antipho. i. 24: τιμωρήσω τῷ τε πατρὶ τῷ ἡμετέρῳ καὶ τοῖς νόμοις τοῖς ὑμετέροις); *O. T.* 220: τοῦ πραχθέντος (cf. Antipho. i. 6, 13); *O. T.* 227: τοὐπίκλημ' (cf. Antipho. 3 a. 1, β. 5, 9, etc.: ἐπικαλεῖν); *O. T.* 249: οἴκοισιν εἰ ξυνέστιος . . . (cf. Pl. *Euthphr.* 4b, c: ἐάνπερ ὁ κτείνας συνέστιός σοι . . . ᾖ . . . ἴσον γὰρ τὸ μίασμα γίγνεται ἐὰν συνῇς τῷ τοιούτῳ συνειδώς); *O. T.* 702: τὸ νεῖκος ἐγκαλῶν (cf. D. xli. 7, 11; Antipho. 2. δ. 11: ἔγκλημα, so ibid. 3. β. 9, γ. 11); *O. T.* 705: εἰσπέμψας (cf. Pl. *Euthd.* 305b); *O. T.* 677: ἐν δὲ τοῖσδ'. (cf. Earle's note ad loc.) Very interesting in this respect is the variant recorded by the scholium at 134: γράφε τήνδε θεσπίζει γραφήν. This would make good sense: "very properly does Phoebus (and you too) advise from the oracle this suit on the dead man's behalf."

190. *O. T.* 1193: τὸν σόν τοι παράδειγμ' ἔχων, τὸν σὸν δαίμονα. Th. ii. 37 παράδειγμα δὲ μᾶλλον αὐτοὶ ὄντες (cf. Lycurg. *In Leocr.* 83). Cf. also Th. v. 90 (Melians to Athenians): σφαλέντες ἂν τοῖς ἄλλοις παράδειγμα γένοισθε.

191. Published in *Textos y Estudios*, Instituto de lenguas clasicas, Ministerio de Educacion, Universidad Nacional de la ciudad Eva Perón, Eva Perón (La Plata), Argentina, 1952. Cf. p. 57: "sinteticemos nuestra tesis: el estasimo segundo . . . se refiere a Layo y se refiere solamente a Layo."

192. Ibid., pp. 79 ff.

193. 874: ὑπερπλησθῇ. This same word is used in the preceding scene (779) of drunkenness: ὑπερπλησθεὶς μέθης. Cf. Hp. *Morb.* ii. 53: ἀπεχέσθω θωρηξίων καὶ μὴ ὑπερπίμπλασθαι. Pl. *R.* iii. 426a: μεθύων καὶ ἐμπιμπλάμενος. . . .

194. Ehrenberg (2) discusses the passage and the fifth-century use of the term *prostatês* at some length (pp. 99-103). He concludes that in 882 "there is no idea of opposing the divine *prostatês* to a human political leader." But though he proves beyond much doubt that the term *prostatês* was not in any sense an official title in the fifth century, it is still, surely, a word which suggests the democratic state and the position of the leading statesman in it. And in lines 880 ff. I do not see what sense the passage has unless there is a strong contrast between divine and human leadership.

195. 884: πορεύεται. A word associated strongly with the journeyings of Oedipus; cf. 787 and also 801 (ὁδοιπορῶν).

196. Th. ii. 64: ἦν καὶ νῦν ὑπενδῶμέν ποτε (πάντα γὰρ πέφυκε καὶ ἐλλασσοῦσθαι) μνήμη καταλείψεται. . . . The word ὑπενδῶμεν is a strong one; Thucydides uses the form ἐνδιδόναι to describe the Athenian surrender in 404 B.C. (ii. 65).

197. Th. ii, 65. 7.: ἡσυχάζοντας . . . περιέσεσθαι. . . .

NOTES FOR CHAPTER THREE: MAN

1. Cf. Th. ii. 62, 2 (Pericles) and iv. 65. 4 for Athenian confidence.

2. *O. T.* 1197-8: ἐκράτησας τοῦ πάντ' εὐδαίμονος ὄλβου.

3. περὶ τῆς ἐν ἀρχῇ καταστάσεως. Cf. D. L. ix. 55.

4. See Ehrenberg (2), pp. 61 ff.

5. 30: πόριμον ἐξ ἀπόρου. Cf. S. *Ant.* 360: παντόπορος· ἄπορος
ἐπ' οὐδὲν ἔρχεται. . . .

6. *O. T.* 109 ἴχνος . . . δυστέκμαρτον. For the force of παλαιᾶς
cf. X. *Cyn.* vi. 4: ἐξιέναι δὲ πρωὶ ἵνα τῆς ἰχνεύσεως μὴ ἀποστερῶνται
[sc. αἱ κύνες] . . . οὐ γὰρ ἐπιμένει τοῦ ἴχνους ἡ φύσις λεπτὴ
οὖσα . . . For δυστέκμαρτον cf. ibid. viii. 1: εἰ δ' ἐνέσται
μελάγχιμα [i. e. patches of bare ground in the snow] . . .
δυσζήτητος ἔσται [sc. ὁ λαγώς]. For εὑρεθήσεται cf. ibid. vi. 4, 18,
vii. 7, etc.

7. *O. T.* 110-11: τὸ δὲ ζητούμενον ἀλωτόν. The stages of the hunt
are summarized in a famous sentence of Xenophon (*Cyn.* v.
33): "so pleasant is the sight that to see the hare tracked, found,
pursued, and caught, is enough to make a man forget the one
he loves." (ἰχνευόμενον, εὑρισκόμενον, μεταθεόμενον, ἁλισκόμενον).
For ἀλωτόν cf. also ibid. vi. 10, 18; for ζητούμενον ibid. viii. 1,
vi. 19, 24, 25.

8. *O. T.* 221: ἴχνευον . . . μὴ οὐκ ἔχων τι σύμβολον. Cf. Poll.
E. 11: ἴχνος, ἰχνηλασία, σημεῖα ποδῶν, σύμβολα ἐντετυπωμένα τῇ γῇ.

9. "ἐκκινεῖν is used of starting game," says Jebb on this passage,
and compares *El.* 567: ἐξεκίνησεν ποδοῖν . . . ἔλαφον. It is a
favorite Sophoclean metaphor, and peculiarly his; the word
does not seem to occur in any other classical Greek author
except Plutarch. Its other appearances in S. in a metaphorical
sense also suggest its force as a hunting term: *Tr.* 979: κἀκ-
κινήσεις . . . φοιτάδα δεινὴν νόσον (where φοιτάδα reinforces the
hunting context as well as the medical), and ibid. 1242: σὺ
γάρ μ' ἀπ' εὐνασθέντος ἐκκινεῖς κακοῦ, where εὐνασθέντος suggests
the lair of the wild beast. Cf. X. *Cyn. passim* for this sense of
εὐνή, and especially ix. 3: εὐνάσειν (of a dam bedding down
her fawn) and ix. 4: τὸν νεβρὸν . . . εὐνασθέντα.

10. 475-6 τὸν ἄδηλον ἄνδρα πάντ' ἰχνεύειν. ἄδηλος is the hunting
term for a vanished track; cf. X. *Cyn.* viii. 6: ἕτερον δὲ ζητεῖν
πρὶν τὰ ἴχνη ἄδηλα γένεσθαι (contrast viii. 1: τὰ ἴχνη . . . δῆλα.

Notes for CHAPTER THREE: MAN

Cf. now J. C. Kamerbeek, *The Plays of Sophocles, Part I, Ajax* (Leiden, 1953), p. 24 (on 31).

11. 468: πόδα, 479: ποδί. For a discussion of the whole complex of puns on the name of Oedipus see Chap 4, pp. 182-4.

12. 541-3: τυραννίδα θηρᾶν . . . ἁλίσκεται.

13. 1255: φοιτᾷ γὰρ. . . . Cf. 476: φοιτᾷ γὰρ . . . ὁ ταῦρος. Earle (on 1254: περιπολοῦντ'), sees this suggestion in the language, and remarks: "Seneca tastelessly expresses what Sophocles implies (qualis per arva Libycus insanit leo etc. Sen. Oed. 918 ff.)" For φοιτᾶν cf. Kamerbeek, p. 30 (on 59).

14. 1265: δεινὰ βρυχηθεὶς. For βρυχᾶσθαι used of the bull cf. S. *Aj.* 322: ταῦρος ὣς βρυχώμενος, Theoc. xxv. 137, E. *Hel.* 1557, Hes. *Th.* 832.

15. 1451: ἔα με ναίειν ὄρεσιν. Other words which reinforce the image of the hunter are: ἄγριος (344 of Oedipus' anger, 476 of the wild wood where the bull ranges, cf. also 1205, 1349), ματεύω (1052, 1061, cf. S. *Ichneutae* 13), and possibly ἐκτρέπεσθαι (851: εἰ δ' οὖν τι κἀκτρέποιτο τοῦ πρόσθεν λόγου, cf. Plu. *De cur.* 11, 520 E: καθάπερ οἱ κυνηγοὶ τοὺς σκύλακας οὐκ ἐῶσιν ἐκτρέπεσθαι καὶ διώκειν πᾶσαν ὀδμήν).

16. 4: θυμιαμάτων γέμει. . . . For γέμω v. Liddell and Scott s. v.

17. 22-4: σαλεύει κἀνακουφίσαι κάρα βυθῶν ἔτ' οὐχ οἷα τε φοινίου σάλου. Contrast the successful seafarer in the stasimon of the *Antigone*, χωρεῖ περιβρυχίοισιν περῶν ὑπ' οἴδμασιν (336-7).

18. 101: χείμαζον. For ἡγεμών, "captain," cf. Poll. A. 98: ὁ τῆς νεὼς ἡγεμών, Th. vii. 50: τοῦ πλοῦ ἡγεμόνας, "pilots," and for ἀπευθύνειν Pl. *Criti.* 109c: ἐκ πρύμνης ἀπευθύνοντες οἷον οἴακι.

19. 694 ff. reading (with Pearson) σαλεύουσαν for the ἀλύουσαν of the MSS.

20. 1207 ff.: μέγας λιμήν. For λιμήν in a sexual sense cf. Diels-

235

Kranz, Empedocles B 98. 3: Κύπριδος ὁρμισθεῖσα τελείοις ἐν λιμένεσσιν.

21. It is common in prose too: cf. the legal formula ἐπὶ παίδων γνησίων ἀρότῳ (quoted by M. Nilsson (2), p. 120).

22. T. Mitchell, *The Oedipus Tyrannus of Sophocles* (Oxford, 1841), note on 1208.

23. Such metaphors, however, are sometimes more horrifying than the plainest imaginable speech. The language of Leontes in *The Winter's Tale*, for example ("sluiced," "fishpond," etc.), reveals the disease of his mind more eloquently than any combination of four-letter words could do it.

24. Cf. Earle (p. 144): "the forms of blight . . . described may be regarded as a symbolical judgment on the incestuous marriage."

25. *Od.* xix. 109-14. Cf. Sir James G. Frazer, *The Golden Bough* (3d ed., London, 1935), vol. 2: *The Magic Art*, Chap. 11, especially p. 115.

26. Cf. Frazer, 2, 135-41. For more evidence (but a different estimate) see L. R. Farnell, *Cults of the Greek States* (Oxford, 1896-1909), *1*, 184-92 (Zeus and Hera), *3*, 176 (Eleusis), *5*, 217 ff. Dionysus). Cf. also Nilsson (2), pp. 121-2, 429-30, (Hera), 661-2 (Eleusis).

27. Cf. Farnell, 5, 217 ff., L. Deubner, *Attische Feste* (Berlin, 1932), pp. 104 ff., A. W. Pickard-Cambridge, *The Dramatic Festivals of Athens* (Oxford, Clarendon Press, 1953), p. 11: "It was doubtless a piece of fertility-magic, and symbolized the union of the god of fruitfulness with the community represented by the wife of its religious head."

28. 1405: ἀνεῖτε ταὐτοῦ σπέρμα (with Jebb). For ἀνεῖτε cf. 270: μήτ' ἄροτον αὐτοῖς γῆς ἀνιέναι τινὰ μήτ' οὖν γυναικῶν παῖδας and the Homeric hymn to Demeter, 332: γῆς καρπὸν ἀνήσειν.

29. Cf. also 717: βλάστας, 1376: βλαστοῦσ' ὅπως ἔβλαστε and χέρσους 1502 (on which see Earle, ad loc.).

30. Diels-Kranz, B8. τὸ αἴνιγμα γνῶναι (so the MSS). Diels' emendation, πλίγμα (retained, with a question mark, in the latest edition), is high-handed and unnecessary; cf. Kathleen Freeman's discussion of it (1), p. 362. For γνῶναι τὸ αἴνιγμα in the sense of "solve the riddle" cf. Anaxilas ap. Ath. xiii. 558d: ἀλλ' ἐν αἰνιγμοῖς τισιν . . . εἶθ' ὃ μὲν γνοὺς ταῦτ' ἀπῆλθεν εὐθὺς ὥσπερ Οἰδίπους. Cf. also E. *Ph.* 1506; μέλος ἔγνω Σφιγγός, ibid. 1759.

31. The text of the riddle and its answer, though preserved in full only in a late writer, were familiar to the fifth-century audience. The riddle is clearly alluded to in Aesch. *Agam.* 80-1 (see E. Fraenkel, *The Agamemnon of Aeschylus*, Oxford, 1950, ad loc. and on 1258) and in E. *Tr.* 275. Further, Creon's reference to the Sphinx in the *O. T.* (as Hermann saw) alludes to the content of the riddle: ἡ . . . Σφὶγξ τὸ πρὸς ποσὶ σκοπεῖν . . . ἡμᾶς . . . προσήγετο (130). Earle sees in ῥαψῳδὸς . . . κύων (391) a reference to the hexameter form of the riddle.

32. ζητεῖν and its cognates are much more frequent in the *O. T.* than in the other Sophoclean plays: eight occurrences in the *O. T.*, three in the *Ajax*, two in the *O. C.*, one in *Trach.* In the fragments only 843: τὰ δ' εὑρετὰ ζητῶ.

33. It occurs only once in Homer (and in the literal sense)— *Il.* xiv. 258: ἐμὲ . . . ζήτει. Not in Pindar, only once in Hesiod (*Op.* 400). In Aeschylus it occurs only in *P.V.* (262, 316, 776).

34. Pl. *Ap.* 19b: ζητῶν τά τε ὑπὸ γῆς καὶ οὐράνια. . . .

35. Ar. *Nu.* 171-2 (Socrates), 188 (pupils). Cf. also ibid. 761, 1398.

36. Cf. also Pl. *Sph.* 224c, *Plt.* 261e, *Men.* 79d, *R.* vii. 528c.

37. *Plu. De fortuna* 98a, quotes these lines together with S. Fr.

759, as the expression of an attitude which would be meaningless if the universe were governed by blind chance.

38. Diels-Kranz, B3. ἐξευρεῖν δὲ μὴ ζατοῦντα ἄπορον καὶ σπάνιον, ζατοῦντα δὲ εὔπορον καὶ ῥάδιον. The translation follows Kathleen Freeman, *Ancilla to the Pre-Socratic Philosophers* (Cambridge, Harvard Univ. Press, 1948), p. 80. This sentence is quoted as an encouragement to the mathematician by Iamb. *Comm. Math.* xi. p. 45, ll. 10 ff.

39. Cf. R. iii. 411d, ii. 368c, *Tht.* 191a, *Cra.* 421a, *Sph.* 221c, etc.

40. Hp. *V. M.* 3 (translated by W. H. S. Jones, *Hippocrates*, London, Loeb Classical Library, 1923): τῷ δὲ εὑρήματι τούτῳ καὶ ζητήματι. Cf. ibid. 5: οἱ δὲ ζητήσαντες καὶ εὑρόντες ἰητρικήν. The word ζητεῖν is used throughout this work in the sense of "research": see especially 2 (on proper scientific method).

41. Th. i. 20: ἡ ζήτησις τῆς ἀληθείας. . .

42. *Plu. de cur.* 522c: ζητῶν γὰρ ἑαυτὸν ὡς οὐκ ὄντα Κορίνθιον ἀλλὰ ξένον . . . καὶ πάλιν ἑαυτὸν ἐζήτει.

43. Cf. also (ζητεῖν) 362, 450, 658, 659, 1112. With 1112: ὅνπερ πάλαι ζητοῦμεν, cf. Pl. *R.* iii. 392b, iv 420b, *Crat.* 424a.

44. i. 21. 2. Cf. also i. 22: τὸ σαφὲς σκοπεῖν, ii. 48, v. 20, etc.; Ar. *Nu.* 231: τἄνω κάτωθεν ἐσκόπουν, ibid. 742: ὀρθῶς διαιρῶν καὶ σκοπῶν. Aristotle (*Metaph.* 3. 1005ᵃ31) defines the "object of the speculations" of the φυσικοί as περὶ τῆς ὅλης φύσεως σκοπεῖν. (Quoted by Werner Jaeger, *The Theology of the Early Greek Philosophers*, Oxford, Clarendon Press, 1947, p. 198, n. 4). Cf. also Hp. *Aer.* 3: σκοπεῖν καὶ βασανίζειν. Ar. *Ra.* 974 ff.

45. Cf. also 130: τὸ πρὸς ποσὶ σκοπεῖν (Creon), 286: σκοπῶν . . . ἐκμάθοι.

46. See J. Schweighaeuser, *Lexicon Herodoteum* s. v., J. E. Powell, *A Lexicon to Herodotus*, Cambridge, 1938, s. v.: ἱστο-

ῥεῖν ἱστορίη. Cf. M. Croiset, *Histoire de la littérature grecque* (3rd ed. Paris, 1913), 2, 613 (quoted in How and Wells, *A Commentary on Herodotus*, Oxford, 1912, 1, 53): "Le mot ἱστορίη . . . implique et signale une révolution littéraire. . . ."

47. For a statistical study of the questions in the *O. T.* as compared with other Sophoclean plays see John P. Carroll, "Some Remarks on the Questions in the Oedipus Tyrannus," *CJ*, 32, No. 7 (April 1937), 406-16. Carroll attributes Oedipus' penchant for asking questions to his heredity; he develops the idea that Laius, too, was much given to asking questions.

48. 954: οὗτος δὲ τίς ποτ᾽ ἐστὶ καὶ τί μοι λέγει;

49. 1173-4: καὶ τοῦτο τοὐπιχώριον ἀτεχνῶς ἐπανθεῖ τὸ τί λέγεις σύ.

50. πᾶσαν προσφέρων ἀνάγκην as Plutarch puts it (*de cur.* 522c).

51. 1165: μὴ πρὸς θεῶν μὴ δέσποθ᾽ ἱστόρει πλέον. For ἱστορεῖν cf. also 1144, 1150, 1156.

52. The questioning was broken off and Oedipus intervened in person when the shepherd refused to admit that he had given a child to the Corinthian messenger (1150; οὐκ ἐννέπων τὸν παῖδ᾽ ὃν οὗτος ἱστορεῖ). The shepherd's final admission of the truth is so phrased as to recall the words with which Oedipus first intervened: εἰ γὰρ οὗτος εἶ ὃν φησιν οὗτος . . . (1180-1).

53. Hdt. i. 57: εἰ δὲ χρεόν ἐστι τεκμαιρόμενον λέγειν τοῖσι νῦν ἔτι ἐοῦσι Πελασγῶν. . . . Cf. ibid. ii. 33: τοῖσι ἐμφανέσι τὰ μὴ γινωσκόμενα τεκμαιρόμενος . . . E. *Fr.* 574; Th. i. 1: ἐλπίσας μέγαν τε ἔσεσθαι . . . τεκμαιρόμενος ὅτι. . . .

54. Cf. Hp. *Prog.* 24, *Acut.* 68.

55. Diels-Kranz, B1: σαφήνειαν μὲν θεοὶ ἔχοντι, ὣς δὲ ἀνθρώποις τεκμαίρεσθαι. On this passage see Hermann Fränkel, *Dichtung und Philosophie des Frühen Griechentums* (New York, 1951), p. 439, n. 2. "Der neue Sinn in dem es [das Verbum] Alkmaion verwendete, blieb von nun an an dem Wort haften."

56. δυστέκμαρτος only here in S.; in A. only in *P.V.* 497: δυστέκμαρτον εἰς τέχνην ὥδωσα θνητούς— a technique "difficult to infer," the technique of prophecy. Cf. E. *Hel.* 711-12: ὁ θεὸς . . . ποικίλον καὶ δυστέκμαρτον.

57. οὐδ' ὁποῖ' ἀνὴρ ἔννους τὰ καινὰ τοῖς πάλαι τεκμαίρεται. This word is found elsewhere in S. only in Fr. 330; in A. only at *P.V.* 336.

58. Hp. *Prorrh.* ii. 1: ἐγὼ οὐ . . . μαντεύσομαι, σημεῖα δὲ γράφω οἷσι χρὴ τεκμαίρεσθαι. . . .

59. Oedipus makes the same contrast, though in a more reverent spirit, in the later *O.C.* (403: κἄνευ θεοῦ τις τοῦτό γ' ἂν γνώμῃ μάθοι). For the same contrast (γνώμη versus prophecy) see also X. *Mem.* i. 1. 7-9. For γνώμη opposed to chance (τύχη) cf. Th. i. 144; A. Fr. 389. In the Hippocratic writings the opposition of γνώμη to σῶμα is common (cf. *V. M.* 10, *de Arte* 7, *Flat.* 1). Cf. also Hp. *de Arte* 2. where a contrast is made between things perceived by the eyes and those perceived by γνώμη.

60. The play contains a number of words related to γιγνώσκειν which are rarely found in the other Sophoclean plays: γνωτός, 58, 396 (elsewhere only in Fr. 282; not in A.); ἄγνωτος, 58 (not elsewhere in S.; not in A.); γνωστός, 361 (elsewhere only in Fr. 203; cf. Hp. *V. M.* 2.: γνωστὰ λέγειν τοῖσι δημότῃσι); γνωρίζω, 538 (only here in S.; in A. only at *P.V.* 487).

61. εἴθε μήποτε γνοίης ὃς εἶ.

62. οὓς δ' ἔχρῃζεν οὐ γνωσοίατο. I follow Jebb's interpretation of this enigmatic sentence.

63. μάντις . . . καὶ κατὰ γνώμαν ἴδρις. Cf. *El.* 472 ff. for the same collocation of the mantic and the "secular" mode of cognition.

64. τυφλὸς τά τ' ὦτα τόν τε νοῦν τά τ' ὄμματ' εἶ. Epicharmus (Diels-Kranz, B12): νοῦς ὁρῆι καὶ νοῦς ἀκούει. τἆλλα κωφὰ καὶ

240

τυφλά. With the second half of this phrase cf. *O.T.* 290: καὶ μὴν τά γ' ἄλλα κωφὰ καὶ παλαί' ἔπη.

65. Diels-Kranz, B24: οὖλος ὁρᾶι, οὖλος δὲ νοεῖ, οὖλος δέ τ' ἀκούει. For τυφλός cf. also Democritus (Diels-Kranz B175): διὰ νοῦ τυφλότητα.

66. E. *Ba.* 1269: γίγνομαι δέ πως ἔννους, μετασταθεῖσα τῶν πάρος φρενῶν. Pl. *Ti.* 71e: οὐδεὶς γὰρ ἔννους ἐφάπτεται μαντικῆς ἐνθέου καὶ ἀληθοῦς.

67. νηπίους ὄντας τὸ πρὶν ἔννους ἔθηκα. Cf. Democritus (Diels-Kranz, A111): ζητήσεως δὲ τὴν ἔννοιαν [εἶναι κριτήριον.]

68. τοῦ νοῦ τῆς τε συμφορᾶς ἴσον. See Jebb's perceptive note on this line.

69. ὁδοὺς . . . φροντίδος.

70. φροντιστήριον (*Nu.* 94); φροντίδ' ἐξήμβλωκας ἐξηυρημένην (ibid. 137). Cf. also ibid. 101: μεριμνοφροντισταί, 155: φρόντισμα, 226: φροντιστῇ, and 414, 695, 700, 723, 735, 763, 1345. The *Connos* of Ameipsias, produced in the same year as *The Clouds*, had a chorus of φροντισταί. Cf. Eupolis, Fr. 352: μισῶ δὲ καὶ τὸν Σωκράτην . . . ὃς τἄλλα μὲν πεφρόντικεν, ὁπόθεν δὲ καταφαγεῖν ἔχοι τούτου κατημέληκεν.

71. *Nu.* 229: τὸ νόημα καὶ τὴν φροντίδα. Burnet's statement (p. 76) that "the use of φροντίς for 'thought' . . . is Ionic rather than Attic" and that the word "struck Athenian ears as odd" seems exaggerated in view of the many passages in Aeschylus where φροντίς seems to mean "thought" rather than "care" or "heed" (which Burnet claims is the Attic sense of the word). Cf. A. *Pers.* 142, A. 912, 1530, Supp. 407, 417.

72. νοσεῖ . . . πρόπας στόλος, οὐδ' ἔνι φροντίδος ἔγχος ᾧ τις ἀλέξεται. The metaphorical ἔγχος may have been suggested by the military connotations of the preceding στόλος.

73. τὸ γὰρ τὴν φροντίδ' ἔξω τῶν κακῶν οἰκεῖν γλυκύ.

74] . g. 59, 105; and cf. 129 where he reproaches Creon for not attaining full knowledge of the circumstances of Laius' murder.

75. ὁ μηδὲν εἰδὼς Οἰδίπους. He is adapting the priest's admiring phrase, οὐδὲν ἐξειδὼς πλέον (37).

76. 1008: οὐκ εἰδὼς, 1014: ἆρ' οἶσθα . . . 1022: ἴσθι, 1181: ἴσθι δύσποτμος γεγώς.

77. The source of this famous story seems to be Vitruvius, *De architectura* ix. (preface) 10: *nudus vadens domum . . . currens . . . graece exclamabat* ευρηκα, ευρηκα.

78. Cf. e. g. Hdt. i. 25: σιδήρου κόλλησιν ἐξεῦρε, ibid. 94, ii. 4, Pl. *Phdr.* 267a on Euenus (πρῶτος ηὗρεν), and other rhetorical "inventors." See A. Kleingünther, "Πρῶτος εὑρέτης," *Phil. Suppl.*, 26 (1933). Heft 1. Virgil makes use of this Greek formula in *Aen.* vi. 663: inventas aut qui vitam excoluere per artis.

79. i. 21. 1. For εὑρίσκειν used of historical discovery cf. also ibid. i. 1. 3.

80. Cf. also ibid. 469, and 59, 267, 475.

81. *Palamedes:* Fr. 479. 3: ἐφηῦρε. *Nauplius,* Fr. 432.1: ηὗρε, 2: εὑρήματα, 5: ηὗρε, 8: ἐφηῦρε.

82. Hp. *V. M.* 2: ἀρχὴ καὶ ὁδὸς εὑρημένη, καθ' ἣν τὰ εὑρημένα πολλά τε καὶ καλῶς ἔχοντα εὕρηται ἐν πολλῷ χρόνῳ, καὶ τὰ λοιπὰ εὑρεθήσεται, ἤν τις ἱκανός τε ἐὼν καὶ τὰ εὑρημένα εἰδὼς ἐκ τούτων ὁρμώμενος ζητῇ. With εὑρεθήσεται cf. *O. T.* 108.

83. Cf. ηὑρῆσθαι in Th. i. 21.

84. It may indeed be, as Robert (p. 76) says, a "rudimentärer Rest einer älteren Sagenversion," but it is also dramatically effective, and typical of the unscrupulous opportunism of the Corinthian messenger.

85. Jebb's note shows how strained is the use of the word

εὕρημα in this passage. The context shows clearly that Oedipus is thought of as the son of Dionysus and one of the nymphs, but the word εὕρημα seems to contradict this idea. Its presence in this passage suggests the intrusive force of the metaphorical significance of εὑρεῖν throughout the play

86. 13: τοὺς τῶν μετεωρολόγων λόγους οἵτινες . . . τὰ ἄπιστα καὶ ἄδηλα φαίνεσθαι τοῖς τῆς δόξης ὄμμασιν ἐποίησαν. Cf. Hp. *V. M.* xx: τοιαύτην δὴ βούλομαι ἀληθείην καὶ περὶ τῶν ἄλλων φανῆναι.

87. τάδ' ἤδη διαφανῆ. Only here in tragedy. In Ar. *Nu.* 768 it is used to describe the transparent crystal with which Strepsiades proposes to melt the wax tablet on which is written the accusation against him. For its use in the Hippocratic writings see Liddell and Scott s. v.

88. σάφα (σαφής only in the *Hymn to Hermes* 208).

89. i. 22. Cf. also iii. 29, vi. 60. Liddell and Scott do not recognize this meaning of σαφής except for "seers, oracles, prophets" (s. v. 2). But they instance (and I quote their translations) Antipho. i. 13: τῶν πραχθέντων τὴν σαφήνειαν πυθέσθαι, "the plain truth"; Pi. *O.* 10 (11). 55: τὸ σαφηνές, "the plain truth"; and the Thucydidean passage quoted above, τῶν γενομένων τὸ σαφές, "the clear truth." Cf. also the Empedoclean opposites Νημερτής (truth) and Ἀσάφεια (obscurity) Diels-Kranz, B. 122, 4.

90. Cf. Hp. *V. M.* xx: περὶ φύσιος γνῶναί τι σαφές. E. *Or.* 397: σοφόν τοι τὸ σαφές, οὐ τὸ μὴ σαφές.

91. Cf. Hdt. viii. 77, where he singles out for mention as exempt from criticism those oracles which "speak clearly" (ἐναργέως λέγοντας).

92. See Jebb, ad. loc. and for ἐξήκοι cf. Hdt. vi. 80: ἐξήκειν μοι τὸ χρηστήριον.

93. Aeschylus' Prometheus describes his revelations to mankind with the word ἔδειξα (458, 482). Cf. Pl. *Ti.* 49e: ὅσα δεικνύντες

. . . δηλοῦν ἡγούμεθά τι, and see Arist. *Metaph*. B4. 1000ᵃ. 20, where a contrast is drawn between οἱ θεολόγοι and οἱ δι' ἀπο-δείξεως λέγοντες.

94. See Jebb, ad loc. for the force of this word.

95. For Athens as σωτήρ cf. Isoc. 4. 80, 7. 84; Hdt. vii. 139. 5.

96. For sophistic rhetoric as "savior" see Pl. *Grg*. 511c and cf. the words of Strepsiades to Pheidippides after he emerges as a graduate of the sophistic school (Ar. *Nu*. 1177): ὅπως σώσεις μ'.

97. 1350: ἔλυτο (with recc. and Jebb) . . . κἀνέσωσεν. Oedipus also says ἔρυτο, and this verb follows the same pattern, for in the beginning he himself was the rescuer (τήνδε ῥυσαίμην πόλιν, 72).

98. A. P. V. 478 ff.: τὸ μὲν μέγιστον is his prefatory phrase.

99. Hp. V. M. 2. See n. 82, above.

100. Hp. V. M. 9: δεῖ γὰρ μέτρου τινὸς στοχάσασθαι· μέτρον δὲ οὔτε ἀριθμὸν οὔτε σταθμὸν ἄλλον πρὸς ὃ ἀναφέρων εἴσῃ τὸ ἀκριβές, οὐκ ἂν εὕροις ἀλλ' ἢ τοῦ σώματος τὴν αἴσθησιν.

101. The word suggests "lightening" the ship, i. e. jettisoning cargo. Cf. Hdt. viii. 118: καὶ τὴν νέα ἐπικουφισθεῖσαν οὕτω δὴ ἀποσωθῆναι.

102. Hp. *Epid*. i. 7; cf. in the same chapter [πυρετοί] ὑποκου-φίζοντες and σμικρὰ διακουφίζοντες. Cf. also *Epid*. i. 2 and Case x; ἐκούφισεν ὀλίγῳ, Case vi: πάντων ἐκουφίσθη, *Int*. 53, *Morb*. iii, 15, 16, Thphr. *Sens*. 45: ἀνακουφίζεσθαι τῆς λύπης, Aret. ii. 8. 9: ἀνεκουφίσθησαν. The word ἀνακούφισις occurs only here in S. See D. L. Page's note (*Euripides, Medea*, Oxford, 1938) on E. *Med*. 473 (cf. Arist. *Prob*. 894ᵃ. 23). For lists and discussion of Hippocratic "technical terms" in S. see H. W. Miller, "Medical Terminology in Tragedy," *TAPhA*, 75 (1944) 156-67. Euripides uses ἀποκουφίζειν in a similar sense;

cf. *Hec.* 104: παθέων ἀποκουφίζουσ' *Or.* 43: ὅταν μὲν σῶμα κουφισθῇ νόσου (cf. ibid. 218).

Two other words in the opening lines of the priest's speech have medical connotations. σαλεύειν (cf. *O. T.* 23) is used to describe the gait of people with malformed hip joints ("rolling") in Hp. *Art.* 56 and Plato (*Lg.* 923b) speaks of people "rolling" (σαλεύοντας) "in disease or old age." For γέμειν cf. Arist. *Prob.* (ἰατρικά) 861a: τὰ δὲ κάτω πολλῆς γέμει περιττώσεως καὶ εὐσήπτου, and Hp. *Flat.* 10: ὅταν αἱ . . . φλέβες γεμισθῶσιν ἠέρος.

103. Cf. Hp. *Epid.* ii. 5. 6, *Aph.* v. 59, *Aer.* 22; Arist. *GA.* 726ª. 9; Thphr. *Od.* 62. The word does not occur in Aeschylus.

104. Cf. Hp. *de Arte* 8, *Fract.* 3, *Art.* 9, *Medic.* 14, *Decent.* 11.

105. For ἴασις cf. Hp. *de Arte* 6, *Aer.* 22 (ἐν ταύτῃ τῇ ἰήσει, "in this method of treatment"), *Decent.* 9, *Morb. Sacr.* 1, 2, etc., *Int.* 26, and see Miller's article referred to above.

106. This is a very common word in the doctors; cf. Hp. *Epid.* iii. 1 γ', *Acut.* 54, *Epid.* i. 26 η', *Aph.* ii 13, *Liqu.* 1, etc.

107. Hp. *Prog.* 24: ἄρχονται μὲν πονεῖσθαι τριταῖοι, χειμάζονται δὲ μάλιστα πεμπταῖοι. Cf. S. *Ichneutae* 267: ἰσχὺς ἐν νόσῳ χειμάζεται where see Pearson's note. Creon's word πλησιαζόντων (91), which occurs only here in S., is frequent in medical contexts; cf. Hp. *Acut.* 41, and Arist. *Prob.* vii. 887a: ὀφθαλμίας καὶ ψώρας οἱ πλησιάζοντες . . . ὁ πλησιάζων τοιοῦτον ἀναπνεῖ. Creon's use of ἀρωγός in 127 recalls the frequent occurrence of ἀρήγειν, used to describe the doctor's action, in the Hippocratic writings: cf. Hp. *Aer.* 10, (ἀρωγά), *Acut.* 29, 41, 60, 65, 67, *Art.* 16, and also Pl. *Lg.* 919c: νόσου . . . ἀρωγή.

108. Cf. Hp. *Morb. Sacr.* 14, *Morb.* ii. 66, iii. 7, *V. M.* 19, *V. C.* 15, etc., and φλόγωσις in Th. ii. 48. D. L. Page, in his article "Thucydides' Description of the Great Plague," *CQ,* 47 (1953), 97-119, has established the fact that this description "is expressed in the standard terms of contemporary medical science." Cf. also *Aret.* i. 7. 4, iv. 2. 2: πυριφλεγέες δίψαι.

109. Cf. Hp. *Art.* 48, Arist. *Prob* i (ἰατρικά). 865ᵃ, *PA.* iii. 9. 672ᵃ: ὀδύναι θανατηφόροι. The chorus also uses the words ἀλεξίμοροι (163) and ἀλέξεται (171), which recall Prometheus' word for the function of medicine (*P. V.* 479: οὐκ ἦν ἀλέξημ' οὐδὲν). Cf. also Hp. *Salubr.* 1: ἀλέξασθαι, *Acut.* 54: ἀλεξητήρια, *Mul.* ii, 212: ἀλέξημα, A. R., ii. 519: λοιμοῦ ἀλεξητῆρα, and the title of Nicander's treatise: ἀλεξιφάρμακα.

110. Cf. Hp. *Fract.* 27 ἕλκος . . . μέλαν ἐπὶ πολὺ ἢ ἀκάθαρτον, *Epid.* vi. 3, 1, *Aer.* 6 (of "impure" air), *Morb.* ii. 16, 41, 43, iii. 16, *Aff.* 38. This word is found nowhere else in tragedy except in the *Oedipus* of Achaeus (Nauck, Fr. 30) where Hesychius says it means μανιώδες. For ἀκάθαρτον . . . ἐᾶν cf. Hp. *Ulc.* 1: ἀνεπίδετον . . . ἐᾶν, *Haem.* 2: ἐᾶσαι ἄκαυστον.

111. Cf. especially πάθημα, 554 (cf. 1240). This is a common Hippocratic term (cf. e. g. Hp. *V. M.* 2, 14, 22, 23, *Prog.* 1, etc.) which does not occur in Aeschylus, and which S. uses in the *Philoctetes* in the medical sense (cf. 193). The word ἀποκρίνας (640) occurs nowhere else in S. and does not occur at all in A. It is common in the Hippocratic writings (although usually in the passive), in the sense required by the context here—"to separate out"; cf. Hp. *Morb. Sacr.* 1 13, 21, *Prog.* 23, *V. M.* 14, 16, *Aer.* 6, 9, etc. and Th. ii. 49. Page (1) 107 comments: "This verb is a standard technical term in the doctors, especially signifying the secession of an element from a compound, of a unit from a plurality."

112. Cf. Hp. *Aer.* 4. Also ibid. 7: τὰς τοιαύτας φύσιας οὐκ οἷόν τε μακροβίους εἶναι . . . ταῦτα δὲ τὰ νοσεύματα μηκυνθέντα τὰς τοιαύτας φύσιας ἐς ὕδρωπας καθίστησι.

113. For κομίζειν cf. Hp. *Morb.* ii. 71: πρὸς τὴν αἰθρίην κομίζειν, "move the patient into the open air"; *Epid.* iv. 3: ἀπὸ πυλέων μετακομισθεὶς παρ' ἀγορήν.

114. Cf. Hp. *Medic.* 1: πρὸς δὲ ἰητρὸν οὐ μικρὰ συναλλάγματα τοῖς νοσέουσιν ἐστιν. Jones (2, 213) translates this: "intimacy between physician and patient is close."

115. 961: σμικρὰ παλαιὰ σώματ' εὐνάζει ῥοπή. For ῥοπή cf. Hp. *Epid* i. 26: ῥοπὰς ἐπὶ τὸ ἄμεινον ἢ τὸ χεῖρον, *Epid*. i. 24 and ii. 1.6 (ῥέπειν), Gal. on Hp. *Prog.* i. 14 (59): μικρά τις . . . ῥοπή, *idem, de vict. acut.* iv. 78 (856): βραχεῖαν . . . ῥοπήν, Arist *Prob.* i (ἰατρικά). 861a (discussing the aged): μικρᾶς . . . ῥοπῆς. Aret. iii. 12 is an almost exact parallel: κοτὲ καὶ γέροντες ἁλῶναι ῥηΐδιοι καὶ ἀπόφρικτοι ἁλόντες ὅσον βραχείης ῥοπῆς ἐς εὐνὴν θανάτου χρέος. For εὐνάζω cf. E. *Or.* 151: χρόνια γὰρ πεσὼν . . . εὐνάζεται.

116. Hp. *Epid.* i. 11: προλέγειν τὰ ἐσόμενα. μελετᾶν ταῦτα. Cf. also Prog. 1: προγινώσκων γὰρ καὶ προλέγων, ibid. 23, *V. C.* 19, *Fract.* 35, *Art.* 13, Prorrh. ii. 7.

117. Hp. *Prog.* 1: πρόνοιαν ἐπιτηδεύειν. Cf. ibid.: τὴν πρόνοιαν ἐκμανθάνειν, *de Arte* 6. See Galen on Hp. *Prog.* I. 4 for a discussion of πρόνοια in Hippocrates and its antithesis to τύχη.

118. *Loc. Hom.* 46 (Littré, vol. 6). Since I have not seen this brilliant passage quoted elsewhere, I quote the Greek text in full: Βέβηκε γὰρ ἰητρικὴ πᾶσα, καὶ φαίνεται τῶν σοφισμάτων τὰ κάλλιστα ἐν αὐτῇ συγκείμενα ἐλάχιστα τύχης δεῖσθαι. ἡ γὰρ τύχη αὐτοκρατὴς καὶ οὐκ ἄρχεται . . . ἡ δὲ ἐπιστήμη ἄρχεταί τε καὶ εὐτυχής ἐστιν ὁπόταν βούληται ὁ ἐπιστάμενος χρῆσθαι. Ἔπειτα τί καὶ δεῖται ἰητρικὴ τύχης; εἰ μὲν γὰρ ἐστι τῶν νοσημάτων φάρμακα σαφῆ, οὐκ ἐπιμένει τὴν τύχην τὰ φάρμακα ὑγιᾶ ποιῆσαι τὰ νοσήματα. . . . The whole of this chapter in this little-known work is an extraordinarily clear and dignified statement of the empirical attitude of the Ionian physicians.

119. Hp. *de Arte* 4: ἐγὼ δὲ οὐκ ἀποστερέω μὲν οὐδ' αὐτὸς τὴν τύχην ἔργου οὐδενός. ἡγεῦμαι δὲ τοῖσι μὲν κακῶς θεραπευομένοισι νοσήμασι τὰ πολλὰ τὴν ἀτυχίην ἕπεσθαι, τοῖσι δὲ εὖ, τὴν εὐτυχίην.

120. Ibid. 4: τὸ μὲν γὰρ τῆς τύχης εἶδος ψιλὸν οὐκ ἐβουλήθησαν θεήσασθαι. . . .

121. εἰκῆ only here in S.; in A. only in P.V. 450 (v. infra) and 885. Some of its connotations are illustrated by the following examples: Ar. Nu. 43-4, the easy, unorganized (and dirty) life of the countryman, ἄγροικος . . . βίος . . . ἀκόρητος,

εἰκῇ κείμενος. Arist. *Metaph.* A3, 984ᵇ. 17, Anaxagoras seemed like a sober man among drunken babblers, νήφων ἐφάνη παρ' εἰκῇ λέγοντας. Heraclitus (Diels-Kranz B. 124), the universe a dust-heap piled up at random, ὥσπερ σάρμα εἰκῇ κεχυμένων ὁ κάλλιστος . . . κόσμος. Pl. *Phlb.* 28d a universe governed by irrational chance, πότερον . . . τὰ σύμπαντα καὶ τόδε·τὸ ὅλον καλούμενον ἐπιτροπεύειν φῶμεν τὴν τοῦ ἀλόγου καὶ εἰκῇ δύναμιν καὶ τὸ ὅπη ἔτυχεν ἢ τἀναντία . . . νοῦν καὶ φρόνησίν τινα . . . ; Aeschin. 3, 187 εἰκῇ opposed to ἀκριβῶς. For the line as a whole cf. E. *El.* 379.

122. Hp. *Epid.* i. 19: οἱ εἰκῇ καὶ ἐπὶ τὸ ῥᾴθυμον βεβιωκότες. In *Epid.* vii. 9 (quoted by Liddell and Scott) εἰκῇ is an emendation for ἐκεῖ (v. Littré ad loc.).

123. 1075: τῆς σιωπῆς τῆσδ'. A real silence surely, not the "silence" of Jocasta's last speech ("reticence" says Jebb in the note ad loc.) and see Carlo Diano, "Edipo figlio della Tyche," *Dioniso, 15* (1952) 56-89. Earle understands "the silence implied in ἄλλο . . . ὕστερον." For the Sophoclean use of dramatic silences compare the first speech of Philoctetes. There are surely pauses (and certainly a failure to answer on the part of the chorus and Neoptolemus) after each of his appeals to them to say something. This is shown by the climactic progress of his requests for an answer: φωνῆς δ' ἀκοῦσαι βούλομαι (225), φωνήσατ' (229), ἀλλ' ἀνταμείψασθ' (230).

124. Cf. Arist. *Mir.* 846ᵃ: τῶν ἐν Αἴτνῃ κρατήρων ἀναρραγέντων *Met.* 386ᵃ: ὕδατα ἀνερράγη γιγνομένων σεισμῶν.

125. Hp. *Fract.* 11: ὀχλώδεα καὶ πολλάκις ἀναρρηγνύμενα . . . , *Flat.* 7: ἀὴρ ὁκόταν ἀναρρήξῃ τὰς πομφόλυγας, ibid. 10: τὸ φλέγμα . . . ἀναρρηγνύει τὰς φλέβας, ibid.: διὰ τί δήποτε τὸ ῥεῦμα ἀναρρήγνυται, ibid.: τὸ αἷμα . . . ἀναρρηγνύει τοὺς πόρους. Cf. ibid. 11: τὰ . . . ῥήγματα, *Morb.* i. 21: ἀναρρήγνυται. The simple verb ῥηγνύειν and other compounds are very common in the Hippocratic texts, often applied to the "bursting" of an infection: e. g. *Epid.* ii. 2. 5, ibid. 3. 3, *Int.* 1: ῥαγῇ . . . συρραγέωσιν . . . καταρ-

ρήγνυνται . . . ἀνάρρηξις, ibid. 8: ἀναρράγῃ, ἀναρρήγνυται, 18: ὀδύνη
. . . ῥαγεῖσα, *Prorrh.* ii. 7, etc. ἐκρήγνυμι (which Jebb cites as a
parallel for his interpretation of the metaphor as drawn from
the storm) is also common in the medical texts: cf. *Epid.* i. 5:
λημία . . . ἐκρηγνύμενα, Hdt. iii. 133: φῦμα . . . ἐκραγέν (cf. Hp.
Aph. iv. 82, *Fist.* 1, Hp. *Morb.* ii. 31, 47, *Int.* 32).

126. μυδώσας (1278) is a medical term (see Miller's article and
references there, to which add Hp. *V. C.* 15: σάρκα . . . μυδῶσαν,
ibid. 21, and idem, *Ulc.* 10). For σταγών (only here in S.)
cf. Hp. *Flat.* 8 and for χάλαζα (1279) cf. Hp. *Morb.* ii. 49.

127. Jebb's text.

128. 1293: τὸ γὰρ νόσημα μεῖζον ἢ φέρειν. Cf. Hp. *Prog.* vi:
φέροντα τὸ νόσημα, ibid. 9, 15, *Int.* 12. νόσημα (which occurs
also at 307) is, according to Page (1), a more specific term in
the doctors than νόσος: ". . . most often used when a particular
malady is under consideration. It is noticeable that the word
occurs in Thucydides only with reference to the plague."

129. φραγμός, Hp. *Flat.* 10 (cf. Arist. *PA* 672^b). Cf. also Hp.
Flat. 7: ἐμφραχθείσης . . . κοιλίης, *Aer.* 9: ὁ στόμαχος . . . συμ-
πέφρακται, *Int.* 13: ἀποφραχθῇ. For ἀποκλῆσαι cf. Hp. *Art.* 11:
ἀποκλείουσι γὰρ τῆς ἄνω εὐρυχωρίης τὴν κεφαλὴν τοῦ βραχίονος—
"they shut out the head of the humerus from the space above
it." He is speaking of cauteries. Cf. also ibid. 30: τῷ ὑπὸ τὸ οὖς
ὀστέῳ . . . ὅπερ ἀποκλείει τὰς κεφαλὰς τῆς κάτω γνάθου. For metaphorical use of this word in the doctors cf. Hp. *Vict.* iii. 81,
Int. 1, *Off.* 24, Gal. *Mixt.* iii. 687. For πηγῆς (1387) cf. Hp.
Flat. 7 πηγαὶ . . . τοῦ αἵματος, Gal. on Hp. *Prog.* 164.

130. For metaphorical use of ὕπουλος in Attic see Jebb ad loc.;
for medical usage cf. Hp. *Medic.* 11, Arist. *Prob.* i. 863^a, Pl. *Ti.*
72d, Plu. *De san. tuend.* 137c, Gal. *Vict. Att.* 1. 2.

131. Additional instances of words with medical connotations:
φρίκη, 1306. (Not in A., in S. only here and Fr. 875.) For
medical contexts see Liddell and Scott and add Hp. *Flat.* 7, 8,

Int. 38, 48 etc., *Morb.* iii. 16. ὀχλεῖς, 446. (Only here in S., in A. only at *P. V.* 1001.) Its collocation with ἀλγύναις (446) suggests a medical metaphor here; ὀχλεῖν and ὀχλωδής occur frequently in Hp. *Fract.* in the sense of "trouble, irritate, troublesome" (e. g. 7, 11, 13, 18, 31; οὐδὲν δεῖ μάτην ὀχλεῖν καὶ ὀχλεῖσθαι. See also medical references in Liddell and Scott s.v.). ἐπίκουρος, 497. ἐπικουρίη is used in Hp. *de Arte* 8 with the meaning "treatment, aid"; cf. also E. *Or.* 211: ἐπίκουρον νόσου, and X. *Mem.* i. 4. 13: νόσοις ἐπικουρῆσαι. The word is common in the later medical writers. Jocasta's phrase ἄρθρα . . . ποδοῖν (718, cf. 1032) is medically exact; cf. Hp. *Art.* 62, 63.

132. Aesch. *P. V.* 59-60: καὶ μὴν ἀριθμόν, ἔξοχον σοφισμάτων ἐξηῦρον αὐτοῖς.

133. S. Fr. 432: οὗτος ἐφηῦρε . . . σταθμῶν ἀριθμῶν καὶ μέτρων εὑρήματα . . . ἔτευξε πρῶτος ἐξ ἑνὸς δέκα κἀκ τῶν δέκ' αὖθις ηὗρε πεντηκοντάδας, ὃς χίλι' εὐθύς. . . . Cf. Gorg. *Pal.* 30: εὑρὼν . . . ἀριθμόν τε χρημάτων φύλακα.

134. Diels-Kranz, Philolaus B4: πάντα γα μὰν τὰ γιγνωσκόμενα ἀριθμὸν ἔχοντι· οὐ γὰρ οἷόν τε οὐδὲν οὔτε νοηθῆμεν οὔτε γνωσθῆμεν ἄνευ τούτου. The translation is Kathleen Freeman's (2), p. 74. Cf. the (forged) Epicharmus fragment, Diels-Kranz, B56: ὁ βίος ἀνθρώποις λογισμοῦ κἀριθμοῦ δεῖται πάνυ· ζῶμεν [δὲ] ἀριθμῷ καὶ λογισμῷ· ταῦτα γὰρ σῴζει βροτούς.

135. Arist. *Top.* 6. 142ᵇ: εἴ τις τὸν ἄνθρωπον ὁρίσαιτο τὸ ἐπιστάμενον ἀριθμεῖν.

136. Pl. *Grg.* 508a: ἡ ἰσότης ἡ γεωμετρικὴ καὶ ἐν θεοῖς καὶ ἐν ἀνθρώποις μέγα δύναται.

137. E. *Ph.* 541-2: καὶ γὰρ μέτρ' ἀνθρώποισι καὶ μέρη σταθμῶν ἰσότης ἔταξε κἀριθμὸν διώρισε. Jocasta, in this great speech, is of course really concerned with political equality, but the reference in these lines is clearly to the mathematical concept. For a mathematical definition of equality see Nicom. *Ar.* p. 44, 13 ff.

138. A typical example is Diophantus vi. α. ἐὰν οὖν ϳᾱ↑Μ̄β̄ ἰσώσωμεν κύβῳ, λύσομεν τὸ ζητούμενον. The words ἰσοῦν and ἐξισοῦν are not used by A., and in S. they are found, outside the O.T., only in the *Electra* (ἰσοῦν: 686; ἐξισοῦν: 738, 1072, 1194). For examples of these words used in a mathematical sense by nonmathematical authors cf. Hdt. ii. 34, Pl. *Phdr.* 239a: οὔτε δὴ κρείττω οὔτε ἰσούμενον, *Prm.* 156b: αὐξάνεσθαι τε καὶ φθίνειν καὶ ἰσοῦσθαι (cf. 157b), ibid. 144e. ἐξισοῦσθον δύο ὄντε. The words ἴσος, ἰσοῦν, etc. occur with extraordinary freqency in the O.T. (cf., in addition to the many passages quoted below), 611, 627, 677, 810, 1347, 1498.

139. This is Jebb's literal translation in the note on 84. For συμμετρέω cf. also 963.

140. It has even been compared, by Sigmund Freud, to the process of psychoanalysis (*Interpretation of Dreams*, chap. 5, p. 307): ". . . the disclosure, approached step by step and artistically delayed (and comparable to the work of a psychoanalysis). . . ."

141. This atmosphere is emphasized by the profusion of numerical phrases in the play; every character is at great pains to be arithmetically precise. Cf. (in addition to the passages discussed below) εἷς: 62, 122, 247, 281, 374, 615, 748, 753, 846, 1335, 1380; δύο, etc.: 581, 640, 1280, 1373, 1505; τρεῖς: 718, 1136, 1398; πέντε: 752; ἐκμήνους: 1137; ἁπλοῦς: 519, 606; διπλοῦς: 20, 809, 938, 1135, 1249, 1257, 1261, 1320 (twice); δεύτερος: 282; τριπλοῦς: 716, 730, 800, 1399; τρίτος: 283, 581, 1062; τρισσοί: 163; τρίδουλος: 1063; πολλάκις τε κοὐχ ἅπαξ: 1275; τὸν αὐτὸν ἀριθμόν: 844. προσθήκη θεοῦ (38) seems to be colored by the same metaphorical context; προστιθέναι is the normal term for the operation of addition; cf. Thgn. 809, Zeno, (Diels-Kranz A21), Hdt. vii, 184, Pl. *R.* vii. 527a ff., *Phd.* 96e, etc. For προσθήκη itself cf. Iamb. *Comm. Math.* xxx. p. 92. 9. προσθήκη only here in S. In A. *A.* 500 it seems to mean "addition" (so translated by Paley and accepted by Fraenkel). Cf.

Pl. *R*. i. 339b, *Lg*. iii. 696e. *O. T*. 232: χή χάρις προσκείσεται—
"will be added"—gives us a passive of προστιθέναι.

142. For ἀνάριθμος in a "scientific" context cf. Melissos (Diels-
Kranz, A. 5, 976a 30): τί κωλύει πολλὰ καὶ ἀνάριθμα τοιαῦτα
εἶναι;

143. I believe (with Jebb) that "the vulgate is sound"; not
only sound but magnificent. See Pearson (3) for his defense
of his adoption of Wilamowitz' ὅσ' ἐξισώσεις.

144. For λογίζομαι as a mathematical term cf. Pl. *Men*. 82d:
Πόσοι οὖν εἰσιν οἱ δύο δὶς πόδες; λογισάμενος εἰπέ. Hdt. ii. 36:
λογίζονται ψήφοισι Ἕλληνες μὲν ἀπὸ τῶν ἀριστερῶν ἐπὶ τὰ δεξιὰ,
ibid. 16, i. 137, Plato, *Lg*. 817e: λογισμοὶ μὲν καὶ τὰ περὶ ἀριθμούς,
Euthphr. 7b, Ar. *Ach*. 31, *Nu*. 20. For ψεύδεσθαι in a mathematical sense cf. Arist. *Phys*. A. 185ª: ὅσα ἐκ τῶν ἀρχῶν τις
ἐπιδεικνὺς ψεύδεται.

145. For διώρισαν cf. the Euripides passage quoted above (n.
137). S. uses the word only here and 1083 of this play. Aeschylus uses it only in *P. V*. (440, 489) and the lost *Palamedes*
(Nauck 182). It is a central word of the new scientific vocabulary. διορισμός later appears as a technical term in Euclidean
geometry (see Liddell and Scott). For διορίζω in mathematical
writings cf. Iamb. *Comm. Math*. p. 12. 3, 19. 7, 36. 14 etc. The
word ξύμπαντες (752 and 813) is a form of πᾶς which in later
mathematical writers is used to denote a total.

146. For ἐκμετρεῖν cf. Hero *Metr*. ii. 20. Idem, *Dioptr*. 34-5 is
concerned with the mensuration of large distances over land
(34) and over land and sea (35). A typical formula is as
follows (35): δέον δὲ ἔστω . . . τὴν μεταξὺ Ἀλεξανδρείας καὶ
Ῥώμης ὁδὸν ἐκμετρῆσαι. The method employed in this case is
based on the observation of a lunar eclipse.

147. Creon (122) said λῃστὰς and Oedipus (124) corrected
him: πῶς οὖν ὁ λῃστής . . . ;

Notes for CHAPTER THREE: MAN

148. 845: οὐ γὰρ γένοιτ' ἂν εἰς γε τοῖς πολλοῖς ἴσος. Cf. Diels-Kranz, Democritus A37, 20 (Simplicius quoting Aristotle on Democritus): κομιδῇ γὰρ εὔηθες εἶναι τὸ δύο ἢ τὰ πλείονα γένεσθαι ἄν ποτε ἕν. Ibid. Xenophanes (A28. 977ᵇ.7): τὸ δὲ ἓν οὔτε τῷ οὐκ ὄντι οὔτε τοῖς πολλοῖς ὠμοιῶσθαι, 977ᵇ.17, οὔτε γὰρ τῷ μὴ ὄντι οὔτε τοῖς πολλοῖς ὅμοιον εἶναι. Melissos A5. 974ᵃ. 21: κατὰ πάντα γὰρ ταῦτα πολλά τε τὸ ἓν γίγνεσθαι καὶ τὸ μὴ ὂν τεκνοῦσθαι . . . ταῦτα δὲ ἀδύνατα εἶναι. The Sophoclean line is perhaps parodied in Ar. Nu. 1181-2: οὐ γὰρ ἔσθ' ὅπως / μί' ἡμέρα γένοιτ' ἂν ἡμέρα δύο.

149. For the meaning of these words see Chap. 1, n. 96 above.

150. Jebb takes ἴσως in its common sense of "perhaps," but the obsessive repetition of ἴσος and similar words throughout the play suggests the literal meaning here. And in any case it makes better dramatic sense. Why should the messenger announce the death of Oedipus' father to Jocasta with such a preface as "You will certainly rejoice—and you might perhaps feel grief"? It may be a true estimate but it is hardly a tactful expression, and the messenger is a man who is looking for a reward (cf. 1005-6).

151. Jocasta's question and the messenger's answer (943-4) have been the subject of many attempts to remove the ἀντιλαβή in 943. LA recc. read:

943　Ιο.　πῶς εἶπας; ἢ τέθνηκε Πόλυβος; Αγγ. εἰ δὲ μὴ
944　λέγω γ' ἐγὼ τἀληθές, ἀξιῶ θανεῖν.

For 944 some of the recc. give the following variations: εἰ μὴ λέγω τἀληθὲς, εἰ δὲ μὴ λέγω, εἰ μὴ λέγω γ' ἐγώ. Most editors have suppressed the messenger's εἰ δὲ μὴ in 943 and substituted a phrase which they attribute to Jocasta: ὦ γέρον (Bothe, accepted by Jebb), or (with the suppression of Πόλυβος), Οἰδίπου πατήρ (Nauck). But surely this violent and sudden ἀντιλαβή is precisely what we should expect from Sophocles at this moment of high excitement. "Par cette coupe extraordinaire," says Masqueray (p. xxviii), "Sophocle . . . marque le violent émoi de Jocaste." Masqueray prints the reading of LA recc. A better solution would perhaps be to combine the reading of LA recc. for 943 with one of the variant readings for 944:

Ιο. πῶς εἶπας; ἢ τέθνηκε Πόλυβος; Αγγ. εἰ δὲ μὴ
εἰ μὴ λέγω τἀληθές, ἀξιῶ θανεῖν.

Such a repetition (εἰ δὲ μὴ, εἰ μὴ) is characteristic of excited emphatic protestation. Compare Pythonicus' denunciation of Alcibiades' parody of the mysteries quoted by Andocides (i. 11): Θεράπων ὑμῖν ἑνὸς ἐνθάδε ἀνδρῶν ἀμύητος ὢν ἐρεῖ τὰ μυστήρια (a statement that must have been greeted with expressions of incredulous surprise, like Jocasta's πῶς εἶπας;)—εἰ δὲ μὴ, χρῆσθέ μοι ὅ τι ἂν ὑμῖν δοκῇ, ἐὰν μὴ τἀληθῆ λέγω. The ending εἰ δὲ μὴ and the beginning of the next line εἰ μὴ might easily have given rise to the unmetrical εἰ δὲ μὴ λέγω found in some of the recc.; the version of LA recc. (λέγω γ' ἐγώ, etc.) may be a later attempt to restore the meter.

152. εἰκῇ, "at random," describes a state of affairs unacceptable to the mathematician above all others. Cf. Cebes, Tabula (7): [τύχη] . . . εἰκῇ δίδωσιν (31) οὐδὲν γὰρ ποιεῖ μετὰ λογισμοῦ ἀλλ' εἰκῇ καὶ ὡς ἔτυχε πάντα. Iamb. In Nic. 23: οὐκ εἰκῇ παρὰ τοῦ τυχόντος λαβόντες τῷ τυχόντι ἀποδώσομεν, ἀλλὰ κατὰ τὴν αὐτὴν ἀναλογίαν, γνώμονι χρώμενοι καὶ οἷον κανόνι. . . .

153. For οὐδὲν as "zero" cf. Nicom. Ar. ii. 6. 3: ὥσπερ εἴ τις τὸ οὐδὲν οὐδενὶ συντεθὲν σκέπτοιτο, οὐδὲν γὰρ ποιεῖ . . . Iamb. In Nic. 24: ἀπὸ δὲ τοῦ πέντε ἀφελόντες οὐδὲν . . . τοῦ γὰρ δύο καὶ τοῦ οὐδὲν ἥμισυ τὸ ἕν (25) οὐδενάκι θ' οὐδὲν. And see O. T. 1187: ἴσα καὶ τὸ μηδὲν. . . .

154. And, as Earle (on 1447, τῆς μὲν κατ' οἴκους) points out, "Oedipus has no name for Jocasta."

155. μῆνες with μικρὸν καὶ μέγαν suggests an implicit comparison between the fortunes of Oedipus and the waning and waxing of the moon. For a similar comparison made explicit cf. S. Fr. 871. For the expression μικρὸν καὶ μέγαν cf. Pl. Epin. 978d: τὴν σελήνην . . . ἢ τοτὲ μὲν μείζων φαινομένη, τοτὲ δὲ ἐλάττων. . . .

156. Literally, "to weigh." This is the third of the triad ἀριθμός, μέτρα, σταθμά, for which see X. *Smp.* iv. 43, 45, Hp. *V. M.* 9, Pl. *Lg.* vi. 757b, and the Palamedes references in n. 133 above.

NOTES FOR CHAPTER FOUR: GOD

1. ὡς γὰρ ἐπὶ θεοῦ βωμοὺς πάρεισιν ἐπὶ τοὺς πρὸ τῶν βασιλείων ἱδρυμένους.

2. See Earle ad loc.

3. See W. Ax, "Die Parodos des Oidipus Tyrannos," *Hermes*, 67 (1932) 413-37, especially 421: "Die Liturgische Form des Inhalts."

4. 216-18: αἰτεῖς· ἃ δ' αἰτεῖς . . . λάβοις ἄν. For the religious connotations of αἰτεῖν cf. Euthyphro's definition of prayer (Pl. *Euthphr.* 14c): τὸ δ' εὔχεσθαι αἰτεῖν τοὺς θεούς.

5. Hdt. i. 66.: ἡ δὲ Πυθίη σφι χρᾷ τάδε. 'Αρκαδίην μ' αἰτεῖς; μέγα μ' αἰτεῖς· οὔ τοι δώσω. Eus. *P.E.*, 5, 27: ἥκεις δ' εὐνομίην αἰτεύμενος· αὐτὰρ ἐγώ τοι δώσω. Cf. the oracles supposed to have been given to Laius (*O. T. Hypothesis* iii, Anth. Pal. xiv. 67): Λάιε Λαβδακίδη παίδων γένος ὄλβιον αἰτεῖς, and to Alcmaeon (*Ath.* vi. 232 f.): τιμῆέν μ' αἰτεῖς δῶρον. . . . Cf. also P. *Isthm.* 6.52.

6. Pl. *R.* viii. 568b: ἰσόθεον . . . τυραννίδα, ibid. ii. 360c: ἐν τοῖς ἀνθρώποις ἰσόθεον ὄντα. Cf. also Pl. *Phdr.* 258c: βασιλεὺς . . . ἆρ' οὐκ ἰσόθεον ἡγεῖται αὐτός τε αὐτὸν ἔτι ζῶν; E. *Tr.* 1169: ἰσοθέου τυραννίδος.

7. It appears in the summary of Pericles' financial report (ii. 13, 5) but in a reference to the removable gold on the statue of the goddess Athena, which Pericles tells the Athenians they can make use of if other sources of revenue run short: αὐτῆς

τῆς θεοῦ τοῖς περικειμένοις χρυσίοις. In striking contrast to the absence of the word θεός from the Periclean speeches is its frequent occurrence in the speeches attributed to the Spartans (e. g. Brasidas iv. 87, Archidamus ii. 74, Sthenelaidas i. 86), the Plataeans (iii. 58, 59, ii. 71), the Corinthians (i. 71, 123), the Boeotians (Pagondas iv. 92), and Nicias (vii. 69, 77). On the other hand, the word is never attributed to Cleon, Diodotus, or Alcibiades.

8. Th. ii. 41. Pericles speaks of his praise of Athens as a ὕμνος: ibid. 42: ἃ γὰρ τὴν πόλιν ὕμνησα. . . .

9. Cf. Eupolis, Fr. 117 (Δῆμοι) 6 ff.: ἀλλ᾽ ἦσαν ἡμῖν τῇ πόλει πρῶτον μὲν οἱ στρατηγοὶ ἐκ τῶν μεγίστων οἰκιῶν πλούτῳ γένει τε πρῶτοι, οἷς ὡσπερεὶ θεοῖσιν ηὐχόμεσθα· καὶ γὰρ ἦσαν.

10. Hp. Aph. 1: ὁ βίος βραχύς, ἡ δὲ τέχνη μακρή. Diels-Kranz, Protagoras B4: βραχὺς ὢν ὁ βίος τοῦ ἀνθρώπου.

11. Pl. Tht. 162d: θεούς τε εἰς τὸ μέσον ἄγοντες, οὓς ἐγὼ ἔκ τε τοῦ λέγειν καὶ τοῦ γράφειν περὶ αὐτῶν ὡς εἰσὶν ἢ ὡς οὐκ εἰσίν, ἐξαιρῶ. This corresponds very well with the opening statement of Protagoras' book On the Gods; it is difficult to see how Plato could have squared this with the highly theological account of human progress which he attributes to the sophist in the Protagoras.

12. Hp. Decent. 5: ἰητρὸς γὰρ φιλόσοφος ἰσόθεος. Cf. Pl. Tht. 161c: ἡμεῖς μὲν αὐτὸν [sc. Protagoras] ὥσπερ θεὸν ἐθαυμάζομεν ἐπὶ σοφίᾳ.

13. Th. i. 140: τὴν τύχην ὅσα ἂν παρὰ λόγον ξυμβῇ εἰώθαμεν αἰτιᾶσθαι. Cf. Diels-Kranz, Democritus B119: ἄνθρωποι τύχης εἴδωλον ἐπλάσαντο πρόφασιν ἰδίης ἀβουλίης.

14. Th. ii. 61: τὸ αἰφνίδιον καὶ ἀπροσδόκητον καὶ τὸ πλείστῳ παραλόγῳ ξυμβαῖνον.

15. The word παράλογος (which expresses this characteristic of the events of the war) is very common in Th.; cf. ii. 61 (the

plague), ii. 85 (Phormio's victory), iii. 16 (the Athenian expedition against the Peloponnese), vii. 55 (the Athenian naval defeat at Syracuse), vii. 28 (the Athenian expedition against Sicily while under Peloponnesian attack), vii. 61 (Nicias reminds the Athenians of the unpredictability of war), viii. 24 (the miscalculations of the Chians).

16. E. *Alc.* 785-6, 788-9.

17. Idem, *H. F.* 1357: νῦν δ' ὡς ἔοικε τῇ τύχῃ δουλευτέον.

18. Idem, *Or.* 715-16: νῦν δ' ἀναγκαίως ἔχει, δούλοισιν εἶναι τοῖς σοφοῖσι τῆς τύχης. Menelaus is speaking of the impossibility of predicting the reaction of the Argive popular assembly, which he is about to address on behalf of Orestes.

19. Idem, *Tr.* 1203-5: αἱ τύχαι, ἔμπληκτος ὡς ἄνθρωπος. . . . Cf. Chaeremon Fr. 2 (Nauck²): τύχη τὰ θνητῶν πράγματ' οὐκ εὐβουλία.

20. E. *Ion.* 1512 ff.

21. The word τύχη does not of course occur in Homer (*h. Hom.* ii. 420 is certainly late). Its first appearance seems to be Archil. 8. Diehl³.

22. Cf. also Hdt. i. 126: θείῃ τύχῃ γεγονώς (Cyrus), Pl. *R.* ix. 592a, *Lg.* vi. 759c.

23. P. O. xii. 1-2. According to Pausanias (vii. 26. 8) Pindar stated also that Chance was one of the Fates (Μοιρῶν) and more powerful than her sisters.

24. Diehl, Fr. 44: Εὐνομίας ⟨τε⟩ καὶ Πειθῶς ἀδελφὰ καὶ Προμαθείας θυγάτηρ. (Tyche as sister of Peitho appears also in Hes. *Th.* 360; they are both daughters of Oceanus and Tethys). Pausanias (iv. 30) mentions a statue of Tyche made by Bupalus, who is usually assigned to the sixth century. Cf. Greene (1), p. 66.

25. E. *Cyc.* 603-7. The last two lines run; ἢ τὴν τύχην μὲν δαίμον'

ἡγεῖσθαι χρεών, τὰ δαιμόνων δὲ τῆς τύχης ἐλάσσονα. Cf. Nauck, adesp. 169: εἰ μὲν θεοὶ σθένουσιν, οὐκ ἐστιν τύχη. εἰ δ' οὐ σθένουσιν οὐδὲν, ἐστιν ἡ τύχη. (Nauck's comma after σθένουσιν in 2 makes nonsense of the lines, and G. Wolff's correction ἐστιν ἢ τύχη is unnecessary). Cf. also ibid adesp. 506, E. *Hec.* 488 ff., Fr. 901: εἴτε τύχα εἴτε δαίμων τὰ βρότεια κραίνει. . . .

26. Pl. *Lg.* 709a-b: τύχας δ' εἶναι σχεδὸν ἅπαντα τὰ ἀνθρώπινα πράγματα . . . θεὸς μὲν πάντα καὶ μετὰ θεοῦ τύχη καὶ καιρὸς τἀνθρώπινα διακυβερνῶσι σύμπαντα. For Pl. and θεία τύχη see references in n. 22 above.

27. W. S. Ferguson, "The Leading Ideas of the New Period," *CAH* VII (Cambridge Univ. Press) p. 2. He uses the phrase of the third century, but it applies equally well to the fourth; no better description can be found of the apathetic spirit against which Demosthenes wages so valiant a struggle. Cf. D. ii. 22 on τύχη and for the fourth-century Athenian "sense of drift" cf. D. iv. 10-11, 40-2.

28. This is clear from the comedies of Menander. On this subject cf. C. F. Angus, *CAH*, VII, pp. 226, 229, and (e. g.) Menander, Koerte-Thierfelder, 1959, Fr. 249, 296, 395, 420, 630, etc. Fr. 417 (from the *Hypobolimaeus*) reads like an expansion of Jocasta's speech; cf. especially 5-6 on πρόνοια.

29. Plb. xxix. 21: ἡ πρὸς τὸν βίον ἡμῶν ἀσύνθετος τύχη καὶ πάντα παρὰ τὸν λογισμὸν τὸν ἡμέτερον καινοποιοῦσα καὶ τὴν αὑτῆς δύναμιν ἐν τοῖς παραδόξοις ἐνδεικνυμένη. . . .

30. She was the patron goddess of Antioch in Hellenistic times. For lists and discussion of the cults of Tyche see L. Ruhl, "Tyche: Kult," in Roscher's *Lexikon*, 5, 1344-56.

31. This was written before I saw Werner Jaeger's *Theology of the Early Greek Philosophers*, in which he speaks (p. 174) of "the higher stage of the spiral cycle," and refers the reader to his 1943 Aquinas Lecture (in *Humanism and Theology*, p. 54) for his discussion of "the spiral as the most fitting symbol

of the historical development of Greek philosophical thought."
The "descending spiral" which I speak of is of course a symbol
not so much of the development of philosophical thought as of
the vulgar philosophical-religious feeling of the ordinary man;
the advances made by the philosophers in the fourth and third
centuries correspond to (and were an attempt to arrest) the
retreat from reason which was the dominant mood of the Greek
population at large.

32. According to Plutarch (*Per.* xxi) he led an expedition
against the Delphians and restored to the Athenians their προ-
μαντεία, the right to consult the oracle first. (For the interpretation "right of consulting the oracle on behalf of others
also" [B. Perrin, trans., *Plutarch's Lives*, London, Loeb Classical Library, 3 (1916), 65] see the discussion and bibliography
in How and Wells, *Commentary on Herodotus*, 1, p. 75.)

33. Plu. *Per.* viii: ἀθανάτους ἔλεγε γεγονέναι καθάπερ τοὺς θεούς·
οὐ γὰρ ἐκείνους αὐτοὺς ὁρῶμεν ἀλλὰ ταῖς τιμαῖς ἃς ἔχουσι καὶ τοῖς
ἀγαθοῖς ἃ παρέχουσιν ἀθανάτους εἶναι τεκμαιρόμεθα.

34. *O. T.* 387-9: μάγον . . . μηχανορράφον, δόλιον ἀγύρτην, ὅστις
ἐν τοῖς κέρδεσιν μόνον δέδορκε. . . . Some of these epithets are
found in the Hippocratic treatise *The Sacred Disease*, where
they are applied to quack doctors who claim magic powers of
healing and use incantations. Cf. especially 2: μάγοι τε καὶ
καθάρται καὶ ἀγύρται καὶ ἀλαζόνες, 3: περικαθαίρων . . . καὶ μαγεύων
. . . τοιαῦτα . . . μηχανώμενοι . . . 4: μαγεύων καὶ θύων . . . ἄνθρωποι
βίου δεόμενοι πολλὰ καὶ παντοῖα τεχνῶνται. Cf. also Pl. R. ii.
364b: ἀγύρται δὲ καὶ μάντεις. . . .

35. Cf. Hdt. ii. 133: ἐλθεῖν οἱ [i. e. Mycerinus] μαντήιον ἐκ
Βουτοῦς πόλιος, viii. 114: χρηστήριον ἐληλύθεε ἐκ Δελφῶν Λακε-
δαιμονίοισι. . . . Paus. ix. 5. 10: μάντευμα ἦλθεν ἐκ Δελφῶν. . . .

36. φῆμαι (723) is the proper word for this.

37. 853-4: ὅν γε Λοξίας διεῖπε χρῆναι παιδὸς ἐξ ἐμοῦ θανεῖν.

38. Jebb's commentary on this scene performs prodigies of subtlety in an attempt to defend the basic piety of Jocasta. "In 853 (ὅν γε Λοξίας διεῖπε)," he says in his note on 711, "the name of the god merely stands for that of his Delphian priesthood." With the word "merely" Jebb begs the question in truly Olympian fashion, for the distinction between the god and his Delphian priesthood is fundamental for his view of Jocasta's attitude. (See his note on 708: ". . . a deep and bitter conviction that no mortal, be he priest or seer, shares the divine foreknowledge.")

39. καλῶς νομίζεις, 859, immediately after her most general and far-reaching denunciation of prophecy.

40. 909: κοὐδαμοῦ τιμαῖς Ἀπόλλων ἐμφανής. Cf. the Periclean "proof" of the immortality of the gods: τοὺς θεοὺς . . . ταῖς τιμαῖς ἃς ἔχουσιν . . . ἀθανάτους εἶναι τεκμαιρόμεθα (Plu. Per. viii).

41. Cf. 922.

42. 919: ἄγχιστος γὰρ εἶ. Cf. Σ. πρὸ τῶν θυρῶν γὰρ ἵδρυτο.

43. Cf. 916: τὰ καινὰ τοῖς πάλαι. . . .

44. Jebb's note (on 946) to the effect that "Jocasta's scorn is pointed not at the gods themselves but at the μάντεις who profess to speak in their name" and his statement (note on 708) that "in 946, 953, θεῶν μαντεύματα are oracles which professed to come from the gods" will not hold water. Jocasta is talking about a prophecy which Oedipus attributes unequivocally to Apollo himself (788 ff.).

45. I read παρόντα with the MSS. Oedipus means that the "present" prophecies (i.e. the prophecies given to him by Apollo) are proved worthless by the natural death of Polybus, as worthless as the "old" prophecies given to Laius; he is talking in terms of Jocasta's distinction between τὰ καινά and τὰ πάλαι.

46. The same phrase (τὰ τῆς τύχης) is found in Th. iv. 55, 3.

Cf. ibid. 18.3: τὸ τῆς τύχης. It emphasizes the abstract, un personified nature of this conception of chance. Cf. E. *Alc.* 785: τὸ τῆς τύχης.

47. See Plato's definition of the province of prophecy, *Smp.* 188b: καὶ οἷς μαντικὴ ἐπιστατεῖ—ταῦτα δ' ἐστὶν ἡ περὶ θεούς τε καὶ ἀνθρώπους πρὸς ἀλλήλους κοινωνία. . . .

48. According to Simplicius on Arist. *Ph.* ii. 4, 75, Tyche and Loxias were both invoked at Delphi: ἐν Δελφοῖς δὲ καὶ προκατῆρχεν ἐν ταῖς ἐρωτήσεσιν ᾿Ω τύχη καὶ Λοξία, τῷ δέ τινι θεμιστεύεις ;

49. 263: νῦν δ' ἐς τὸ κείνου κρᾶτ ἐνήλαθ' ἡ τύχη. Cf. Poll. Γ 150: παγκράτιον . . . λὰξ ἐνάλλεσθαι. Plu. *Mor.* (*Non posse suaviter* . . .) 1087b: εἰς τὴν γαστέρα . . . ἐναλεῖσθαι, S. Fr. 756.

50. It depended on Jocasta's mentioning the nature of the place where Laius was killed; this she did not need to do, she "just happened" to mention it.

51. For this meaning cf. Andoc. i. 120: ἡ παῖς τύχῃ χρησαμένη ἀπέθανεν.

52. Cf. S. *El.* 498 ff.: ἤτοι μαντεῖαι βροτῶν οὐκ εἰσὶν ἐν δεινοῖς ὀνείροις οὐδ' ἐν θεσφάτοις, εἰ μὴ τόδε φάσμα νυκτὸς εὖ κατασχήσει. The Hippocratic author of *Vict.* iv takes dreams seriously as prophetic warnings and Aristotle's treatise *On Prophecy in Sleep* (*Parv. Nat.* 426b) begins its discussion of the subject as follows: "It is not easy to dismiss or accept the proposition" (οὔτε καταφρονῆσαι ῥάδιον οὔτε πεισθῆναι) and goes on to admit that "all or most people suppose that dreams have some significance" (ἔχειν τι σημειῶδες).

53. 986: κεἰ καλῶς λέγεις. Cf. his previous καλῶς νομίζεις, 859.

54. He expresses what is almost a wish that she were: ἀλλὰ τῆς ζώσης φόβος, 988.

55. 1080: παῖδα τῆς τύχης. Cf. E. Fr. 989: ὁ τῆς τύχης παῖς κλῆρος. According to Pausanias, there was at Thebes a temple of Tyche with a statue of the goddess carrying her son Ploutos

(ix. 1-2: Τύχης ἐστιν ἱερόν· φέρει μὲν δὴ Πλοῦτον παῖδα . . .
ἐσθεῖναι Πλοῦτον ἐς τὰς χεῖρας ἅτε μητρὶ ἢ τροφῷ τῇ Τύχῃ. Cf.
O. T. 1092). The sculptors were Xenophon the Athenian and
Callistonicus the Theban; the statue can thus be assigned to the
early fourth century, but the conception may well be based on
an old tradition (though Pausanias talks as though it were the
invention of the artists). For Oedipus and Ploutos cf. O. T.
380. Ruhl (in Roscher, Lexicon, 5, 1350) speaks of a "Relief
der Tyche von Melos mit dem Plutos Knaben."

56. 1081: τῆς εὖ διδούσης. For this religious formula cf. Pl. Cra.
404b: Δημήτηρ . . . διδοῦσα, Isoc. 4. 28: Δήμητρος . . . δούσης
δωρεὰς διττάς. . . . E. Alc. 1005: χαῖρ' ὦ πότνι' εὖ δὲ δοίης, idem
Or. 667.

57. μῆνες (1083) may be a reference to the connection between
Tyche and the moon: cf. Roscher, Lexikon, 5, 1330 (CIG
7304), a gem inscribed Τροφίμου. Σελήνη τύχη[ν] [κ]υβερν[ω]σα.
Cf. ibid. 1331 for a discussion of the later identification of
Tyche and Selene (Luna). Strabo (xii. 3. 31) speaks of the
so-called "royal oath" in Pontus, at the temple of the men of
Pharnaces—τύχην βασιλέως καὶ Μῆνα Φαρνάκου—and adds "this
is also the temple of Selene." The scholium on E. Phoen. 26
adds an interesting piece of information: ἔνιοι δὲ καὶ Ἡλίου φασιν
αὐτὸν [i. e. Oedipus] εἶναι παῖδα.

58. On the dramatic motivation of this choral ode see M. Bowra,
Sophoclean Tragedy (Oxford, 1944), p. 199.

59. The enthusiasm of the chorus and also their complete
commitment to the cause of Oedipus are indicated by their
announcement that they will dance (χορεύεσθαι, 1093); before
this scene began they were asking, "Why should I dance?,"
τί δεῖ με χορεύειν; (896). If Oedipus had turned out to be the
son of a god and a nymph, he might have been classed as a
daimon. Cf. Pl. Ap. 27d: εἰ δ' αὖ οἱ δαίμονες θεῶν παῖδές εἰσιν
νόθοι τινες ἢ ἔκ νυμφῶν ἢ ἐκ τινων ἄλλων. . . .

60. I read τεκὼν in 1025 with the MSS. Oedipus fears that the

Corinthian may have been his father; the messenger's enigmatic line 1018 he interprets as a hint in this direction, as is clear from the vehement tone of his reproving answer (1019). The messenger would not have been above lying on this point, if he judged it safe and advantageous; he lies later when he claims to have "found" Oedipus on Cithaeron (εὑρὼν, 1026), a lie which he retracts (1038) only when he realizes that Oedipus wants more information than he can supply. See Campbell's note on this passage.

61. Though the herdsman could corroborate the truth of the matter of Laius' murder, he is never asked to do so; the proof of the truth of the "old" oracles is enough to guarantee the truth of the "new."

62. 1181: ἴσθι δύσποτμος γεγώς.

63. The proper use of this title is suggested by X. *Ages.* xi. 13: οἱ γε μὴν συγκινδυνεύοντες [ἐκάλουν αὐτὸν] μετὰ θεοὺς σωτῆρα.

64. For this antithesis cf. the speech of Iris in E. *H. F.* 841: ἢ θεοὶ μὲν οὐδαμοῦ, τὰ θνητὰ δ' ἔσται μεγάλα, μὴ δόντος δίκην.

65. Σ ad loc. εἰκότως οὖν κέχρηται τῷ τέκνα ὡσπερεὶ πατήρ.

66. Cf. also the θρόνος of Oedipus (237) and the θρόνος of Artemis (161); δεῖ κἀμὲ βουλεύειν (619) and ὦ Ζεῦ τί μου δρᾶσαι βεβούλευσαι πέρι (738); ἐφέστιοι (32) and τὴν Πυθόμαντιν ἑστίαν (965); ξυνίημ' (346) and Ζεὺς ὁ τ' Ἀπόλλων ξυνετοί (498); τὰ Πυθικὰ . . . ὡς πίθοιθ' ὅ τι (70-1); ἀλεξοίμην (539) and ἀλεξίμοροι (163; cf. 171).

67. Such a feeling is not un-Sophoclean; compare the merciless way Athena mocks Ajax in front of his enemy in the prologue of the *Ajax.*

68. Cf. 1033. Francis Fergusson, *The Idea of a Theater* (Princeton, Princeton Univ. Press, 1949), p. 19, has a perceptive comment: "Oedipus' entrance (majestic but for his tell-tale limp). . . ."

69. This is pointed out by Jebb (Preface, p. xix, n. 2): "In v. 397 ὁ μηδὲν εἰδὼς Οἰδίπους suggests a play on οἶδα." Masqueray remarks on 397: "Une étymologie du mot Οἰδίπους. Celle que l'on trouve couramment est donnée au vers 1036. Mais Oedipe n'était-il pas aussi l'homme εἰδὼς τὸ περὶ τῶν ποδῶν αἴνιγμα?" This was anticipated by Earle (p. 40): "As 'Knowfoot' (εἰδὼς τοὺς πόδας) he solves the riddle about feet."

70. Cf. e. g. 43: οἶσθά που, 59: οἶδ' ὅτι, 84, 105, 397, 498, 745, and cf. Chap. 3, pp. 127-8.

71. L recc. read κάτοισθ' ὅπου in 926. This would make the pun even clearer, and may well be what Sophocles wrote. The change of number (the plural is only implied in ὑμῶν ὦ ξένοι, not expressed) is not unusual in addresses to the chorus. (Cf. 7. El. 175: φίλαι. . . . 184: σκέψαι, ibid. 215, 218, 751, 757, etc.)

72. The rhymes have often been noticed, but dismissed. "Probably unintentional" (Earle); "ὅπου at the end of two lines and Οδίπου carelessly rhyming between them" (H. D. F. Kitto, Greek Tragedy, 2d ed. London, Methuen, 1950, p. 182, n. 1). The existence of puns in Sophocles is generally ignored or excused. A. C. Pearson (3) is reluctant to admit them but finds no alternative. On O. T. 70 (Πυθικὰ . . . πύθοιτο) he comments as follows: "It seems strange to us that Sophocles should have had the bad taste to introduce an etymological pun at this stage of the action. But the fact is beyond dispute. . . ."

73. Pl. Lg. iv. 716c: ὁ δὴ θεὸς ἡμῖν πάντων χρημάτων μέτρον ἂν εἴη μάλιστα. . . .

1. With Pearson and many others, I cannot believe that the play ended with the tasteless and hardly intelligible tetrameters of 1524-30. As the scholiast says (on 1523): καὶ αὐτάρκως ἔχει τὸ δρᾶμα· τὰ γὰρ ἑξῆς ἀνοίκεια γνωμολογοῦντος Οἰδίποδος. By which he meant, I take it, that these lines are inappropriate for Oedipus (and in fact all the MSS attribute them to the chorus) and impossibe for the chorus (which could hardly say ὦ πάτρας Θήβης ἔνοικοι, words which are possible only if the chorus does not consist of Thebans, like the chorus of the Euripidean *Phoenissae*). Apart from this obvious indication that these miserable lines were written for the end of the *Phoenissae* (whether Euripides wrote them is another question), the plural αἰνίγματα in 1525 is meaningless, and 1526 and the last three lines defy sense and syntax alike.

2. φέρομαι and φοράδην. For φοράδην see Jebb's note: "in the manner of that which is carried." Jebb comments: "He feels as if his voice was borne from him on the air in a direction over which he has no control."

3. For which the medium is the lyric meter of his opening song after his reappearance on stage: he does not return to the iambic medium of rational speech until he begins to argue in 1369.

4. For the blinding as "deliberate purpose" see Sir Richard Livingstone, "The Exodus of the *Oedipus Tyrannus*," in *Greek Poetry and Life* (Oxford, 1936), p. 160.

5. ἂν προσεῖδον, 1372; ὄψις ἦν, 1375; ἔμελλον . . . ὁρᾶν, 1385. What Oedipus says now about what he thought then is proved exact by the messenger's account of what he said at the time (1271-4).

6. The beggar is shameless in his importunity (κακὸς δ' αἰδοῖος ἀλήτης, says Penelope, *Od*. xvii. 578, "a modest beggar is no

good "'); he compliments the man he hopes to make his patron (Odysseus to Antinous, ibid., 415 ff.); he compares his own miserable circumstances with the splendid prosperity of his patron (ibid. 419 ff.); he calls down blessings on his benefactor's head (Odysseus to Eumaeus, *Od.* xiv. 53-4). Cf. also xvii. 354-5. All these formulas of the beggar are to be found in Oedipus' appeals to Creon.

7. See Jebb's note. The expression is completely ambiguous, for φρονῶ can mean either "understanding" (i. e. "I do not idly speak things I do not understand—and will not understand until I consult the oracle again") or "intention" (in which case it is a definite concession to Oedipus). Yet Jebb is surely right in taking it in the latter sense (as Oedipus evidently does), and there is then no contradiction between this passage and the reference to Oedipus' exile in *O. C.* 765 ff. From the *O. C.* it appears that Creon never did, in fact, consult the oracle of Apollo about the exile of Oedipus; the decision to exile him was made by Creon alone and connived at by Oedipus' sons. The words οὐκ ἤθελες, *O. C.* 767, mean not "refused" but simply "were unwilling," as Creon in the *Oedipus Tyrannus* clearly is.

8. See "Sophocles' Oedipus," in *Tragic Themes in Western Literature*, ed. Cleanth Brooks (New Haven, 1955), pp. 23-9.

9. D. Chr. lxiv. 6 says, of Oedipus: ἡ τύχη γὰρ αὐτῷ τὸ μηδὲν παθεῖν περιποιουμένη τὸ ἀγνοεῖν ἔδωκεν, ὅπερ ὅμοιον ἦν τῷ μὴ παθεῖν. εἶτα ἅμα τῆς εὐτυχίας ἐπαύσατο καὶ τοῦ γιγνώσκειν ἤρξατο.

SUGGESTIONS FOR FURTHER READING

Segal, Charles, *Oedipus Tyrannus: Tragic Heroism and the Limits of Knowledge*, New York, 1993. A handbook for the Greekless reader, covering "literary and historical context" and the author's own sensitive "reading" of the play and offering an extensive bibliography with useful critical remarks on each item.

Bushnell, Rebecca W., *Prophesying Tragedy*, Ithaca, N.Y., 1988, pp. 67–85.

Fagles, Robert, trans., *Sophocles: The Theban Plays*, introduction by Bernard Knox, Harmondsworth, England, 1984, pp. 131–53.

Gellie, G. H., *Sophocles: A Reading*, Melbourne, Australia, 1972, pp. 79–105.

Goldhill, Simon, *Reading Greek Tragedy*, Cambridge, 1986, pp. 199–221.

O'Brian, Michael, ed., *Twentieth-Century Interpretations of the "Oedipus Rex,"* New York, 1968.

Segal, Charles, *Sophocles' Tragic World*, Cambridge, Mass., 1995, pp. 138–212.

Vernant, Jean-Pierre, and Vidal-Naquet, Pierre, *Myth and Tragedy in Ancient Greece*, trans. Janet Lloyd, New York, 1988, pp. 85–140, 207–36, 320–27.

Whitman, Cedric, *Sophocles: A Study of Heroic Humanism*, Cambridge, Mass., 1951, pp. 122–46.

Winnington-Ingram, R. P., *Sophocles: An Interpretation*, Cambridge, 1980, pp. 173–204.

Angus, C. F., "Athens," *Cambridge Ancient History* (Cambridge, University Press, 1928), vol. 7, chap. 7.

Ax, W., "Die Parodos des Oidipus Tyrannos," *Hermes*, 67 (1932), 413-37.

Bonner, R., and Smith, G., *The Administration of Justice from Homer to Aristotle*, Chicago, 1930, 1938.

Bowra, M. *Sophoclean Tragedy*, Oxford, 1944.

Brooks, C., and Heilman, R., *Understanding Drama*, New York, 1948.

Bruhn, E., *Sophokles* (2d ed. Berlin, 1910), vol. 2: *König Oedipus*.

Burnet, J., *Plato's Euthyphro, Apology of Socrates, and Crito*, Oxford, 1924.

Campbell, L., *Sophocles*, London, 1879.

Carroll, J. P., "Some Remarks on the Questions in the Oedipus Tyrannus," *CJ*, 32, No. 7 (April, 1937), 406-16.

Croiset, A. and M., *Histoire de la littérature grecque* (2d ed. Paris, 1898), vol. 2.

Deubner, L., *Attische Feste*, Berlin, 1932.

Diano, C., "Edipo figlio della Tyche," *Dioniso*, 15 (1952), 56-89.

Diehl, E., *Anthologia Lyrica Graeca* (Leipzig, 1925), vol. 2.

Diels, H., and Kranz, W., *Die Fragmente der Vorsokratiker*, 10th ed. Berlin, 1961.

Earle, M. L., *The Oedipus Tyrannus*, New York, 1901.

Ehrenberg, V. (1), *The People of Aristophanes*, 2d ed. Oxford, 1951.

—— (2), *Sophocles and Pericles*, Oxford, 1954.

Errandonea, I., "El estasimo segundo del Edipo Rey," *Textos y Estudios*, Eva Perón (La Plata), Argentina, 1952.

Farnell, L. R., *Cults of the Greek States, Oxford*, 1896-1909.

Ferguson, W. S., "The Leading Ideas of the New Period," *Cambridge Ancient History* (Cambridge University Press, 1928), vol. 7, chap. 1.

269

Fergusson, F., *The Idea of a Theater*, Princeton, 1949.

Fraenkel, E., *Aeschylus Agamemnon*, Oxford, 1950.

Fränkel, H., *Dichtung und Philosophie des Frühen Griechentums*, New York, 1951.

Frazer, Sir James G., *The Golden Bough* (3d ed. London, 1935), vol. 2: *The Magic Art*.

Freeman, K., (1), *The Pre-Socratic Philosophers*, Oxford, 1946.

——— (2), *Ancilla to the Pre-Socratic Philosophers*, Cambridge, Mass., 1948.

Freud, S., *The Interpretation of Dreams*, New York, 1938.

Fritz, Kurt von, "ΝΟΥΣ, ΝΟΕΙΝ, and Their Derivatives," Pt. II, *CP*, 41 (1946), 12-34.

Goodwin, W. W., *Syntax of the Moods and Tenses of the Greek Verb*, Boston, 1890.

Greene, W. C. (1), *Moira*, Cambridge, Mass, 1948.

——— (2), "Fate, Good, and Evil in Pre-Socratic Philosophy," *HSCP*, 47 (1936), 85-129.

Grene, D., *Three Greek Tragedies in Translation*, Chicago, 1942.

Helmbold, W. C., "The Paradox of the *Oedipus*," *AJP*, 72 (1951), 239 ff.

How, W. W., and Wells, J., *A Commentary on Herodotus*, Oxford, 1912.

Jaeger, W., *The Theology of the Early Greek Philosophers*, Oxford, 1947.

Jebb, Sir Richard, *Sophocles, Oedipus Tyrannus*, Cambridge, 1887.

Jones, W. H. S. and Withington, E. T., *Hippocrates*, London, 1923-31.

Kamerbeek, J. C., *The Plays of Sophocles. Part I, Ajax*, Leiden, 1953.

Kitto, H. D. F., *Greek Tragedy*, 2d ed. London, 1950.

Kleingünther, A., πρῶτος εὑρέτης, *Phil. Suppl.*, 26, Heft 1 (Leipzig, 1933).

Knox, B. M. W. (1), "The Date of the *Oedipus Tyrannos*," *AJP* 77 (1956), 133-147.

———— (2), "The *Hippolytus* of Euripides," *YCS*, *13* (1952), 1-31.

———— (3), "Sophocles' Oedipus," in *Tragic Themes in Western Literature*, ed. Cleanth Brooks, New Haven, 1955.

Livingstone, Sir Richard, "The Exodus of the *Oedipus Tyrannus*," in *Greek Poetry and Life*, Oxford, 1936, 158-63.

Maidment, K. J., *Minor Attic Orators* London, 1951, vol. *1*.

Masqueray, P., *Sophocle* (Budé), Paris, 1929.

Meier, M. H. E., and Schömann, G. F., *Der Attische Process*, (Neu bearb. von J. H. Lipsius) Berlin, 1883-87.

Miller, H. W., "Medical Terminology in Tragedy," *TPAPA*, 87 (1944), 156-67.

Mitchell, T., *The Oedipus Tyrannus of Sophocles*, Oxford, 1841.

Murray, G., *The Rise of the Greek Epic*, 3rd ed. Oxford, 1924.

Nestlé, W., "Hippocratica," *Hermes*, 73 (1938), 1-38.

Nilsson, M. (1), *Greek Popular Religion*, New York, 1940.

———— (2), *Geschichte der Griechischen Religion*² (Munich, 1955), vol. *1*.

Pack, R. A., "Fate, Chance, and Tragic Error," *AJP*, 60 (1939), 350-6.

Page, D. L. (1), "Thucydides' Description of the Great Plague," *CQ*, 47 (1953), 97-119.

———— (2), *Euripides. Medea*, Oxford, 1938.

Paley, F. A., *The Tragedies of Aeschylus*⁴, London, 1879.

Pearson, A. C. (1), *Sophoclis Fabulae*, Oxford, 1924.

———— (2), *The Fragments of Sophocles*, Cambridge, 1917.

———— (3), "Sophoclea II," *CQ*, 23 (1929), 87-95.

———— (4), "Sophoclea III," *CQ*, 23 (1929), 164-76.

Pickard-Cambridge, A. W., *The Dramatic Festivals of Athens*, Oxford, 1953.

Powell, J. E., *A Lexicon to Herodotus*, Cambridge, 1938.

Robert, C., *Oidipus*, Berlin, 1915.

Roscher, W. H., ed., *Ausführliches Lexikon der Griechischen und Römischen Mythologie*, Leipzig, 1884-1937.

Sheppard, J. C., *The Oedipus Tyrannus*, Cambridge, 1920.

Thomson, G., *Aeschylus, Prometheus Bound*, Cambridge, 1932.
Waldock, A. J. A., *Sophocles the Dramatist*, Cambridge, 1951.
Whitman, C. H., *Sophocles*, Cambridge, Mass., 1951.
Wormhoudt, A., *The Muse at Length*, Boston, 1953.
Wyse, W., *The Speeches of Isaeus*, Cambridge, 1904.

INDEX

Abae, 46
Abraham, 113
Achaeus, 246
Achilles, 205
Acropolis, the 231
Adeimantus, 160
Aeacus, 70
Aegina, 70
Aegisthus, 60, 124
Aelian, 223
Aeschines, 87, 226–30, 248
Aeschylus, 78, 101, 119, 133, 142, 206, 241, 246, 249, 251; *Oresteia*, 38; *Supp.*, 200, 241; *Pers.*, 241; *Th.* 206; *A.*, 214, 237, 241, 251; *Cho.*, 204, 214; *Eu.*, 61, 223; *P.V.*, 62, 109, 124, 126, 129, 137, 145, 148, 216, 237, 240, 243–4, 246–7, 250, 252; *Palamedes*, 252
Agamemnon, 35, 170
Agave, 125
Agêlatein, 75, 223
Agenor, 56
Agoratus, 85
Ahnfrau, die, 4
Ajax, 35, 263. *See also* Sophocles, *Ajax*
Akathartos, 142, 246
Alcibiades, 23, 44, 97, 219, 224, 254, 256
Alcmaeon, 255
—— of Croton, 123, 239
Alcman, 166
Amazons, 220
Ameipsias, 241
Amphitryon, 62, 216
Anachronism, 61, 63, 215–16
Anarithmos, 151, 252
Anaxagoras, 125, 248
Anaxilas, 237

Andocides, 82, 89, 216, 224–8, 230–1, 254, 261
Anêkeston, 105
Angus, C. F., 258
Anthrôpos tyrannos, 107, 110
Antigone, 212. *See also* Sophocles, *Antigone*.
Antinous, 266
Antioch, 258
Antiphon orator, 85–91, 94, 98, 225–31, 243
—— sophista, 45, 208
Aphienai, 84, 91
Aphrodite, 34
Apokleisai, 147, 249
Apollo, 80, 86, 89, 94, 111, 118, 141, 160, 169, 170, 173, 175, 177, 181, 209, 212, 259, 263, 266; prophecies of, 6, 40, 42, 47, 143, 153, 157, 171–2, 176, 186, 206, 210–11, 260; responsibility of, 7–8, 187, 200; and the plague, 9–10, 200; and Croesus, 36, 38; in the *Oresteia*, 38, 206; and Oedipus, 51, 180, 195; and Laius, 101, 123; and Jocasta, 171–2, 176, 260; A. *mênytês*, 81, 224; "ministers" of, 172–3, 260; in the *Ion*, 45, 207; Lycean A., 159, 176
Apollonius Rhodius, 246
Arcadia, 160, 255
Archê, 66, 182
Archidamus, 64, 217, 219, 256
Archilochus, 213, 257
Archimedes, 128
Archytas, 118
Areopagus, the, 78
Ares, 10, 200
Aretaeus, 244–5, 247
Arginusae, 77

273

RELATED TITLES AVAILABLE FROM YALE UNIVERSITY PRESS

Antigones
How the Antigone Legend Has Endured in Western Literature, Art, and Thought
George Steiner
"[Steiner's] account of the various treatments of the Antigone theme in European languages [is] . . . penetrating and novel." —*New York Times Book Review*

The Death of Tragedy
George Steiner
"This book is important. . . . The very passion and insight with which [Steiner] writes about the tragedies that have moved him prove that the vision still lives and that words can still enlighten and reveal." —R. B. Sewall, *New York Times Book Review*

. . . and in the Hermes Books series

Horace
David Armstrong
"A book that should not be sampled but read through to obtain a view of Horace that is both personal and vivid." —Charles L. Babcock, *Classical Outlook*

Aeschylus
John Herington
"An excellent introduction. . . . Herington's enthusiasm for recapturing the vitality of Aeschylus' drama shows through on every page." —*Choice*

Ovid
Sara Mack
"[This] wonderfully readable account . . . encourages readers to become familiar with the voice of one of the most compelling poets in human history. . . . Masterful." —Maurice B. Cloud, *Bloomsbury Review*

Catullus
Charles Martin
"Martin's book, funny, moving, smart, alive to twentieth-century poetic developments, is now the best book on Catullus in English." —Donald Lyons, *New Criterion*

Homer
Paolo Vivante
"Vivante's book . . . shows us once again that a direct confrontation with the Homeric texts can yield positively exhilarating results." —John E. Rexine, *Plato*

Founded by the distinguished classicist, the late John Herington, the Hermes series is designed to communicate to nonspecialist readers the beauty and relevance of the Greek and Latin masters.